EMERGENCY TELEPHONE NUMBERS

Police _____

Fire _____

Ambulance _____

Poison Control _____

Child Abuse Hot Line _____

Emergency Room _____

Family

_____

_____

_____

Neighbors/Friends

_____

_____

Home Address & Phone

_____

_____

_____

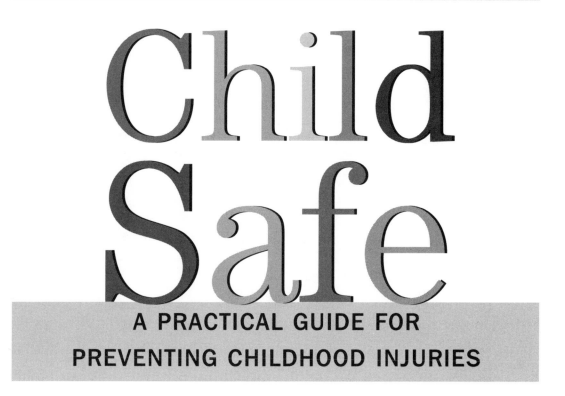

Child Safe

A PRACTICAL GUIDE FOR PREVENTING CHILDHOOD INJURIES

Mark A. Brandenburg, M.D.

THREE RIVERS PRESS
NEW YORK

Though written for parents and grandparents, this book is dedicated to children.
May they all experience the adventure, learning, comforts, and joys that life has to offer.

Copyright © 2000 by Mark A. Brandenburg, M.D.

Published by Three Rivers Press, New York, New York.
Member of the Crown Publishing Group.

Random House, Inc. New York, Toronto, London, Sydney, Auckland
www.randomhouse.com

THREE RIVERS PRESS is a registered trademark of Random House, Inc.

Printed in the United States of America

Design by H. Roberts Design

Library of Congress Cataloging-in-Publication Data

Brandenburg, Mark A.
    Child safe: a practical guide for preventing childhood injuries/Mark A. Brandenburg.
    Includes bibliographical references.
    1. Children's accidents—Prevention. 2. Safety education. I. Title.
    HV675.72.B73 2000
    649'.1—dc21
                                                                99-045740

ISBN 0-609-80412-X
10 9 8 7 6 5 4 3 2 1
First Edition

Acknowledgments

Words cannot fully express the gratitude I have for my loving wife, Kelly, who not only understood my vision for the perfect child-safety book, but who also partook in the dream and toiled with me to see it fulfilled.

I owe a debt of gratitude to my mom and dad, who raised six kids in a child-safe way while still allowing room for individuality and the pursuit of happiness.

Thanks to my sister Joanna Brandenburg, who assisted with the preparation of the manuscript.

I am also grateful to my agents, Nancy Love and Sherrie Sutton, and my editors P.J. Dempsey and Sarah Silbert, for their patience and faith in me as a writer.

Contents

Part II. Age-Related Injuries

Part III. Product Recalls and Resources

So you may see, if you will look
Through the windows of this book,
Another child, far, far away,
And in another garden, play.
But do not think you can at all,
By knocking on the window call
That child to hear you. He intent
Is all on his play-business bent.

ROBERT LOUIS STEVENSON
A Child's Garden of Verses

Introduction

Webster's dictionary defines an accident as "any event that happens unexpectedly." Child injury is no accident. Most of the injuries that occur to children are very predictable and can be anticipated. So if child injuries are not accidents, what are they? Well, they can be viewed as any other childhood disease. Your infant is at great risk of injury or death if not properly buckled into an automobile safety seat when a motor vehicle accident (MVA) occurs. This is predictable. We know with certainty that over four hundred infants will be killed in MVAs this year, most while unrestrained. By properly placing your infant in a safety seat, her risk of injury will be dramatically decreased. Is it an accident then if an unrestrained child is hurt in a MVA? Would it be considered an accident if a young child developed measles because a vaccination was not given?

So, when four hundred infants are killed in MVAs this year, consider them to have been victims of a disease, the disease of child injury—or better yet, the epidemic of child injury. The automobile safety seat is a proven preventive measure for this particular disease—consider it a vaccine. *Child Safe* is full of proven "vaccines" for the prevention of most child injuries. As Louis Pasteur once said, "When meditating over a disease, I never think of finding a remedy for it but, instead, a means of preventing it." Remember, child injury is not an unexpected event. It is not an accident; it is a disease that everybody can and must work to *prevent* rather than simply hope to treat in emergency rooms.

Every year in the United States 25 million children are physically injured. Trauma is the leading cause of death in children older than one year. And each year over twelve thousand children under the age of fourteen years are killed by injury and fifty thousand are permanently disabled. One out of every four children each year will receive medical attention for an injury. The statistics in this book are not meant to scare you, but to teach you about the dangers that children face in the modern world. The bright side of this story is that most of the common injuries affecting children today are preventable.

As an emergency physician, I treat sick and injured children every day. Many wonderful and exciting things happen in the emergency room, but so do some terrible things. The most anguishing moments I experience are when children are badly hurt. In many cases, our attempts to help injured children are successful and there is a happy ending. Too often, however, a child is critically injured or killed. Disability, pain, and suffering afflict these needlessly injured children. And when a child is permanently crippled or killed, not only is that child's life shattered, but so are the lives of family members and friends who suffer huge emotional tolls. What I see in the faces of injured children and their family members is a combination of shock, disbelief, horror, and tremendous grief.

"How could this have happened?"

"Why didn't I see this coming?"

"What should I have done differently?"

These are questions you never want to ask yourself. *Child Safe* was written so you don't have to. This book is for all parents, grandparents, and guardians of children. The inspiration for *Child Safe* came from the many parents who have asked me in the ER, "What could I have done to prevent this?" For obvious reasons, it is difficult to candidly answer that question after having just told a family about their child's injury or death. My belated answer comes in the writing of *Child Safe*. I want parents to be armed with the same information that is already well known to public health researchers and emergency physicians—specifically, how and why children are injured. It made no sense to me that the most important people in society with regard to children—namely you, the parents—didn't have easy access to this information.

How to Use This Book

Children aren't "little adults"; they are different from adults in many, many ways. And to make things more complex, the basic characteristics of a child's physical and mental self evolve as he or she grows up. Only after we understand the unique characteristics of the various stages of childhood can we begin to recognize the situations that are unsafe for children.

Therefore, the many potential dangers discussed in *Child Safe* are organized in a very easy-to-follow format based upon the stages of child growth. The dangers that your child faces will change accordingly as she develops and matures. In early infancy a soft pillow in the crib is deadly. In later infancy the crib gym that hangs above can be a strangulation hazard. During the toddler years a five-gallon bucket of mop water is a drowning hazard. In older children auto-pedestrian and bicycle injuries are common. And, of course, drugs and alcohol also begin to play a role in childhood injuries during the junior high school years. If you are interested in reading about a single type of injury and how it can be prevented in each of the age groups, just follow the cross-references placed throughout the book.

Part I of *Child Safe* contains descriptions of common ways that children of all ages get hurt and how these injuries can be prevented.

Part II is organized into chapters that focus on age-specific injury patterns. Each chapter in Part II pertains to a specific stage of childhood. For the purposes of this book, an infant is between the age of zero and twelve months, a toddler is twelve months to three years, a preschooler is four to five years, and a school-aged child is six to thirteen years old. Throughout this book you will also find many true stories of children I have treated in the emergency room. The names of patients have been changed, but the details of their stories are accurate.

Part III is a comprehensive list of those products that have been recalled in the last four years because they have been found harmful or potentially harmful to children.

Child Safe Is Not Fiction

Reading this book and following the provided guidelines is the absolute best way for you to learn about child injury prevention. But *Child Safe* is not a book to be read once and then discarded. This is a book to be read and reread as your children grow up, and again when a newborn joins the family. First, read *Child Safe* from cover to cover, then read the specific chapters that pertain to your child as she approaches each age group. And periodically review the appropriate chapters when time permits. With each passing day newer products will be marketed that present yet unknown hazards to your child. So use your imagination when searching for possible scenarios that could hurt your child. If you can conceive that an injury might occur in a new and different way or by a new product, trust your instinct and take precautions, because it probably can. And don't be afraid to predict the possible scenarios in which your child might get injured—you're not being paranoid, just smart. If a new idea comes to you, write it down. *If you discover a new way children can be injured, please write and tell me about it. My Internet web site address is www.babyandchildsafety.com.* I am always looking for newer and better ways to protect children. Good luck in raising and caring for your children, and remember—always be *Child Safe.*

Child Safety—It's an Attitude

A Word on the Close Supervision of Young Children

The close supervision of young children is strongly emphasized throughout this book. Supervising young children might be instinctive, but doing it well requires self-discipline and learning. Losing sight of your infant or young child for even a brief moment can be a deadly mistake. Many young children are found dead in bathtubs and pools or get struck by cars or fall down stairs after being left alone for mere minutes. As a guardian of an infant or young toddler, you simply cannot allow one second of unsupervised time, except when your child is safely sleeping in her crib.

Now, I'm not waving a red flag to scare you. Rather, I hope that being aware of potential problems and the steps to prevent them will make you a more confident and safe parent. One of the trickiest things about being a parent is finding the balance between encouraging a child's independence while still safeguarding her welfare. Babies need to continually discover new objects, sensations, sounds, sights, and tastes. Toys that have bright colors, fun sounds, and interesting shapes and designs are wonderful stimulation, so allow plenty of playtime and exploration, but always maintain a watchful eye. Children of all ages need room in their lives for the joy and excitement (and yes, even mischief) that is so inherent in childhood.

A Note to Grandparents

If you are a grandparent with full-time childcare responsibilities you are not alone. Approximately 1.3 million children in the United States are entrusted to the care of their grandparents. The future of your grandchildren has been placed in your hands, and rightfully so; grandparents have a wisdom and maturity that cannot be obtained any other way than by living the years and experiences which you have lived.

As a grandparent, you will probably find yourself in a position of greater responsibility than expected. Did you ever dream that you would again be bottle-feeding or changing the diapers of a little one or chasing after a rebellious toddler? Did you ever imagine you would once again be responsible for the safety of a child? Things have changed since you raised your own children. We have discovered many hazards not recognized twenty or thirty years ago. Air bags, cradles, down comforters, and toy chests are just some of the things from which infants today must be protected. This book lists many more such dangers. In fact, hundreds of individual products have been recalled by manufacturers in recent years after being identified as potentially harmful to infants and children.

Perhaps you are not the full-time guardians of your grandchildren, but are regular or occasional baby-sitters. Your awareness of child safety is no less critical. Your concern must still be ever present. Not only will active participation in child injury prevention directly protect your grandchildren, it will also enable you to educate your own children, who might not take the time to formally learn the rules of child safety. The example you set might just be what is needed to inspire them. The knowledge you pass on could later save a young life. So, to all the grandparents reading this book, good luck and God bless. The courage and virtue you show in once again taking on a task that has already once been accomplished is commendable.

Be Willing to Change

Child Safe is a comprehensive guide to child safety. This book, however, can only show you the way—you must take the necessary steps yourself to prevent your child from being injured. Sometimes preventing injuries in your child simply involves knowing which items not to place in her crib, such as pillows and comforters. On the other hand, following the recommendations in this book might require you to make a complete lifestyle change. For example, consider the couple who has been married for three years and lives in a great home with a ground-level swimming pool in the backyard. They want to have a baby. Before their newborn arrives, this couple could take the many steps necessary in attempts to prevent a drowning, but the safest way to go would be to move to a home without a pool to eliminate the risk completely. Some of these injury prevention steps are not easy to make, but they are the safest.

Trust Your Instincts, Have Courage, and Be a Strong Parent

You might sometimes feel as though certain people in your life are working against your efforts to create a child-safe environment—and you may be right. Count on the fact that some people, whether they mean to or not, will distract you from the responsibility of protecting your child. It might be a neighbor who tells you, "Don't be so uptight all the time, Annie will be all right while she's in our pool." Or it could be the well-meaning grandmother who leaves medications on the kitchen table when visiting. Remember, you are your child's primary protector; if anything, no matter how subconscious, makes you leery, get your child out of that situation. In situations like these you must have the courage to stand up for children and make the sometimes unpopular decisions necessary to prevent injury. Be tactful and polite, but always put your child's safety first.

Planning for Emergencies

Even the most cautious parents will, from time to time, have to deal with child injuries. How you prepare for these circumstances will determine your success in managing them. Basic responses to various possible emergencies should be planned. Use the inside front cover of this book to keep emergency telephone numbers together in a convenient location and keep it close to your telephone. Be sure every capable person in your family remains current in cardiopulmonary resuscitation (CPR) and first-aid skills. Many lives have been saved by parents and older children who were able to quickly administer CPR in an emergency.

Do you know where your child should be taken in the event of a medical emergency? Investigate your local and regional hospitals to determine which are most capable of providing emergency pediatric care. Such a hospital must have emergency physicians and nurses trained in pediatric medicine. Be sure the emergency physicians are board certified by the American Board of Emergency Medicine (ABEM) or the American Board of Osteopathic Emergency Medicine (ABOEM). Know which hospitals have pediatric intensive care units. If you live in a small town, you probably have little choice of emergency rooms, but it helps knowing to which hospital your child should be transferred in the event that specialty care is needed.

PART I

Non-Age-Related Injuries

Automobiles

Motor vehicle accidents (MVAs) claim the lives of nearly 50,000 Americans each year and are responsible for more deaths and serious injury to children than any other cause in the United States. Approximately 8,000 children are killed and 800,000 injured each year in the United States in motor vehicle accidents. In this book, you will find numerous tips on how to prevent your child from being injured while riding in an automobile, but none as important as the recommendation to use seat belts and safety seats. In recent years we have seen a 70 percent decrease in child fatalities as a result of restraint devices and the laws that require their use. By purchasing a safe automobile and always placing your child in the backseat, you can even further reduce your child's risk of injury or death.

BUYING A SAFE CAR

Bigger Is Better

When shopping for a family car, truck, or minivan, consider the size of the automobile. Simply stated, bigger is better. Child passengers of larger cars, trucks, and sport-utility vehicles generally suffer fewer injuries because of protection offered by the added weight and size of the automobile and the fact that these vehicles sit higher off the ground.

There are many factors to consider when looking to purchase a family automobile: style, handling, cargo space, cost, reliability, and so on. Why not check out the safety record of a vehicle? The most precious cargo you will ever transport is your child, so choose an automobile that is worthy of the job. Some automobiles are highly recognized for safety to passengers, while others are recalled for particular dangers. When shopping for a car or truck, find out which automobiles are safe and which are unsafe; your child's life may depend on it.

The following is a list of 1995–97 automobile models that have been recognized by the Highway Loss Data Institute (HLDI) for passenger safety that is substantially better than average.

Four-Door Cars

Very Large
Mercury Grand Marquis
Ford Crown Victoria

Large
Buick Park Avenue
Buick LeSabre
Oldsmobile Eighty-Eight
Chrysler Concorde
Pontiac Bonneville
Eagle Vision
Pontiac Grand Prix

Midsize
Saab 900
Buick Century

Small
Audi A4 Quattro

Station Wagons and Vans

Large
Mercury Sable
Pontiac Trans Sport
GMC Safari 4-wheel drive
Chrysler Town & Country
Chevrolet Venture
Chevrolet Astro 4-wheel drive
Mercury Villager
Ford Taurus
GMC Safari
Ford Aerostar 4-wheel drive

Midsize
Volvo 850

Two-Door Cars

Large
Buick Riviera

Luxury Cars

Very Large
Mercedes S class long wide body
BMW 7 series long wide body
Lincoln Town Car

Large
Lexus LS 400
Cadillac Seville
Lincoln Continental
Cadillac Eldorado
Cadillac DeVille
Oldsmobile Aurora
Acura 3.5 RL
BMW 5 series
Chrysler LHS
Jaguar XJ series
Mercedes E class
Lincoln Mark VII

Midsize
Audi A6/Q6 Quattro 4dr
Lexus SC 300/400
Saab 9000
Volvo 940/960

Pickup Trucks

Large

GMC 2500 series 4x4
Chevrolet 3500 series 4x4
Chevrolet 2500 series
Chevrolet 2500 series 4x4
Ford F-350 series
Ford F-250 series 4x4
GMC 1500 series 4x4
Ford F-350 series 4x4
Ford F-250 series
Chevrolet 3500 series
Chevrolet 1500 series 4x4
Dodge Ram 3500 series
Dodge Ram 2500 series
Dodge Ram 2500 series 4x4
Dodge Ram 3500 series 4x4
Dodge Ram 1500 series 4x4
Ford F-150 series 4x4
GMC 1500 series
Chevrolet 1500 series
Ford F-150 series

Small

GMC Sonoma series 4x4
Chevrolet S10 series 4x4
Dodge Dakota series 4x4

Utility Vehicles

Large

GMC Suburban 1500 4x4

GMC Suburban 1500
Chevrolet Suburban 1500
Chevrolet Suburban 2500 4x4
Ford Expedition
Ford Expedition 4x4

Midsize

Land Rover Range Rover
GMC Yukon 2dr 4x4
GMC Yukon 4dr 4x4
Chevrolet Tahoe 2dr 4x4
Chevrolet Tahoe 4dr 4x4
Chevrolet Tahoe 4dr
GMC Yukon 4dr
Mercury Mountaineer 4x4
Oldsmobile Bravada 4x4
Jeep Grand Cherokee 4x4
Toyota Land Cruiser
Ford Explorer 4dr 4x4
Jeep Cherokee 2dr 4x4

Sports Cars

Midsize

Saab 900 convertible

Small

Porsche 911 Targa/Coupe
Mercedes SL class

Mini

BMW Z3 Roadster

The following is a list of 1995–97 automobile models deemed substantially worse than average with regard to passenger safety by the HLDI are.

Four-Door Cars

Midsize

Mitsubishi Galant
Nissan Altima
Hyundai Sonata

Small

Geo Prizm
Dodge Neon
Ford Escort
Mercury Tracer

Mazda Protégé
Toyota Corolla
Nissan Sentra
Kia Sephia
Hyundai Elantra
Mini
Geo Metro
Toyota Tercel
Ford Aspire
Hyundai Accent

Honda Civic Coupe
Dodge Neon
Mitsubishi Eclipse
Nissan 240SX
Nissan 200SX
Mini
Geo Metro
Toyota Tercel
Ford Aspire
Hyundai Accent

Two-Door Cars
Small
Toyota Celica

Utility Vehicles
Midsize
Isuzu Rodeo 4dr

Features to Look For

These automobile safety features can help prevent injuries to your child.

- *Safety locks and safety windows* in the backseat of your family vehicle are a must. They help prevent toddlers from opening doors or windows when the automobile is moving. New cars are required to have these features when they roll off the assembly line, but older models still on the road may have been built before these safety manufacturing laws were passed.
- *Height-adjustable seat belts* will better fit your child during the growing years after six years of age or when the booster seat is no longer needed.
- *Antilock brakes* decrease the likelihood of skids and provide better maneuverability when the car brakes are hit hard.
- *Built-in child safety seat* will ensure that you are never without this lifesaver. (*See also* "Integrated Safety Seats" in "Toddlers and Preschoolers," page 151.)
- *Rear center lap/shoulder seat belts* will allow you to safely squeeze in that one extra kid who needs a ride.
- *Child safety seat compatibility*—for obvious reasons.

Recalls

Keep an eye out for automobile recalls—your car could be on the list. For example, several child injuries and deaths have been blamed on defective rear-door latches in the 1983–1995 models of Dodge Grand Caravan, Dodge Caravan, and Plymouth Voyager. Once again, the National Highway Traffic Safety Administration (NHTSA) (www.nhtsa.gov) can help you determine if your vehicle has been recalled.

Restraint Devices—Never Let Your Child Ride without One

(See also "Buckle Your Baby" in "Infants," page 108; "Child Seats" in "Toddlers and Preschoolers," page 150; and "Booster Seats" in "Toddlers and Preschoolers," page 152.)

The second collision. When an automobile crashes, two collisions occur. The first is when another car or object is struck. The second collision refers to the impact that the passenger suffers when tossed about the car. It is this second collision that causes personal injury. By proper use of a child restraint device, seat belt, and air bag, the risk to your child in a second collision is nearly eliminated.

It is now required by law that every child be properly secured in a moving vehicle. The proper use of a restraint device, whether an infant seat, a convertible seat, or a booster seat, will significantly reduce your child's risk of a serious injury in an MVA. But these seats must be used properly. A slight error in securing a seat can make the difference between life and death. With so many types of seats on the market today, parents are often stymied by the differences in various models. The NHTSA reports that up to 80 percent of children are placed improperly in automobile restraint devices. Fortunately, help is on the way. A recent ruling by the Department of Transportation will require automobile makers, beginning on September 1, 2002, to outfit all new cars with a single anchoring device that will be simple to use and universal for all child safety seats. This device will make use of a rigid metal bar situated just behind the rear seats.

Throughout this book you will find further discussions about the appropriate use of safety seats, booster seats, and seat belts pertinent to the age of your child.

Dangerous Seats

In 1995, Consumers Union crash tested every model of child safety seat on the market. Of the twenty-five seats tested, three failed and were deemed "not acceptable." The seats that failed were the Century 590, the Evenflo On My Way 206, and the Kolcraft Traveler 700. Many other safety seats have since been recalled by the Consumer Product Safety Commission (CPSC) because of design defects. Before making a purchase, always check the product recall chapter at the back of this book and with the CPSC. *(See also "Child Safety Seats" in "Product Recalls," pages 191.)*

Backseat Positioning

(See also "Positioning Your Baby's Seat" in "Infants," page 109; "Positioning for Safety" in "Toddlers and Preschoolers," page 153; and "Where Should Your Kids Sit?" in "School-Age Children," page 180.)

Children are always safer when they ride in the backseat of an automobile. Regardless of whether air bags are present, children should not ride up front until they are at least twelve years old.

AIR BAGS

Automobile air bags are credited with saving over three thousand lives and preventing many thousands of injuries since their introduction in 1986. In 1998, over five hundred passenger lives were saved by air bags during motor vehicle accidents. As of 1997, driver and passenger side air bags are standard equipment in new cars and trucks sold in the United States. It is important to note, however, that air bag effectiveness is greatest when the driver and passenger are properly restrained.

Preventing Air Bag Injuries

Air bags are not perfect; they do not always protect passengers and they can even hurt or kill young children. Air bags open up with speeds of 200 to 300 miles per hour. Sometimes they deploy unnecessarily during slow-speed accidents and cause injury to child passengers. Air bags have been implicated in the deaths of forty-nine children and thirty-eight adults since 1986. But there's more to this story. Recently, the National Highway Traffic Safety Administration completed a study that found air bags are dangerous to children who are not properly positioned or seat-belted. Most children injured or killed by air bags were improperly restrained or not restrained at all and were sitting in the front seat of the vehicle during an accident. The truth is that anyone sitting too close to a deploying air bag can be hurt or killed, but a child's small body is much more vulnerable.

- Be sure your infant always rides in a safety seat that faces backward and always in the backseat of the car.
- Be sure your toddler always rides in a safety seat in the backseat of the car.
- Be sure all children under the age of twelve years ride in the backseat to avoid injuries from deploying air bags.
- If a child must ride up front, such as in a pickup or a sports car, be sure the seat is pushed as far back as it will go and that she sits as far back in the seat as possible. And never let her sit at the edge of her seat—this will put her dangerously close to the air bag module.

"On/Off Switches"

In December 1997, the NHTSA began allowing certain vehicle owners in high-risk categories to install keyhole "on/off switches" for passenger side air bags. A person must either have a front-seat-only vehicle (i.e., pickup truck or sports car) or be in a situation that makes it impossible to avoid putting children less than twelve years old up front (i.e., carpools or numerous children in one family). For permission to obtain an air bag cutoff switch, you must first fill out an application. To receive the necessary information send a postcard to the NHTSA, Attention—Airbag Switch Requests, 400 7th St. SW, Washington, DC 20590-1000. Applications can also be obtained by calling NHTSA at

800-424-9393 or on the NHTSA web site at (http://www.nhtsa.dot.gov). Once approved, the NHTSA will send a letter stating that you may have an authorized mechanic install the switch. The best place to have an on/off switch installed is at a dealership where you can get one that is custom-made for your car. The cost of installation is about $150.

DOES YOUR DRIVING PUT CHILDREN IN DANGER?

(See also "Chaos in the Car" in "Toddlers and Preschoolers," page 153; and "Be a Good Role Model" in "School-Age Children," page 181.)

There's no question about it, children in a vehicle being driven by an aggressive driver are at greater risk of being injured or killed in an accident. Be careful not to let the annoyances of heavy traffic and inconsiderate drivers get to you. When your frustrations mount and you are tempted to show that tailgater who he's messing with, take a deep breath and think of that wonderful child in the seat behind you. Your child's safety is all you should be concerned about. A few other points are also worth remembering:

- When somebody is tailgating, don't get angry and slow down, just get out of the way as soon as possible.
- Avoid yelling at, gesturing to, or even making eye contact with aggressive drivers. Road rage can turn violent and it can harm you or your child.
- Don't follow other cars too closely.
- Don't rush—give yourself plenty of time when going to scheduled events.
- Never speed—even when late.
- Never attempt to reprimand or discipline a child while driving.
- Always keep your eyes on the road and both hands on the wheel.

PICKUP TRUCK BEDS—CHILDREN AREN'T CARGO

In a time when so much attention is given to automobile safety, it is unbelievable that some people still allow children to ride in the beds of pickup trucks. A simple ten-mile-per-hour fender bender can be deadly to a child riding in a pickup truck bed (or the back of a station wagon, for that matter). In many states it is illegal to have an unrestrained child inside a moving vehicle, yet legal to let a child ride in the bed of a pickup. In some Oklahoma jurisdictions, it is against the law to put an unrestrained dog in the back of a pickup, but perfectly acceptable and legal to do so with a child. Every year thousands of children are seriously injured while riding in pickup truck beds, and around thirty to forty are killed this way. Never allow anybody, particularly a child, to ride in the back of a pickup truck.

Contrary to the belief of some misinformed legislators, a camper shell does not protect children in a pickup truck bed if an accident occurs. Not only this, but children riding in the back of a pickup truck are exposed to much higher levels of automobile exhaust. Many cases of carbon monoxide poisoning in children have been attributed to camper shells that were placed over the beds of pickup trucks.

ALONE IN THE CAR

There are so many reasons why young children should never be left alone in a vehicle. In warm weather, heat can build up inside your vehicle. The temperature in a parked car can rise to 120 degrees Fahrenheit in minutes. A child will succumb to heatstroke under these conditions. During cold months, frostbite and hypothermia can set in quickly. A baby left alone is also a target for child predators. I know one mother who left her baby in a minivan for just a few minutes when she dropped her second grader off at school. During that time two car thieves took off with the vehicle. Fortunately, when the thieves realized they had also kidnapped a baby, they parked the car and ran off; the infant was not hurt. Never leave your young child alone in a vehicle even for a short period of time. And if you ever notice a young child alone in a vehicle, notify the police immediately.

- Never leave a child less than twelve years of age alone in a vehicle.
- Don't let yourself fall into the trap of believing that:
  - you will be back to your car in "just a few minutes" and that your child will be safe when left alone. Distractions may keep you from getting back as quickly as you thought.
  - if you crack the windows it won't get too hot for your child. The heat in a parked car will build up just as quickly.

MOTORCYCLES

Motorcycles and young children are a deadly combination. When your child is an adolescent, and you wish to introduce him to the sport of motocross—then maybe. But don't for a second consider placing your child on the back of a motorcycle. By doing this you have made the decision that your child's well-being and life is worth risking for a little thrill.

PROTECTING YOUR UNBORN CHILD

Your baby will take countless rides in the family car even before birth. During pregnancy, be extra careful while driving. Because your baby sits so close to the steering wheel and dash there is a great risk of injury if an air bag deploys or if you are thrown forward.

How you wear the seat belt is very important. If placed improperly over your abdomen, a lap belt can cause harm to your unborn baby in an accident.

- Always place the lap belt below your abdomen at the level of your hips.
- Run the shoulder belt along the side of your abdomen, between your breasts and over your shoulder.

Air Bags during Pregnancy

In late pregnancy, riding in the front seat of an automobile can be dangerous if an air bag is present. Remember, the closer you sit to an air bag the more likely you are to be injured in an accident. Because of a pregnant woman's size, it may be impossible to sit farther than the recommended ten inches away from an air bag.

- Sit in the backseat of a car as often as you can, rather than driving or riding up front, during the third trimester of pregnancy.
- If you must drive or ride up front during your pregnancy, pull the seat as far back from the dashboard as it will go.

Bunk Beds

Bunk beds are attractive to families with multiple children because they are wonderfully space-efficient. But they do pose a significant risk to young children. Approximately thirty-four thousand children each year are injured on bunk beds in the United States, and nearly 90 percent of these children are less than fifteen years of age. The younger the child, the greater the risk of injury. Most injuries result from falls, usually from the top bunk or ladder.

- Never let a child less than six years of age sleep or play on a bunk bed.
- Routinely inspect the ladder to make sure that it is stable and that the rungs are not loosening.
- Sleeping on a top bunk should not be considered if your child has a medical disorder (i.e. seizures, diabetes) that makes falling more likely to occur.
- Routinely inspect the top mattress supports and guardrails.

THE DANGERS OF BUNK BEDS

There are several situations involving bunk beds that can injure your child:

- A child can roll off the top bunk while sleeping, especially if a guardrail is not present. Be sure a guardrail that extends at least five inches above the mattress is present on each side of the bed, even if one of the sides is against a wall. The guardrails should be firmly attached to the bed so your child cannot dislodge them.
- A child can roll off and get wedged between the bed and the wall and be suffocated.

To prevent this, position the bunk bed so it is either well away from any wall or firmly up against a wall.

- A child's head can get trapped between the guardrail and mattress and strangulation can occur. Be sure the space between the guardrail and mattress is less than 3.5 inches (or 8.9 centimeters) to eliminate this risk.

- Some bunk beds are made with inadequate support for the top mattress. Serious injury can occur if the top mattress falls through while a child is sleeping below. If your bunk bed does not possess such support, place cross beams and/or wires beneath the top mattress to prevent such an accident. Visit the retailer where you purchased your child's bunk bed and ask for a modification kit, or write to Bunk Bed Kit, P.O. Box 2436, High Point, NC 27261, for instructions on how to modify your bunk bed.

Make Sure You Buy the Proper Size Mattress

Bunk beds come in two sizes, regular and extra long. The regular mattress is five inches shorter than the extra long. If a regular mattress is mistakenly placed on an extra-long frame, it may fall through and injure a child below. Remember, a mattress too small for the top bed frame is a death trap. Be sure you have the correct mattress sizes for your child's bunk bed.

Rules to Follow When Using Bunk Beds

- Never allow your child to play on bunk beds. Many children fall from bunk beds when playing on the top bunk or when climbing up or down.
- Move all other bedroom furniture and large toys at least six feet from a bunk bed. By doing this you decrease the chances that your child will be injured during a fall.
- Do not place a bunk bed near a ceiling fan.
- Be sure the ladder is well secured to the bed frame.
- Make sure the ceiling is high enough for a bunk bed, so your child isn't constantly knocking his head.
- Install a night-light in your child's room to improve visibility and prevent stumbling when climbing to and from the top bunk. Negotiating a ladder in the dark is difficult, especially when a child is tired.

Carbon Monoxide

WHAT IS IT?

Carbon monoxide (CO) is an odorless, colorless gas produced by burning fossil fuels such as gasoline, kerosene, propane, natural gas, and wood. The gas is emitted from automobiles, furnaces, gas ranges, fireplaces, charcoal grills, and oil-burning appliances. Often called the "silent killer," CO cannot be smelled, seen, or touched and is deadly when inhaled. It can sneak up on unwary victims and strike without notice.

HOW CO POISONS THE BODY

From the lungs, CO enters a person's bloodstream and prevents hemoglobin in the red blood cells from carrying oxygen to other vital organs. In high concentrations, CO will completely shut down the body's ability to utilize oxygen. A lack of oxygen for more than a few minutes causes permanent damage to the brain and heart, causing victims of severe CO poisoning to essentially suffocate from within.

WHOM DOES IT USUALLY HURT?

At least half of the 1,200 poisoning deaths in the United States each year are caused by carbon monoxide. Another 5,000 people are injured by CO and require treatment in emergency rooms. Children represent a large percentage of CO victims. Over 300 children under the age of five years are killed each year by CO poisoning. These deaths usually occur in the home, the most common place that people are exposed to CO.

HOW MIGHT CO GET INTO MY HOME?

Carbon monoxide can enter your home through an attached garage if an automobile is left running, but it can enter a home by many other routes. Any appliance that uses natural fuel has the potential to release CO into the air. Most cases of CO poisoning occur during the colder months of the year when gas furnaces and fireplaces are used.

- An old furnace with holes from rusting or breakage can leak CO into your home, as can a fireplace that leaks or is poorly ventilated. Look for cracks or missing mortar in the bricks of your fireplace. This can be a point of entry for CO.
- Water heaters, stoves, and space heaters are other appliances that can release CO.
- Never let the ventilation duct of your gas oven empty into the attic. Be sure your duct travels to the exterior of your home. The same holds true for wood-burning stoves and other such appliances. Vent them outside and not into any area of your home.

HTPV Pipes

Some gas furnaces manufactured within the last ten years use high-temperature plastic venting (HTPV) pipes that can crack and allow CO into your home. Investigations by the Consumer Product Safety Commission are ongoing. Ask a heating and air specialist to look for this material in your home.

Dangers Signs for CO

While it is true that CO is colorless and odorless, there are some clues that can tell you if you are at risk. Some signs that an appliance could be releasing CO into the air you breathe are:

- a burning smell (while it is true that pure CO is odorless, smoke from a fire can be easily detected)
- cracking, rusting, or sooting of a ventilation device, whether a chimney or vent
- a low-efficiency furnace or hot water heater
- missing or loose furnace panel or ventilation connections
- moisture forming on the inside of home windows
- chimney masonry that is loosening or falling apart

Enclosed Spaces Can Kill

Using heaters, lanterns, or stoves inside a building or automobile can be deadly. Camping-related CO poisoning sometimes occurs when a fuel-burning appliance is used inside a tent. Burning charcoal in enclosed spaces is responsible for over twenty-five deaths each year in the United States. Never use a fuel-burning appliance in an enclosed space. Automobiles with obstructed exhaust pipes due to snow or other debris can also lead to CO poisoning. Always turn the engine of an automobile or recreational vehicle off when sleeping inside.

THE SYMPTOMS

The early signs of CO poisoning are often unrecognized by victims and can be misdiagnosed by physicians because they are so vague. Most people associate the symptoms of mild CO poisoning with common illnesses such as the flu. If these symptoms are experienced on a recurring basis, always consider CO poisoning. Because CO levels can rise quickly and without warning in your home, the nighttime hours (when your family is sleeping) can be the most dangerous. If you suspect CO poisoning, have the local gas company check your home, workplace, or automobile for a CO leak. This service is usually free and takes only a few minutes to perform. Visit your physician or local ER if you suspect that you or your child is a victim of CO poisoning. A blood test can quickly measure the level of CO in the body. Here are the symptoms:

Mild CO Poisoning

- headaches
- nausea
- vomiting
- dizziness
- weakness
- chest pains
- shortness of breath
- rapid heartbeat

Moderate CO Poisoning

- sleepiness
- confusion

Severe CO Poisoning

- loss of consciousness
- death

The Posts' Story

One morning while working in the ER, I took a call from a small-town fire station—a family had been severely poisoned by CO and the survivors were being transferred to us for treatment. Apparently, Mr. and Mrs. Post and their two children, three-year-old

Misty and four-year-old Jason, returned from a trip after the Thanksgiving holiday. The weather was cold and it was late in the evening when they pulled into the driveway. After unloading the luggage, Mr. Post lit the gas furnace for the first time that year. The tired, unwary family went to bed. Sadly, the ventilation duct of the furnace had developed a hole since the previous winter and deadly CO began leaking into their home. In a state of confusion and weakness, Mr. Post got up to go to the bathroom a few hours later. He was so disoriented he didn't stop to wonder why Misty's lifeless body was lying in the bathtub. He went back to bed. Mrs. Post fell from the bed to the floor and died. A relative found them later that morning. Mr. Post and Jason were the only survivors.

A SURE WAY TO PROTECT YOUR FAMILY

The absolute best way to protect from CO poisoning is to install CO detectors in your home. These detectors sound an alarm if CO reaches a detectable level. Place several monitors evenly throughout your home. The International Association of Fire Chiefs (IAFC) recommends that at least one CO detector be placed in each level of your home, in each bedroom, and on the ceiling above every fuel-burning appliance. Detectors can be found in most local hardware or discount stores. Be sure the one you purchase meets the Underwriters Laboratories (UL) Standard 2034. The price for a CO detector ranges from $35 to $80.

Child Abuse

The laws of our land are based upon the principles of freedom, which were meant to extend deep into our personal lives. These laws were structured to grant parents the right to raise children in the manner of their choosing, regardless of religion, race, or cultural differences. But children were not meant to be property. Parents do not have the right to harm their children. In 1873 Henry Bergh, a prominent attorney, brought before the court of New York City a child named Mary Ellen who was being physically abused by her parents. Her bruises and broken bones were proof that she was being physically abused, while her frail, malnourished body was obvious evidence of cruel neglect. But she was initially denied assistance from the city under the premise that her parents had the right to raise her in the fashion of their choosing, no matter what physical injury resulted. Henry Bergh was appalled. He was also persistent. As the founder and president of the Society for the Prevention of Cruelty to Animals, Mr. Bergh argued in court that Mary Ellen, though she may not be protected as a human, should at least be given the same consideration that other animals receive. It was against the law to abuse animals, so why not children? Mr. Bergh and his young client prevailed, and Mary Ellen was entitled to legal protection under the laws already passed for the protection of animals. Mary Ellen was the first American child to be taken from her abusive parents. And the Society for the Prevention of Cruelty to Children was formed the very next year.

Our legislators have since passed an array of laws that protect abused children. In 1974 the Child Abuse Prevention and Treatment Act was signed into law. This federal law has channeled millions of dollars into states, cities, and smaller communities to provide a myriad of services for the prevention and treatment of child abuse. Under this law child abuse and neglect is defined as

the physical or mental injury, sexual abuse or exploitation, negligent treatment or maltreatment

. . . of a child under the age of 18 or except in the case of sexual abuse, the age specified by the child protection law of the state . . .

. . . by a person (including any employee of a residential facility or any staff person providing out-of-home care) who is responsible for the child's welfare . . .

. . . under circumstances that would indicate that the child's health or welfare is harmed or threatened.

This act defined sexual abuse as

the use of persuasion, or coercion of any child to engage in any sexually explicit conduct (or any simulation of such conduct) for the purpose of

producing an individual depiction of such conduct, or

rape, molestation, prostitution, or

incest with children.

How and why a person could purposely harm a child most of us will never understand. But the abuse and neglect of children is now epidemic in the United States. The problem has become so pervasive that most Americans are barely moved by the evening news when a local child is murdered. Child abuse is a national disgrace, and the problem only continues to worsen. In 1998, over 1.5 million children were physically abused or neglected in the United States. Most of these children were permanently injured, crippled, or emotionally scarred by the abuse that was inflicted upon them. Nearly 3,000 children were killed by physical abuse or neglect. We can expect even more cases of the same next year.

Understanding child abuse is not a simple task; it comes in various types and grades of severity. In this chapter, I describe the various types of child abuse and how you can recognize them. I also stress the importance of reporting suspected abuse. Early reporting is the most important intervention anybody can take to protect abused children. Recognizing the physical signs of abuse and immediately referring these children to authorities can save young lives. A child who exhibits the signs of abuse must be recognized and reported. If not, that child has a 25 percent chance of being seriously injured and a 5 percent chance of being killed. In almost every case of abuse, the suspicion is present long before authorities are notified. Sometimes it is too late and a child dies before effective action can be taken. In fact, most children killed by abusive parents had early visible signs of injury that others should have reported. Friends, teachers, clergy, coaches, and counselors are usually the first people outside the family to see and recognize the signs of abuse in children. But all too often the abuse goes unreported and is allowed to continue.

Not only is it critical for the child that you report suspected abuse, it is mandatory by law. Every state now has statutes that require ordinary citizens to report a suspicion of child abuse. A person can even be held legally responsible for the injury or death of an abused child if the suspicion of abuse is not reported.

Abuse of the Unborn Child

Cigarettes, Alcohol, and Other Drugs

Even before a baby is born, child abuse can occur. Lifelong injury and disability can result to the child of a woman who abuses or neglects her own body while pregnant. A pregnant woman who smokes, drinks alcohol, or uses illicit drugs is the most common example. Man-made diseases such as fetal alcohol syndrome and crack baby syndrome result when a pregnant mother uses alcohol or crack cocaine. Withdrawal symptoms can also occur to a newborn who becomes addicted as a result of a pregnant mother's drug habit. Clinical trials have shown that smoking while pregnant increases the risk of premature delivery and low birth weight. If you know a pregnant woman who has a smoking, alcohol, or drug problem, help her find a physician or a support group who specializes in drug addiction.

Emotional Abuse

Emotional abuse is a form of mistreatment that is psychologically damaging to a child. It is also one of the most difficult to identify. Millions of children have been subjected to emotional abuse and live with hidden scars for the rest of their lives. Any behavior by a parent that causes a child to have low self-esteem, guilt, depression, anxiety, or fear is emotional abuse.

Not only is emotional abuse difficult to identify, it is even more difficult to stop. Few, if any, laws protect children from emotional abuse. These children often turn to drugs or alcohol or early departure from the home as a means of escape. If you know a child who is being emotionally abused you may be able to help. But be very careful;

families are usually reluctant to open themselves up for assistance. Directing these children to licensed counselors is probably the best and only step you can take when confronted with this problem in somebody else's family. If you recognize ongoing emotional abuse in your own family, seek a licensed counselor or psychologist for assistance.

FAILURE TO THRIVE

"Failure to thrive" is the diagnosis given to infants who exhibit a delay in growth and development. Sometimes real medical reasons are responsible for slow growth in a child, but often it is the result of nutritional or emotional neglect by parents. Hospitalization of a growth-retarded child is usually necessary to give doctors an opportunity to provide intravenous (IV) fluids and nutrition while the parents are taught how to prevent the problem from happening again. Education, counseling, and encouragement of parents will often turn these frightening situations around. If identified and corrected early, a child who is failing to thrive can quickly catch up to peers in weight and stature if proper nutrition and care are resumed.

NEGLECT

Child neglect is an even bigger problem than physical abuse and is also very difficult to identify and correct. Neglect can occur in several forms, specifically physical neglect, emotional neglect, educational neglect, and medical neglect. The general definition of child neglect is a failure to provide for the basic needs of a child. Nearly 400,000 children are physically neglected and 200,000 are emotionally neglected each year in the United States. Though child neglect can be an ongoing problem, if the proper steps are taken by authorities it can be stopped.

Nutritional Neglect
One type of physical neglect is the failure to provide adequate nutrition to a child. I once asked a young girl what her mother had in the refrigerator at home. She replied, "A cookie that is two weeks old and lots of beer." It turned out to be true; this girl hadn't been eating well because her alcoholic mom wasn't providing the proper foods at home. This is an obvious example of nutritional neglect.

Poor Supervision
Another type of physical neglect occurs when a parent doesn't take the necessary steps to prevent a likely injury from occurring to a child. An obvious example of poor supervision would be a parent who allows a two-year-old toddler to play on the side of a highway. This is overdramatized, but you get the point. A more likely example would be leaving that same toddler at home alone for any period of time. Usually parents are not

charged under the law for neglect unless a child is seriously injured or killed. And even then, it rarely leads to punishment.

Emotional Neglect

Emotional neglect occurs when a child's basic emotional needs are not met. A baby not held, nurtured, and loved is an emotionally neglected baby who grows up to suffer permanent psychological problems. This type of abuse often puts a child on the road to drug abuse and results in other types of deviant, antisocial behavior. Though not legally required, parents do have a moral obligation to provide a certain degree of nurturing and love to their children.

Educational Neglect

Educational neglect occurs when a child does not receive proper schooling. A lack of attention to a child's school attendance is one such example. We are just beginning to realize the importance of educational neglect in the United States. Some cities are now holding parents responsible for their child's truancy from school.

Medical Neglect

Medical neglect occurs when a parent or guardian fails to provide adequate health care for a child. It is defined in the Child Abuse Prevention and Treatment Act as:

> *the failure to respond to the infant's life threatening conditions by providing treatment (including appropriate nutrition, hydration, and medication) which in the treating physician's or physicians' reasonable medical judgment, will most likely be effective in the meliorating or correcting all such conditions.*

Children with medical conditions that require close supervision and specific treatment regimens are sometimes neglected by their parents and suffer complications as a result. I come across many families who, for various reasons, fail to follow the instructions for the treatment of an ill child given by their physician. Sometimes medicines are not given, appointments are not kept, or sick children are not brought to the doctor in a timely fashion. These are examples of neglect. The overzealous religious or moral convictions of parents may supersede their desire to have a child treated with standard medical therapy. This, too, is against the law today. Parents cannot legally withhold medical treatment for their children even for religious convictions.

There are many cultural boundaries that must be respected when investigating parental behavior. Distinguishing between child neglect and the normal lifestyle of a family from a particular culture or socioeconomic class can sometimes be difficult. For instance, not bathing a child for a week seems unsanitary. But in some cultures this is quite acceptable and is not necessarily considered child neglect by our laws. Remember, neglect by the legal definition does not occur until the health of a child has been endangered or compromised or if a child goes without the basic provisions necessary to live in reasonable comfort.

PHYSICAL ABUSE

Physical abuse occurs to approximately 400,000 children in the United States each year and is the single most common cause of infant death between the ages of six months and twelve months. Approximately 2,000 children die each year from physical abuse. Any purposeful action that results in the physical injury of a child is abusive.

Common types of physically abusive behavior include punching, slapping, kicking, or burning a child. Physical abuse is the easiest form of child abuse to identify because it often results in visible injuries. Unfortunately, many abused children go without help because the suspicion of abuse is never reported—until it is too late.

In order to identify children who are being physically abused you must first learn to recognize the type of injuries associated with abuse. Some injuries should immediately arouse suspicion. For instance, children less than two years of age have very flexible bones that are rarely broken by accident. A strong bending or twisting motion is usually required before an infant's bone will break. Therefore, a broken arm or leg in an infant is usually cause for suspicion of abuse. This is not to say that abuse has definitely occurred when an infant's bone is broken, only that it is likely. Such injuries usually get reported by a physician, but sometimes even physicians fail to perform their obligation to notify authorities. Never assume somebody else will do what's right—do it yourself.

When a child enters the tumultuous toddler years, physical abuse can take the form of what a frustrated parent might call "punishment." These injuries can be obvious, as in the case of linear marks or bruising across a child's back or legs, the result of a harsh lashing with a tree limb or belt. On the other hand, physical signs of abuse might be small, such as cigarette burns, abrasions, scars, and bruises.

Parental behavior can provide clues, too. A parent who violently shakes or screams loudly at an infant or young child is generally a parent more likely to abuse. What may seem to be a harmless statement made by a parent can also be a clue that child abuse is occurring. A parent heard to make an inappropriate statement such as "When I catch up to that kid I'm going to kill him" is obviously having difficulty dealing with frustration and anger.

Some parents abuse their children by burning them. Lighters, hot irons, hot water, and cigarettes are the typical instruments used. Cigarette burns appear as circular wounds or scars, often on hands or feet. Immersion burns typically involve the feet, legs, buttocks, and sometimes even extend all the way up to the abdomen or chest and arms. A parent who commits these crimes often believes he/she is punishing the child for crying or for other unwanted behavior.

Shaken Baby Syndrome

A crying infant is exhausting and frustrating to parents and caretakers, but to those who are young and already under great stress it can seem overwhelming. Irrational feelings of anger can even occur. Parents who have dysfunctional ways for coping with frustration and anger might displace this anger and shake a baby. Shaken baby syndrome occurs when a young child is jerked back and forth so violently that brain damage results. These parents are often young, financially struggling, and poorly educated. They are often not aware of the dangers involved with shaking a baby. If you know somebody who has shaken a baby, report it to authorities before further injury results. If you ever experience a desire to shake your baby, immediately pick up the phone and call a friend, family member, clergy, or health care professional for help. Corrective action and counseling can always be given before it is too late.

Once a baby has been shaken, the damage can be permanent. Symptoms of shaken baby syndrome range from irritability, sleepiness, feeding disturbances, and constant crying to seizures and mental retardation and will vary depending upon the severity of brain injury. Death occurs in approximately 15 percent of infants with shaken baby syndrome, and permanent disability often results in those who survive.

Medical Conditions That Resemble Physical Abuse

All children suffer bruises, scrapes, and cuts from time to time and some will even get broken bones. This is a part of everyday life for growing children. Just as important as recognizing the signs of physical abuse is understanding the typical injury patterns not related to abuse. These injuries are usually minor and will vary by age. Cuts and scrapes to the knees, shins, hands, and elbows from innocent play activities are quite common in young children and do not indicate the presence of abuse. Older children may sustain broken bones as they begin to ride bicycles, use skateboards, and participate in contact sports. Sometimes it will be difficult to tell what is normal and what is abuse; a physician's examination can be helpful in making that determination. X rays and other studies might even by necessary.

Certain medical conditions frequently generate a suspicion of physical abuse.

Mongolian spots. These are skin spots of bluish discoloration found across the back and buttocks of some African American, Asian American, and Native American infants. These areas of pigmented skin are normal and not related to injury. Mongolian spots go away with time, but they can be mistaken for bruising, which in an infant might raise the question of abuse. Doctors who regularly treat infants can, however, easily differentiate these spots from bruises.

Osteogenesis imperfecta (OI). This is a disease of poor bone formation that leads to frequent fractures in young children. Children with this disease have weak and brittle bones that fracture easily during normal activities. Osteogenesis imperfecta is sometimes responsible for false accusations of abuse by concerned adults. A thorough investigation by a physician and the local child welfare department is usually necessary before abuse can be ruled out.

SEXUAL ABUSE

Sexual abuse includes those actions that involve fondling a child's genitals, intercourse, rape, or exhibitionism. Allowing a child to be used for prostitution or the production of pornographic material is also sexual abuse. Most cases of sexual abuse in the home involve a male father figure who abuses his son or daughter. But other situations can exist, such as when the perpetrator is an uncle, cousin, older brother, or occasionally even a mother. The sex offender is usually known to the child, thus taking advantage of a developed trust. The long-term effects and implications to the victimized child are always devastating. Sexually abused children grow up with troubling psychological issues. Always, immediately report any abuse that you suspect is occurring. The sooner that corrective action is taken the less likely a child will suffer long-term emotional damage.

A Growing Problem
The incidence of sexual abuse in the United States has been on the rise for the last few decades, and we do not expect a decline anytime soon. As many as 500,000 cases of sexual abuse occur in the United States each year. Believe it or not, most acts of sexual abuse are against young children from two to six years of age. And over half of sexual abuse incidents occur within the victim's own home.

Clues to Ongoing Sexual Abuse
When should you suspect that a child is being molested? Several clues may be evident.

- *Child play.* How a child interacts with other children can be the first clue of abuse. A child who continually attempts to play with the genitals of other children is engaging in promiscuous behavior, which is often manifested by sexually abused children.
- *Child talk.* If a young child brings up the subject of sex or acts out in a sexually explicit manner, take notice and don't be afraid to ask that child where the behavior was learned. You may be surprised by the answers.

Questions that you might ask such a child include:

- "Has anyone ever touched you there [pointing to a doll's genital region]?"
- "Show me with these dolls how you play with your daddy [or uncle . . .]?"

Any further interviewing of such a child should be performed by a physician or child counselor.

A child who won't go home. Children might also exhibit anxiety and sadness when forced back into an environment of ongoing molestation. Often a child will refuse to go home if the abuse is occurring there.

Genital injury. Bleeding from the vagina, penis, or rectum should raise immediate suspicion, but never attempt to examine a child yourself. This must only be done by an experienced physician. Genital injury may be recognized by complaints of pain or bleeding in the genitalia or anus.

Miscellaneous clues. A sudden onset of bed-wetting and behavior changes may signal the presence of abuse. Victims will sometimes spend long periods of time alone, locked in a bathroom or bedroom, as well.

What to Teach Your Child
It is very difficult to identify those people capable of molesting a child, but fortunately there are several steps you can take in preventing such predators from ever bringing harm to your child.

- First, explain to your child that some people try to hurt children or take them away from their family.
- Teach your child what "private places" are so there is no misunderstanding, and explain that nobody should ever touch her there.
- Teach your child to yell, scream, kick, and escape quickly when somebody tries to hurt her, take her away, or touch her in a "private place."
- Role-playing is a great way to teach your child about sexual advances. Show your child the more subtle moves that a molester might try: a hand on a leg or shoulders, aggressive holding, or frequent requests to sit on a person's lap.

Sexual abuse is usually perpetrated by close family members and friends. If you are a single mom, be extra careful when seeking out a person to be a "male role model" for your child; unfortunately, even husbands, fathers, boyfriends, uncles, and brothers can molest children. In fact, if one of these people does not have your absolute trust, whether it's because you don't know him extremely well or because your instinct is trying to tell you something, never leave him alone with your child. Even with your absolute trust, however, do not let this "male role model" spend time alone with your child until she is at least twelve or thirteen years old and has been taught how to resist sexual advances. Exercise great caution before allowing any adult male to spend time alone with your child unless he is your trusted husband.

- Don't be in denial! If you suspect that molestation may be occurring, immediately look into the matter. Ask your child about it and tell your spouse, too.

- Notify authorities! If you find any evidence to support your concerns about sexual abuse, act first and ask more questions later. Immediately call your local child welfare department and/or police for help.
- If you suspect your own child has been molested, ask her about it. Then, if you are still concerned, call your pediatrician or take your child directly to a local emergency room.

A WORD ABOUT DOMESTIC ABUSE

One thing that researchers have learned in their studies of domestic violence is that a family member who abuses a spouse is also very likely to abuse any children in that home. Whenever I discover that a child is living in a home where another family member is being physically abused, I file a report to the local child welfare office that child abuse is suspected. I recommend you do the same.

CRUELTY TO ANIMALS—IS THERE A LINK?

Absolutely—yes! We now know that people who abuse animals are much more likely than others to also abuse children. If you become aware of somebody who neglects or tortures animals, contact your local Humane Society and be on the alert for child abuse. The American Humane Association (303-792-9900) distributes free literature about the association between the abuse of children and animals.

A CITIZEN'S RESPONSIBILITY TO CHILDREN

Remember, your responsibility is not to prove abuse. Determining whether sexual abuse occurred and by whom is the job of police officers, child welfare workers, physicians, judges, and juries. As a citizen, you are only required to suspect abuse in order to report it to authorities. When reporting, you can remain anonymous. If you need further information or assistance with a situation involving a child that you suspect is being molested, call 800-55-NCPCA for free counseling and advice.

Day Care Centers and Baby-sitters

Over 5 million infants and toddlers spend a portion of their days in day care centers, or with baby-sitters or nannies, while their parents go to work. Fortunately, most children receive very good care from caretakers outside the home. Injuries occur no more frequently than they do at home when parents are supervising. But, of course, this does not mean that injuries don't occur. Your child's safety depends on her caretaker's ability to prevent injury.

DAY CARE CENTERS

What to Look for in Your Day Care Center

Many types of day care centers exist. Some are small, private enterprises, while others are large complexes associated with corporations and restricted to employees of particular businesses. It is impossible to make generalizations about which types of day care facilities are safe and which are not. Each center must be judged on its own merits. As a parent you must thoroughly research any center before leaving your child there. Be sure to read this book and diligently search for injury traps at your child's day care center. Never hesitate to bring your concerns to the attention of the director, and if your instinct tells you a particular day care center is unsafe, take your child out of there.

Staff Members

Are there enough? First examine the staff/child ratio and take into account the average age of most of the children at the facility. Look for a day care center that has at least one employee for every three children under two years of age. The younger the children, the more staff members are needed to safely watch over them. With preschoolers, no more than eight children should be present for every staff person.

Employee education. Remember, not everybody is cut out to be a day care center employee. There are few restrictions on hiring, and sometimes poorly qualified individuals wind up as caretakers. Find out if your center has hiring requirements, and if so, what they are. Be sure each employee at your child's day care center is well versed in child safety and holds a certificate of training in first aid and cardiopulmonary resuscitation (CPR).

Are criminals kept out? Be sure each employee at your child's facility has undergone a criminal background check before being hired. While it's true that day care center employees are responsible for only about 1 percent of the child abuse in the United States, you can't be too careful.

Meet and interview. Before deciding on a day care center, interview the manager and several staff members. Be sure they practice the same safety measures you've been reading about in this book. And don't hesitate to ask tough questions about the care your child will receive. If the answers you get are not satisfactory or you feel uneasy about the interview, trust your intuition and try another facility.

Listen to your child. If your infant or young toddler cries each time you bring her to the facility, ask yourself why. Periodically question your older toddler about the facility's staff and pay attention to the response. Your child's general mood is also very important, and if you find her consistently sad or upset when returning from daycare, find out why. If the answer cannot be found, find another facility.

Punishment issues. If any punishment is administered by the staff, it should involve no more than a brief "time-out" from play activities. Withholding of food, rest, or use of the bathroom is clearly out of line and should be reported to authorities. Any physical means of punishment is also a serious infraction. Report it.

Choosing a Facility

Check with your licensing bureau. A day care center must be licensed by the state in which it exists, but this does not guarantee your child's safety. Just recently in Oklahoma, a two-year-old boy was killed when he wandered from a facility's play area after being left unsupervised. He walked right into a street and was hit by an oncoming car. The day care center was fully licensed, but was under investigation by the state. So, check with your state and local licensing agencies to find out if there is or has been an investigation of the day care center for possible safety violations.

Drop by unannounced. Every day care facility is required to abide by specific safety codes set forth by the state. Local inspectors periodically make unannounced visits to be sure all is safe for the children. And a personal inspection of the facility by you is also in order before your child is left there. You can tour the facility when your child is present and occasionally drop by to see how things are going when not expected.

How clean is your day care center? Every day care center should be clean and tidy. If clutter and toys are strewn about and the center looks generally unkempt, then ask yourself what else (or who else) is not being tended to. Be sure to examine the floors, sinks, toilets, potty chairs, sleeping areas, eating areas, refrigerators, and play areas.

BABY-SITTERS

Choosing a Sitter

Baby-sitters are not subject to licensing or any other type of regulations. Consequently, the responsibility of selecting a quality baby-sitter is upon you. Your instinct and comfort level will play an important role in deciding whom to hire. An infant can be very trying and demanding to a baby-sitter. Be very careful about whom you hire. This person should be mature and trusting. I recommend that you only allow an adult with previous child care experience to sit with your infant, and only when absolutely necessary. Follow several other rules when searching for a baby-sitter.

- Give preference to someone you know well, who is recommended by others, and who has trustworthy friends or relatives nearby that can be called upon in the event of trouble.
- If you do not already know the person you are interviewing, ask for references from previous clients. Don't hesitate to contact some of these people for their opinions about your prospect. (I highly recommend that you never let a stranger, even with background checks, baby-sit your child.)
- Look for somebody who has experience and is mature.
- Never hire a baby-sitter younger than thirteen years of age to look after your toddler or preschooler.
- Get to know as much as you can about the person you are considering to hire as a baby-sitter.

Educating Your Sitter

Once you have made a choice, sit down with the baby-sitter to discuss in great detail your concerns about safety. Expect your baby-sitter to have much less knowledge about child safety than you, and spend at least a few hours reviewing home safety measures.

- Regularly provide educational material and review it together.
- Encourage attendance at a CPR course and other educational courses relating to child care.
- Don't forget to pay for the time your baby-sitter spends learning about child safety. The cost of these educational efforts will more than pay for itself by keeping your child safe when you aren't around.
- Show your sitter around the home and teach her the fire escape routes and how to use the extinguishers.
- Do not allow the baby-sitter to bathe your baby or take your toddler swimming; these activities are simply unnecessary, and the risks are obvious.
- Teach your baby-sitter to never leave the kids unsupervised even when answering the telephone or door. And teach her to keep all doors and windows locked, to never let a stranger know she is there alone, and to not answer the door unless the guest is *known and expected.*
- Your baby-sitter should also know never to take your children outside of the home while you are gone.
- Tell your sitter exactly what foods and drinks your child can have and make everything strictly off-limits.

Baby-sitting is a Job, Not a Form of Entertainment

Remember, your baby-sitter is working for the sake of your children—not to entertain his/herself or friends. Never allow your baby-sitter to have guests in your home when you are away. This distraction could be all it takes to leave your child briefly unsupervised.

In an Emergency

Keep a list of phone numbers and addresses in a convenient location for your baby-sitter. Be sure the list includes emergency numbers, the phone number and address where you can be reached, your beeper or cellular phone number, and the numbers of trustworthy neighbors. Also, in an emergency your baby-sitter might forget your home phone number and address, so keep it readily available with the others.

Dog Bites

Children and cute, cuddly pooches and kitties naturally go together. But it is difficult to predict the behavior of some pets when they get near children. Even a docile pet can become vicious when a rambunctious child enters the room. Children interact with dogs frequently and, consequently, they do tend to get bitten.

Nearly 4 million children suffer dog bites each year and 900,000 require medical treatment in the United States, according to the Centers for Disease Control and Prevention. Nearly 90 percent of all animal bite injuries are a result of dog attacks, while cats are responsible for only about 5 percent. Every year in the United States about 20 children are killed by dog attacks. And children, because of their inexperience and small size, are particularly prone to serious injury from animal attacks—nearly 60 percent of dog bite fatalities are children less than ten years old. The same bite to the leg of an adult could cause life-threatening injury to the face and neck of an infant or toddler. A child is more likely to be bitten in the head or neck because the attacking dog's mouth can easily reach her face. Dogs are also prone to biting children more so than adults because they sense that they are being challenged when a child approaches at eye-to-eye level.

Are Some Breeds More Dangerous Than Others?
Your furry friend has probably never bitten anyone, but this does not mean it can't happen. Every dog has the capacity to bite a child. Under the right circumstances, your four-legged family member can become jealous, frustrated, nervous, or even scared, particularly around active children who sometimes do not understand the nature of dogs.

But any breed genetically engineered by man or nature to be vicious and territorial is certainly more likely to produce a dog that will attack with little or no provocation. These dogs are also more likely to severely injure a child because their ability to tear and crush human tissue is great. The force exerted by the jaws of some such dogs can approach 450 pounds per square inch. In recent studies, shepherds, rottweilers, pit bulls, huskies, malamutes, and wolf mixes were found more likely to attack children. Beware of other breeds such as the chow and the collie. I like to call dogs from these breeds "potentially vicious," but making generalizations about the behavior of specific dog breeds is inexact. Although certain larger dogs attract notoriety when they attack, don't let this fool you. Smaller dogs can be just as likely to bite. Remember, it is best to treat every dog around your child with caution. Never let your child near a potentially vicious or unknown dog.

Searching for a Family Dog

Choosing a dog that is child-friendly is paramount to preventing a dog attack. Do your homework and you will find a magnificent variety of gentle, fun-loving, and, most importantly, safe dog breeds from which to choose your child's best friend. A terrific book on this subject is *The Perfect Puppy: How to Choose Your Dog by Its Behavior,* by Dr. Benjamin L. Hart and Linette A. Hart (W. H. Freeman). This book evaluates fifty-six dog breeds based on the opinions of expert veterinarians and obedience judges. Each dog was evaluated on characteristics such as "snapping at children," "excitability," and "destructiveness," among others.

When looking for a family pet, always consider the age of your child. If you have a child less than two years of age or you are expecting a baby, it is not the best time to introduce a dog into the home. It is difficult to focus the appropriate amount of attention required for both a baby and a new dog at the same time.

- Never leave a baby or toddler alone with a dog.
- Enroll your dog and yourself into puppy socialization and obedience classes.
- Consider having your dog neutered—this often tempers aggressiveness.
- Keep your dog's food bowl where your child cannot get to it.
- Always supervise young children (less than six years of age) around your dog.
- Never allow your pet to roam freely about the house when your infant or toddler is outside of the crib.

What to Teach Your Child

- Exercise caution if confronted by a family pet when visiting someone else's home.
- Always avoid stray dogs and never pet an unfamiliar dog.
- Never surprise a dog by sneaking up on it.

- Avoid running past a strange dog.
- Remain calm if ever confronted by a strange dog; don't stare into the dog's eyes and don't run away. Teach your child not to run, but to stand very still. If she is knocked to the ground or falls, she should curl into a ball while using her hands and arms to protect her face and neck.
- Never tease or harass the family pet.
- Never pull a toy or bone away from a dog.
- Never disturb a dog when it is eating or sleeping.
- Never bother a mother dog with puppies.

Obedience Training

Another very important aspect of dog safety involves proper training and obedience. A dog that completes obedience training is less likely to attack without provocation. A trained dog is usually a happy and well-adjusted dog. Never roughhouse or encourage aggressive behavior (like tug-of-war with toys) with your dog, either; he may not be able to make the distinction between playing and fighting. Your dog will always require a certain amount of exercise and attention each day; without this, he is more likely to act out in aggression. If you cannot provide some amount of daily attention to your dog, don't have one in the first place.

What to Do in Case of Dog or Cat Bites

If your child gets bitten, seek immediate treatment in a local emergency room. The saliva of dogs and cats have bacteria in high concentrations. The incidence of infections from bites is therefore very high—as much as 10 percent of dog bites and 75 percent of cat bites if the wound does not receive appropriate medical care. These bite wounds require thorough cleaning. Animal bite wounds may be left open with sterile packing rather than closed with stitches. This will decrease the chances that an infection sets in. A wound left open can be stitched by your physician two or three days later or left to heal on its own. All wounds from pet bites should be treated with antibiotics as soon as possible after the injury has occurred.

Preventing Rabies

Rabies is a viral infection from which all people must be protected. Just about any mammal (i.e., dogs, cats, cows, horses, raccoons, skunks, etc.) can transmit rabies to humans through saliva. If a dog bites and is not known to have been vaccinated for rabies, it should be quarantined ten days to be sure it does not develop the symptoms and signs of the disease. If it escapes or cannot be quarantined, your child will need to begin a rabies vaccination series immediately. Don't worry, though; these shots are not any more painful than other vaccinations, although they must be given in a series over several weeks.

Farms

There are many wonderful attributes to country living that over 1 million children are fortunate enough to experience—friendly neighbors, quiet country roads, and the star-filled sky on clear evenings are just a few of the benefits. But there are also some very serious dangers that parents must be aware of when raising children on a farm. Statistics show that farm kids are three times more likely to be seriously injured than non–farm kids. Fifty percent of children injured on farms are less than five years old. Approximately five thousand children are seriously injured and three hundred kids are killed each year in farm accidents in the United States.

Heavy equipment used for commercial and farm work presents a unique danger to children, because the operator has poor visibility around the vehicle. The force created by this equipment is also extreme and likely to kill any child that gets in its path. Many children are crippled or killed each year by large tractors or other pieces of farm equipment. Children can also be injured when they fall from moving tractors. Even a fall from a stationary tractor can result in injury since the seat is high off the ground. Farm equipment is large and dangerous and should be off-limits to kids. Examples of highly dangerous equipment are:

- tractors
- power take-offs (PTOs)—rapidly turning shafts that transfer power from a tractor to other implements such as mowers, augers, or feed grinders
- grain augers
- grain bins
- silos

- hydraulic machines
- *pickup trucks*—especially riding in the beds *(see also "Pickup Truck Beds—Children Aren't Cargo," in "Automobiles," page 17)*

Other reasons for farm injuries to children include:

- livestock
- ponds *(see also "Ponds, Troughs, and Wells" in "Toddlers and Preschoolers," page 148)*
- electricity
- chemicals and poisons *(see also "Poisoning" in "Toddlers and Preschoolers," page 154)*

Some basic farm safety rules to follow are:

- Never let your child sit on a piece of farm equipment, even when not in operation.
- Never let your child play near any farm machinery.
- Direct your child to play only in designated safe areas.
- Teach your child as early as possible about the dangers of farm equipment.
- Give your child only age-appropriate tasks around the farm.
- Always use a machine's protective shield, so that its working parts are not exposed.
- Keep your machinery in good repair.
- When not in use, place the brakes on and take the keys out of farm vehicles.
- Be sure appropriate lights, reflectors, and warning decals are present on your machinery.
- When starting up a machine, know exactly where your kids are.
- Always check completely around and beneath a vehicle before starting it up.
- Be sure all electrical boxes, cords, and outlets are locked up.
- Keep ladders put up and out of your child's reach.

If your family lives on a farm and you would like to know more about how to prevent farm injuries, contact Farm Safety 4 Just Kids (a national organization that distributes detailed pamphlets and videos on this subject) at 110 S. Chestnut Ave., P.O. Box 458, Earlham, IA 50072, or by telephone at 515-758-2827, or on the Internet at www.fs4jk.org.

Firearms

Our society is very gun oriented. Over 44 million Americans own 192 million guns, 65 million of which are handguns. Like it or not, the private ownership of guns is a way of life in the United States. Unfortunately, firearms pose enormous danger to children everywhere. This scenario leads to an all-too-common tragedy—that of an exploring child who finds a handgun and inadvertently shoots himself or another child. You may not think this will happen in your home, but just keep in mind that a gun is fifty times more likely to injure someone in your family than to be used in self-defense. In the ten-to-thirteen-year-old age group, one out of every eight deaths is firearm related. Most of these shooting deaths are unintentional and occur when another child inadvertently pulls the trigger. And don't think a gun can be hidden from your child. Studies show that three out of four children whose parents own a gun know where the gun is kept. In fact, 40 percent of handguns in the home are not even locked up.

As your child grows up, the likelihood of seeking out a gun that you own increases dramatically. Your child may only want to touch and hold it, but he may even desire to pull the trigger. Your child could also gain access to a gun while playing in someone else's home. A troubled child may bring a gun to school for showing off or intimidating others. Gun recreation such as hunting and target shooting also put children at risk, because some children are not taught the necessary safety skills. For all these reasons, it is no wonder that a great many children are killed every year by guns.

You should also know that many states now consider it a crime when a child is hurt or killed by a gun left in the home. The person who is charged in this circumstance is the owner of the gun or the parent responsible for making the gun accessible to a child.

AIR RIFLES

Unfortunately, many parents fail to take seriously the dangers of air rifles. Pellet guns and BB guns should never be dismissed as harmless. The truth is that thousands of children are injured every year by these less-powerful weapons. Some of these gunshot wounds even lead to death when they involve the chest, neck, or head. As a young patient named Karin found out, a BB gun wound can be extremely painful. Her injury occurred when another child purposely shot her in an attempt to be funny. You see, when parents don't teach the dangers of firearms, their children don't learn them.

GUN SAFETY TIPS

- Always unload a gun before bringing it into your home.
- If you have a gun in your home, always keep it locked in a safe.
- Store the ammunition in a secure place, separate from the gun.
- When cleaning your gun, never leave it unattended.
- Be especially alert when other children are playing in your home. And remember, children who have friends over are more likely to break house rules.
- Educate your child about injury prevention. Even if you don't own a gun, your child may still be at risk. Given the prevalence of guns today, chances are good that your child will come across a firearm at some time in his life.
- Teach your child never to touch a gun and to tell you or another adult if one is ever found.
- If you decide to let your child be involved in a shooting sport, a gun safety course should be taken first. This can safely be done as early as eight years of age.

Home Fires

(See also "Fourth of July," page 52; "Burns/Fires" in "Infants," page 101, in "Toddlers and Preschoolers," page 141, and in "School-Age Children," page 171.)

A home fire is tragic to any family, but is devastating when somebody is hurt or killed. Nearly half a million home fires occur in the United States each year, injuring twenty thousand persons—five thousand of whom are children. Residential fires are the number one cause of burn-related deaths in children. Several preventive measures must be taken to decrease the likelihood of a fire occurring in your home. And further steps can be taken to help your family get out if a fire ever does start.

A home fire can happen to any family. Yours is no exception. Understanding the hows and whys of these tragedies will help you diminish the chances that a fire ever breaks out in your home. Toddlers and preschoolers are at greater risk in a home fire than older children because they are very likely to panic and hide in closets or under beds rather than escape. If a fire does occur in your home, it is important to have a plan.

WHAT ARE THE COMMON CAUSES OF HOME FIRES?

Home fires can occur as a result of:

• faulty wiring
• heaters

- stoves (kitchen flames are responsible for most home fires)
- fireplaces
- smoldering cigarettes, cigarette lighters, and matches
- children who play with fire

Keep young children away from flammable materials at all times.

Flame-Retardant Clothing

Your child's clothing can mean the difference between life and death if a fire breaks out. Manufacturers are required by law to use flame-retardant material in children's sleepwear up to size 14. These garments are not fireproof, but are slow to catch fire and will stop burning when pulled away from a flame. One thing to remember: this material will gradually lose its flame-retardant property as it ages, so when your child's garments begin to show wear and tear, replace them immediately.

Loose-fitting clothing, especially when made of cotton, is much more likely to catch fire and burn a child than snug-fitting garments. More than two hundred children each year are treated for burns that occur when loose clothing ignites. Why does baggy clothing catch fire more easily? Two reasons. First, the fabric is more likely to hang down over a flame or space heater and catch fire. Second, because more oxygen, necessary to fuel a flame, is present between the garment and a child's skin, a flame can quickly grow.

- Be sure your infant or young child wears only snug-fitting pajamas during the evening and bedtime hours.
- Be sure your infant always wears flame-retardant clothing.
- Be sure your toddler sleeps with flame-retardant pajamas at night.
- After numerous washings, the special chemicals on this clothing can lose their effectiveness, so replace sleepwear periodically.
- Be sure your older child wears snug-fitting clothing during the evening and nighttime hours. Loose-fitting garments such as oversized T-shirts, robes, and gowns are more likely to catch fire and lead to burn injuries.

Have an Escape Plan

Nobody wants to think about their home burning, but preparation and planning is an important part of fire safety. Every family should have an escape plan with alternate routes. Fire drills should be run at least twice a year. The primary rule your child should know at this age is to dial 911 and immediately leave the home if a fire starts.

- During the preschool years, it is especially important to teach your child what to do in the event of a home fire and include him in family fire drills.
- Place a smoke detector in each bedroom and on each floor of your home, so everybody can be alerted if a fire starts.

How Fires Start

Cigarettes

Most fatal fires occur between the hours of 10:00 P.M. and 6:00 A.M., when families are sleeping. The single most common cause of deadly home fires is the smoldering cigarette, often dropped when a smoker falls asleep. Smoking in your home should be forbidden, especially when the smoker is lying down in bed, on a recliner, or a sofa.

Cigarette Lighters

One of the biggest causes of home fires is children who play with lighters. In previous years, young children playing with cigarette lighters have sparked over 5,500 home fires leading to the deaths of 150 people and many more injuries. A mandatory standard for manufacturing child-resistant cigarette lighters took effect in July 1994. Lighters are now made in such a way that prevents children less than five years old from being able to operate them. As expected, the incidence of fires due to children playing with lighters has decreased significantly since the passage of this law. However, many dangerous lighters still make their way into homes every year, so be on the lookout and always keep these dangerous products out of your home. Fireplace lighters can be dangerous to curious kids, too. All lighters should be kept away from your child.

Flammable Materials

Flammable materials, such as dust rags, newspapers, gasoline containers, and gunpowder, increase the odds of a fire occurring. Such fire hazards are usually found in the garage or in closets.

- Always throw away rags that have been soaked with furniture oil or gasoline—they are highly flammable.
- Store flammable items in a shed or barn placed well away from your house.
- Prohibit smoking near a site where flammable materials are kept.

Indoor Flames

In winter months the incidence of home fires tends to rise because fireplaces, portable space heaters, and wood-burning stoves are being used.

- If your home has a fireplace, clean it regularly and have the chimney swept out each fall by a licensed chimney sweep.
- Use a screen or window across the hearth of your fireplace to prevent sparks and flames from jumping into the room.
- If you own a space heater or wood-burning stove, always keep it at least three feet away from curtains, furniture, walls, or other flammable items.

Electrical Outlets

- Replace appliances and repair outlets when necessary. Sparks may shoot out from old or worn electrical cords and outlets.
- Never overload electrical outlets. This can spark and ignite nearby flammable material.
- Allow only licensed electricians to work on your home. An unqualified person may put your family at risk.

Smoke Detectors

The most common reason children die in home fires is not flames, but smoke and carbon monoxide (see also "Carbon Monoxide," page 22). The use of smoke detectors has become a standard home safety measure. Detectors are affordable and can be found in hardware stores everywhere. But remember, just because you have a smoke detector doesn't mean it will work. Approximately 20 percent of households have smoke detectors that don't work, usually because the batteries are dead. Never forget, a dead battery can lead to tragedy.

- Place a smoke detector on each level of your home (including the basement) and in each bedroom. Each smoke detector should be placed on the ceiling or six to twelve inches from the ceiling.
- Each month, check all the detectors in your home to be sure they are functioning properly.
- If you have short-life batteries, change them twice a year. Make it a habit to do this at each daylight saving time change and you will be less likely to forget.
- Lithium batteries with ten-year lives have recently become available and are the best way to keep smoke detectors working.

Fire Extinguishers

If a small fire ever does break out, a properly used fire extinguisher can help save your home and everybody in it. There are several types of extinguishers on the market today; know which type you have and how to use it. It is ideal to have an A-B-C fire extinguisher as it will put out most types of home fires, including wood, plastic, clothing, gasoline, kitchen grease, and electrical. Look, too, for the Underwriters Laboratories (UL) label on your extinguisher to ensure its quality.

- Keep a fire extinguisher in your kitchen. This is the most likely place for a fire to start.
- Keep an extinguisher near the sleeping areas of your home and in the garage.
- Make sure the fire extinguisher is in working order. Once used, a fire extinguisher may not function well, so avoid practicing with it in your home. Instead, visit your local

fire department for a demonstration and a practice session with your type of extinguisher.

Devise a Family Escape Plan

It is unlikely that you and your family will ever be forced to evacuate your home because of fire, but it can happen—and if it does, every second will count. A well-rehearsed escape plan can be lifesaving for everyone in your family. Children of all ages can participate in home fire drills, their rolls changing as they grow older. So always include your child in the practice drills.

- Practice a workable escape plan with the whole family at least twice a year.
- Plan two escape routes from your home.
- Designate a doorway on the first floor to be the primary exit.
- Designate a specific location outside your home as a meeting place should an escape from the home be necessary.
- Equip one window in each bedroom on the second floor with an escape ladder in case an upstairs window must be used as an alternate route. Be sure the ladder you purchase is approved by Underwriters Laboratories (UL).

Holidays

Holidays are a time of joy and excitement for the whole family, but as we relax and reunite with family and friends it is easy to forget about child safety. Whether it's a Fourth of July celebration at a friend's lake house or a Christmas Eve gathering with relatives, children are in greater peril than usual because of the unique dangers and distractions that go hand-in-hand with large get-togethers.

EASTER

The modern-day celebration of Easter involves one important danger—candy. I can still remember my own childhood Easters. We would tear into our baskets of colorful eggs, chocolate candies, and jelly beans, tasting them as we went. While older children do just fine with such treats, younger children (under six) can choke on them. To make Easter fun and exciting yet still safe for younger children, focus on the coloring and hiding of Easter eggs instead of eating candy. When your children are older you can then safely add sweets to the festivities. Just make sure they don't share candy with the little ones. Children, especially those younger than six years, should always be supervised when eating candy.

FOURTH OF JULY

The Fourth of July holiday is another favorite for children. Most families enjoy picnics, cookouts, or backyard parties on Independence Day. Children revel in the excitement and fun that these get-togethers bring. Of course, it is the fireworks that make this day unique. Your child will naturally want to join in on this part of the celebration, so watch him closely. Firecrackers, fireworks, sparklers, and other explosives are particularly dangerous to children. In 1997, over eight thousand fireworks-related burns, usually involving the hands or face, required care in emergency rooms—and nearly 50 percent of these injuries involved children. Firecrackers alone account for 30 percent of these injuries.

Sparklers, Firecrackers, and Firework Dangers

Sparklers are often lit and then handed off to children, who hold them as they light up the night. They seem harmless enough, but sparklers can be quite dangerous. In fact, the most common cause of firework injuries to children less than five years are sparklers. Sparklers heat up to nearly 1,800 degrees Fahrenheit and commonly cause burns to the eyes and face when held too close. Some children are burned when they fall onto a sparkler.

Firecrackers are another common cause of injury to children. Not only are they inexpensive, they are readily available. Firecrackers are considered safer than the larger and more colorful fireworks; consequently, parents are more likely to overlook their children playing with them. But firecrackers cause serious injuries to the eyes, ears, and fingers when they explode prematurely or are held too long after the fuse is lit. Firecrackers are also extremely loud and can cause hearing damage.

As children get older they are increasingly vulnerable to larger fireworks, rockets, and other exploding devices. Injuries usually involve the face, hands, and fingers. Such mishaps often occur when a firework tips over, has a rapid or delayed fuse time, or takes an unexpected flight path.

Even if a child doesn't actually light fireworks, there is a significant risk of injury. Danger lurks when just watching others play with fireworks. Believe it or not, most of the youngsters injured by larger fireworks are bystanders.

- Never let a child less than eight years of age hold a lighted sparkler.
- Be very cautious when young children are near others who are playing with sparklers.
- Never let children younger than fourteen years of age play with firecrackers.
- Never let your child get too close to anyone lighting fireworks.
- Your best bet for a safe Independence Day is to eliminate home fireworks and go out to view one of the many spectacular public displays.

Water Dangers

(See also "Drowning" in "School-Age Children," page 172.)

Did you know that more children drown on the Fourth of July than on any other day of the year? When I work in the emergency room on Independence Day, I can expect to see at least one child who has been involved in a drowning or near drowning. It makes sense when you think about it: millions of Americans celebrate the Fourth of July by picnicking and drinking alcohol at lakes, rivers, and ocean beaches. On this day, activities such as boating, swimming, and water skiing are enjoyed by children everywhere. The single most common reason children drown is poor adult supervision, and alcohol is a major contributing factor. Many of the adults that should be supervising children in or near the water are drinking alcohol. In fact, on the Fourth of July, the average lake in the United States has more boaters who are under the influence of alcohol than not.

- Eliminate alcohol from your celebration and your children will be much safer.
- Have your children swim only in water that is designated for swimming and be sure a lifeguard is on duty.

HALLOWEEN

Children love to dress up in costumes because it lets them express imagination and creativity. Halloween is a day when they can do just that. And getting lots of candy while "trick-or-treating" is a wonderful bonus that further adds to the fun. Halloween does have a few dangers, but none that a few basic safety measures can't eliminate.

Costumes
When planning a safe Halloween, first consider all parts of your child's costume to be sure the clothing and accessories allow for safe trick-or-treating.

- Be sure the costume and accessories (i.e., masks, wigs, beards, and hats) are all made of flame-resistant material and that no flammable objects, such as toy accessories, are included. Also, watch out for flammable decorations. Outdoor jack-o'-lanterns have caught many a kid's costume on fire.
- Masks should be soft and comfortable so as not to abrade a child's face and eyes. It should also be snug enough so it doesn't fall down over her eyes and obstruct vision. A well-fitting mask allows a full field of vision from both eyes.
- Makeup is preferable to a mask because it allows better vision. If you can, avoid a mask altogether.
- Swords, knives, magic wands, and the like should not have sharp edges and should be made of soft flexible material that will not hurt when played with.
- Shoes must be comfortable and properly sized. Your child's tennis shoes are best. Never allow a child to wear adult shoes or high-heeled shoes, which might cause tripping or prevent running away if a stranger approaches.

Pedestrian Accidents
(See also "Auto-Pedestrian Accidents" in "Toddlers and Preschoolers," page 139; "Auto-Pedestrian Accidents" in "School-Age Children," page 167.)

There are several common ways that children are injured during the festive search for candy on Halloween. Auto-pedestrian accidents are clearly some of the most serious accidents. Falls are not as likely to cause major injury, but they are very common.

- A costume should be comfortable and hemmed to a length that won't cause tripping.
- Give your child a flashlight to carry for better visibility; this will also allow others to see her.
- Teach your child to stay on sidewalks or at the curbside and never to dart out into a street.
- Use light-colored and reflective fabric to make costumes—this will allow motorists to better spot kids walking down neighborhood streets or sidewalks.
- Teach your child never to run at night and to stay on lighted sidewalks, streets, and driveways. Instruct kids not to travel across people's yards, where obstacles such as flowerpots, yard tools, stairs, curbs, and other tripping hazards may not be clearly visible.

Stranger Dangers
(See also "Door-to-Door Sales," page 185.)

A child who walks alone on Halloween is vulnerable to predators.

- Always be sure your child travels with a group of other kids (or with you or another trusted adult)—never alone.
- Never let a stranger get within arm's reach. Remind your child to practice the rules of stranger safety and door-to-door sales, and teach your youngster to approach only the homes of families you know well and whose porch lights are turned on.

Candy Safety
The candy received while trick-or-treating can also be dangerous. Follow these few simple rules when the sacks of treats are brought home.

- Instruct your child never to eat Halloween candy until you have inspected it.
- Throw away any unwrapped candy, fruits, or drinks collected by your child—it could be tainted.
- Choking on candy is a real danger, so keep small treats away from children less than six years of age.
- If you have children less than six years old at home, lock the candy up and pass it out at your discretion. Give out only small amounts to lessen the chance that the younger ones get ahold of it.

THANKSGIVING, CHRISTMAS, AND HANUKKAH

Thanksgiving is generally not associated with a higher incidence of injury to children, but a few precautions should nonetheless be taken during this holiday weekend. The busiest travel day of the year is the day before Thanksgiving—often referred to as "Black Wednesday." On this day and over the whole weekend, our nation's highways are packed with motorists scurrying from city to city, making accidents more common.

- Be alert for dangerous items that might inadvertently be brought into your home when guests arrive. Immediately place all purses and coats in a secure location so infants and toddlers cannot get into them.
- If you make visits to other homes during the holiday season, be on the lookout for the various dangers your child might get into.
- Avoid driving on "Black Wednesday" and the following Sunday, if possible. If you must drive, take the necessary precautions discussed throughout this book to protect your child from a motor vehicle accident (MVA) injury.
- Drive safely and be sure every passenger is properly restrained.
- Take the largest and safest of your vehicles to improve everybody's chance of survival if involved in an MVA.

Don't let the excitement of the Christmas and Hanukkah season get your guard down when celebrating with family and friends. There is an increase in child injuries during this season because of the many distractions to parents. Always remember, child safety is paramount to a merry Christmas or a happy Hanukkah. Nothing dampens the holiday spirit like an injured child.

Holiday Goodies
At parties food is often set out where young children can walk up and grab it. Holiday treats such as nuts, candies, fruit, and small pieces of cheese or meat can cause small children to choke. Small foods should be kept out of a young child's reach.

Holiday Plants
Mistletoe leaves, holly berries, and poinsettia plants are poisonous and also present a hazard of choking. Plants should be kept away from the busy hands and fingers of your little ones.

Holiday Decorations
Some of our most precious family heirlooms are those homemade, holiday decorations we like to display on tabletops and mantels, but these can be dangerous to young chil-

dren, especially if they contain tiny parts that can be broken off. Small ornaments can be choking hazards, while glass figurines can break and cut little fingers. Consider using only unbreakable ornaments until your child is older, and keep them out of your child's reach.

Christmas Trees

With all the beautiful decorations and lights on a Christmas tree, need anyone wonder why a toddler would take such great interest? Keep in mind that a large Christmas tree might topple over if your toddler tugs on the branches or ornaments. Such mishaps can lead to cuts, bruises, and eye injuries. Small Christmas lightbulbs can injure a child's mouth or cause serious injury if chewed or swallowed.

When your child is less than six years, use a small tabletop tree rather than a large one that sits on the floor. But be careful here, too; an overhanging tablecloth might enable her to pull a tabletop tree down. Either fold the covers of your tablecloth under or tailor it to fit your table just right.

Holiday Lights

Burn injuries to children are common during the Christmas and Hanukkah seasons. Lightbulbs are hot to touch and candles can catch clothing on fire. Older sets of Christmas lights or an older electric menorah can become worn and may have frayed ends, loosened connections, or defects in the insulation, making them prone to producing a shock or a flame.

* Keep your child away from all holiday bulbs and wires, and keep an eye on wall outlets, too.
* Inspect all electrical wires and outlets each year before lighting up your home or tree.
* Whether it's a menorah or Advent wreath, don't leave candles out where your toddler or infant can reach them.
* A real Christmas tree is highly flammable and is no place for candles.
* When using lighted candles, watch out for tablecloths, napkins, and wrapping paper that might catch fire.

Presents and Wrappings

The beautiful wrapping paper and the trimmings that come with presents can also cause injury to infants and young toddlers. Ribbons and strings can cause strangulation and plastic bags can suffocate. Always pick wrapping material up and throw it away or store it immediately after opening gifts. Certain wrapping papers have also been found to contain toxic dyes that if eaten or chewed, could make a young child sick. Be sure toys are age appropriate and safe to play with. If your child receives an unsafe toy, exchange it. Hurt feelings can be mended much easier than a hurt child.

TRAVELING WITH CHILDREN

Hotel Rooms

When staying in a hotel, be very alert to your surroundings and watch out for child traps. As always, the absolute best method of injury prevention is close supervision of your child.

A hotel room in which kids stay should be child-safe; just be sure the guidelines throughout this book are adhered to. If you discover the staff at your hotel does not consider the safety of your child a top priority, look for another hotel.

- Be sure to never leave your child alone, whether inside the room or out. Child predators sometimes use these areas as their hunting grounds.
- Inspect the furniture (i.e., cribs and high chairs) to ensure against defects that might cause injury to your child.
- Search for choking (i.e., small candies and coins) and strangulation (i.e., drapery cords) hazards.
- Be sure all the windows and doors are secure.
- Check the temperature of the tap water in your room. Many hotels and motels keep the water temperature higher than most of us do in our homes and the water might get very hot, so check it out and be careful when running your child's bathwater.

Safety in the Air

Although it is inherently safer to fly than to drive, there is still one important step you can take to improve the safety of your child when flying on a commercial airliner—the use of proper restraint devices (i.e., seat belts and child seats). Turbulence and rocky landings can toss passengers from their seats. Some airlines do permit passengers to hold young children in their laps, but this is not a safe way to fly. Children, because they weigh far less than adults, are more vulnerable to being thrown if turbulence is experienced. In fact, several preventable deaths have occurred to infants who were not restrained while flying. The Federal Aviation Administration (FAA) recommends that every infant be placed in a car seat that faces backward and is secured into the seat by the plane's seat belt. Be sure your child is properly restrained at all times when flying. A toddler weighing twenty to forty pounds should sit in a forward-facing seat secured by the seat belt. Unfortunately, some commercial airline seats were not constructed to adequately hold child restraint devices. Car seats wider than 16 inches will not fit most airplane seats. Children over forty pounds can safely use the airplane seat belt.

Lawn Mowers

Most of us don't realize just how much damage a power mower can do to a person. The spinning blades of a lawn mower are extremely powerful and dangerous, with a force three times that of a .357 Magnum handgun. Power mowers are responsible for over 100,000 injuries each year in the United States; 8,000 of these victims are children.

A large percentage of these injuries are suffered by children less than fourteen years old, and poor supervision is the primary reason why. Children less than six years of age, because of their small body sizes, are at a greater risk of severe injury by a mower. Riding mowers cause the most severe injuries to children, whose injuries usually involve little hands or feet and sometimes result in amputation of arms or legs.

THREE DANGEROUS SCENARIOS

A child who gets hurt by a power mower is usually in one of the following scenarios:

1. Playing in a yard that is being mowed
2. Riding on the lap of an adult operating a riding mower
3. Actually operating the mower

- The golden rule with lawn mowers is simple—never let a child less than twelve years old be anywhere near a power mower while it is in operation.
- Be sure your mower has a "deadman" control handle that turns the power off when it is let go.
- Never let a child younger than fourteen years of age operate a ride-on mower.

Lead Poisoning

Chronic lead poisoning is a major health hazard to infants and toddlers. Although lead poisoning rarely kills, it can gradually and silently damage a child's brain and body. Nearly 4 million homes in the United States have dangerous lead paint on walls and woodwork and over 12 million children under the age of seven live in older housing that could expose them to lead. It is estimated that one in eleven children today have elevated blood lead levels. And it's not just poor children who are at risk—many middle- and upper-class homes also have dangerous sources of lead. According to the U.S. Census Bureau in 1986, 40 percent of all occupied dwellings in the United States were built before 1950, when indoor lead-based paint was routinely used. During these years indoor paint was sometimes composed of as much as 50 percent lead. In 1977, however, the use of indoor lead-based paint ended when a law banned its use.

THE SYMPTOMS

Lead is one of the basic elements. It can poison every system of the body, especially the brain, blood, kidneys, and gastrointestinal system. Our greatest difficulty in determining which children suffer chronic lead poisoning is that they rarely appear very sick. The symptoms of chronic lead poisoning are often mild, vague, and nonspecific. They include:

- irritability
- fatigue
- fussiness

- decreased IQ
- behavior change
- decreased concentration
- appetite change
- vomiting
- constipation

These symptoms usually are reversible if the problem is corrected in time. Late symptoms, however, are often irreversible and include:

- behavior changes
- mental retardation
- seizures
- blindness
- weakness

LEAD DUST

Lead poisoning is likely to occur if a child eats leaded paint chips found on or near walls, but sometimes dangerous lead comes in the form of simple house dust. In fact, more children are poisoned by lead dust then by paint chips. One of the most common sources of tainted house dust is created when paint cracks, chips, or peels from door hinges and windows. Furniture and walls that have been painted with lead-based paint also create lead dust when they are bumped and scraped. Low concentrations of lead dust can cause chronic poisoning if allowed to build up on furniture and other household surfaces.

Keep dust in your home to a bare minimum by regular dusting and cleaning. By doing this you will decrease the likelihood that your child inhales lead dust. And don't forget about the dust caught by your dust rag. Used rags may contain high concentrations of lead, so keep them away from your child and wash them frequently.

HOW CAN I BE CERTAIN MY CHILD IS SAFE?

The only sure way to know whether or not your child is being poisoned by lead is to check her blood lead level. The Centers for Disease Control recommends that low-risk children be tested at twelve months of age and then again at twenty-four months of age. But if you feel your child may be at risk, begin testing her at six months. The need for future testing can then be determined by your physician based upon her level of risk and previous test results. The cost of a blood screening test for lead is only about $25— a small price to ensure that your child is lead free.

HOME BUYERS BEWARE

In a recent move to ensure that home buyers and renters are made aware of potential lead hazards before a purchase is made, Congress passed the Residential Lead-Based Paint Hazard Reduction Act of 1992, which became law in 1996. The Environmental Protection Agency (EPA) and the Department of Housing and Urban Development (HUD) assisted Congress in the passage of this act. This law holds the seller or landlord of a residence responsible for notifying the buyer or tenant of any known potential lead poisoning hazards that exist. If a danger is not known to the seller or landlord, however, no obligation exists. So most of the responsibility of checking for lead poisoning dangers still goes to the buyer or renter. For specific details or a copy of this law, call the National Lead Information Center Clearinghouse (NLICC) at 800-424-LEAD.

HOW DO I TEST FOR LEAD IN MY HOME?

Concentrations of lead can also be measured in samples of paint, dust, soil, and water from in and around your home. Several home testing kits are currently being evaluated by government researchers, but the accuracy of these tests is uncertain. Professional lab testing is much more reliable. If you suspect lead contamination in or around your home, contact your local health department for information on the nearest EPA-certified lab. To obtain a list of these labs in your area, call the NLICC at 800-424-LEAD and ask for the NLLAP/ELPAT list of labs.

GETTING THE LEAD OUT

If your home was built prior to 1977, lead paint may still be present on the walls. During a remodeling project, lead dust and paint chips can be dispersed and scattered throughout your home, exposing your family. When sanding and stripping, be aware that clouds of dust and debris might contain lead dust which can be dangerous to your child. Take your family to stay with friends or relatives or at a hotel during this phase of the work.

If you plan to remodel and are suspicious that lead paint might be on your walls, consult an EPA-certified expert for specific instructions on how to proceed. You will be safer if a professional does this type of work. The truth is, an even better approach might be to simply paint over some walls that are coated with lead paint.

WORK CLOTHES

If you are exposed to lead at work, be very careful with your dirty clothes because they can be soiled with lead dust. This airborne lead from dirty clothes can be inhaled by your child. If you cannot have your work clothes cleaned at the job site or at an outside cleaner, take them straight to a hamper or washing machine when you get home. Do not lay them where your child might be exposed.

LEAD VINYL MINIBLINDS

Certain vinyl miniblinds manufactured in foreign countries can also cause lead poisoning and have been recalled. Millions of potentially dangerous miniblinds were imported from China, Taiwan, Mexico, and Indonesia in recent years. Lead was present in the raw material used to make these blinds and gradually leaks from the blinds in the form of dust. If you purchased such miniblinds before 1996, have a small piece of the vinyl tested at a certified lab. If the material is found to contain significant amounts of lead, return the miniblinds to the manufacturer or the store from where they came. When shopping for new miniblinds, look for a packaging label that confirms they are lead free.

OLD WALLPAPER

Certain wallpapers made before the 1970s have also been known to contain high concentrations of lead. Lead-containing wallpaper can be hazardous to children if it chips, peels, or cracks, because lead dust can be created. Leaded wallpaper may exist beneath a layer of paint or newer wallpaper, so always be careful when stripping the walls of an older home.

DRINKING WATER

Your water supply can be tainted with lead as it courses through the leaded pipes that are sometimes present in older homes or apartments. According to the Environmental Protection Agency, over 30 million Americans might be drinking water that is poisoned with lead. Have your water tested for lead by an EPA-certified lab to be sure it is safe to drink. Certain water filters can take out most lead contaminants, but don't rely on these products if you know your water may have the presence of lead. In some circumstances a plumber is required to replace older pipes.

SOIL

Approximately 30 million tons of lead have been released into our environment as factory and automobile exhaust. This airborne lead settled into the soil and can be dangerous to children who play in it. The soil in your own yard may even contain toxic levels of lead. Fortunately, the passage of strict pollution regulations and the elimination of leaded gasoline in the 1970s has helped decrease air and soil lead concentrations. Average blood lead levels in the United States have since declined. Nonetheless, the ground near factories and busy streets should still be considered dangerous. Be choosy about where your child plays and consider a soil study to measure the content of lead if you live near a factory or highway.

PLAYGROUND EQUIPMENT

The 1977 consumer ban on lead paint was also intended for playground equipment. Many cities across the United States, however, still use leaded paint on their playgrounds. Although no reports of lead poisoning from playground equipment have been registered, it is important to recognize that children six years and younger are at risk, because they are the most likely to eat paint chips. Young children should not play unsupervised on a public playground. By staying close to your youngster you will be sure to notice the danger and steer him away from any paint chips that might be present.

Playgrounds

PLAYGROUND INJURIES

A playground can be a magnificent place of discovery and fun, providing hours of entertainment for you and your child. But injury can occur if safety is not given top priority. Public playgrounds are generally not suited for children less than five years old. But even children between the ages of five and nine years are frequently injured on playgrounds, both public and private. Approximately 200,000 playground injuries occur every year, nearly 7,000 children require hospitalization, and more than 20 children die as a result. About 70 percent of these injuries occur on public playgrounds, while the rest are associated with home playgrounds. And 75 percent of injuries affect children less than eight years old. Half of these deaths are caused by strangulation from ropes on playground equipment or when a piece of clothing gets snagged. The next most common cause of death to children on playgrounds is falling from the equipment.

Strangulation Injuries

The most serious playground injuries often occur by strangulation, when a piece of clothing or a drawstring is snagged on a piece of equipment. Components to playground structures, such as the S hooks on a swing set, torn pieces of metal, and protruding screws, are clearly dangerous.

Some openings in playground equipment can also entrap or hang children. All spaces on playground structures should be less than 3.5 inches or greater than 9.0 inches to prevent this from happening.

Clothing

The clothing your child wears to the playground is very important, because some garments and accessories are more likely to get caught on playground equipment and cause injury.

- Be sure your child does not wear loose or baggy clothing while on the playground.
- Never let your child wear a necklace or string around her neck while at the playground.
- Be sure drawstrings and shoestrings are no longer than three inches.

Falls

As you can imagine, falls are responsible for the greatest number of playground injuries. About 80 percent of the treated injuries from playgrounds result from falls. Most playground falls are associated with slides, swings, and monkey bars. Here are several features that every piece of playground equipment should have in order to diminish the likelihood of falls.

- Check the height of the structures on your child's playground; they should not be higher than six feet.
- Playground structures should also be at least twelve feet apart for adequate running room.
- Tripping hazards, such as rocks, stumps, tree roots, concrete footings, ditches, and debris, should be removed.
- Playground equipment can even fall onto or swing into playing children, so inspect each structure on the playground to be sure it is well-anchored and stable.

And remember to teach your child how to behave on the playground.

- Never push other children.
- Never crawl up the slide, slide down headfirst, or be on the slide when another child is already on it.
- Be careful when running.
- Never jump from elevated structures.
- Always wear shoes, preferably sneakers, when at the playground.

Check the ground surface. Children usually tumble and fall from time to time when playing. Where they fall and what they fall on determines the severity of injury. Hard surface falls account for a significant percentage of playground injuries. Be sure the ground covering material is at least one foot deep and extends at least six feet around each piece of playground equipment. Adequate ground cover is what constitutes the "fall zone" around each piece of playground equipment. This fall zone should be even larger for tall equipment and swings. No two fall zones should overlap, as this might allow two children to collide. And be sure to pick up and throw away any sharp items such as broken glass, bottle caps, nails, pieces of wood, or metal cans that you come across.

Pay particular attention to the ground surface. Is it hard and more likely to result in injury when a child falls? Packed dirt, grass, and even concrete or asphalt are often used for playgrounds. These surfaces are much too hard. The safest ground surfaces are composed of:

> sand
> mulch
> pea gravel
> soft wood chips

Be careful when infants and toddlers are around some of these ground materials, as the small particles can cause choking.

Cuts, Scratches, and Pinches

Minor injuries such as bruises, cuts, and scratches are very common and sometimes result from defects in playground equipment. When inspecting your child's playground, be on the lookout for sharp metal, pinch surfaces, and exposed screws or nails.

A distant memory. When I was five years old and my sister Gretchen was three, we were enjoying our backyard bench swing one sunny afternoon. In those days, the dangerous pinch surface on the floors of these swings was not recognized. We were not wearing shoes and in a single moment, one of Gretchen's toes slipped between the bars of the floor as they were closing together. Gretchen's toe was instantly amputated. Although these swings are no longer made, pinch surfaces can still be found on some pieces of playground equipment.

EQUIPMENT SAFETY

Swings

Swing sets seem to be a favorite for most children and can provide hours of simple fun. But they are also one of the more dangerous structures on any playground. Nearly 25 percent of all playground injuries are associated with swings. Injury to the face can also occur if a wooden or metal seat strikes a child.

• Be sure the swing set is far enough away from other playground equipment so other children will not be struck.

- Be sure there is a large enough fall zone for swinging children. Any obstacle within twice the length of the swing set might result in a collision. Remember, once a child is swinging, it becomes impossible to stop him quickly.
- Be sure the swings are far enough apart from each other to minimize the possibility that children collide.
- Swings, made of wood or plastic, can cut and bruise your child if she is struck. Look for swings made with pliable materials such as rubber, lightweight plastic, or canvas that will soften the impact if one strikes your child.

Slides

Playground slides are also associated with accidents to children. The most serious injuries occur when a child falls from the very top of a slide. For this reason a slide higher than six feet is dangerous. Deteriorating slides that produce protruding metal can cause strangulation injuries and cuts.

- Be sure that adequate safety rails are present along the full length of the slide, especially the top.
- The slope of a slide should be less than 30 degrees so children will not gain too much speed before hitting the ground.
- Inspect the slide on your child's playground to be sure there are no catch points or jagged edges.
- To ensure that a child sliding down will adequately decelerate before landing, the bottom of the slide should taper off, becoming horizontal to the ground for at least two feet before it ends.
- The ground cover at the end of the slide must also be soft and free of debris to soften the landing.
- Be sure the slide is well secured and cannot be tipped over.

Platform Units

Any equipment that allows a child to stand up at a height greater than three feet is likely to cause significant injury in the event of a fall. Adequate and stable guardrails must be present on all such equipment. Sliding poles should not be greater than twenty inches from the equipment so that children can easily reach them.

- Do not allow children less than six years of age on a platform unit.
- Be sure guardrails are placed on all sides of an elevated platform.
- Any platform above two feet should have a guardrail that is at least three feet high around each side, to prevent a child from falling off.

DANGEROUS EQUIPMENT

Despite all efforts to make them safe, certain pieces of playground equipment are simply too dangerous for children. The following items should never be in a playground:

- heavy swing sets that use animals or other characters as the seat
- multiple occupancy swings
- rope swings
- swinging exercise rings
- trapeze bars
- trampolines

PLAYGROUND LOCATION

Consider the location of your public playground. Children have the tendency to run in and out of playgrounds. The surrounding area must therefore be child-safe. Auto-pedestrian injuries can occur if a playground is too close to a street. Be sure your public playground has a surrounding fence that is at least four feet high and six feet from any equipment. The gate should not open into or near the street. Although a tall fence around such a play area can help prevent injuries, close supervision is still the golden rule.

Consider the path your little one takes to a playground. Auto-pedestrian injuries sometimes occur when children are walking to and from such areas. To keep this from happening, follow some simple rules:

- Be sure a sidewalk is present along the path she takes.
- Be sure all crosswalks are well marked.
- Never allow a child less than eight years of age to walk in a street to the playground.
- Do not let her walk along a street that does not have reasonable speed limits.
- Environmental hazards such as ponds, ditches, and trees with low-lying branches should also be avoided as play areas for kids.

Remember, children love to explore when they play and a certain degree of independence is necessary on the playground. Always closely supervise your toddler, but at the same time allow her some freedom to play alone on the magical toys that await her. Just stay close enough to rescue her should she get into trouble.

HOME PLAYGROUNDS

Although public playgrounds offer children a variety of play activities, you may choose to build a backyard playground for your child. A properly built home playground can be a wonderful place in which she can play, with some unique advantages. Not only can you closely supervise her, you can also control the safety of your playground equipment. In this section, a few basic rules of home playgrounds are discussed. Otherwise, the same principles of public playground safety hold true.

Purchasing Playground Equipment

Home playground equipment is not yet subject to mandatory safety standards. However, the Playground Equipment Manufacturers Associated (PEMA), a consortium of home playground equipment manufacturers, voluntarily conforms to the guidelines set forth by the American Society for Testing and Materials (ASTM).

• Be sure the ASTM label is on each piece of home playground equipment that you purchase.
• Look for equipment that is made of wood and/or plastic material rather than metal. This will help prevent burn injuries that can occur with hot metal surfaces.

Location

The location of your playground is a major safety factor. Follow these rules when choosing the site for your child's home playground.

• Build the play area so it is visible from your home, especially from rooms where you frequently relax or work, such as the family room and kitchen.
• Never build your home playground next to a pool; this will only increase the danger of a drowning.
• To keep children in the play area, construct a fence around your yard. A fence is a major factor in preventing children from darting into the street. (Follow the guidelines for fences in "Swimming Pools" in "Sports and Recreation," page 80.)
• Also try to put your playground in a shady part of the yard. This will prevent your child from being overexposed to the sun and scorched by hot surfaces.

Maintenance

As with public playgrounds, routine inspections and maintenance is mandatory. At least once a month, check to be sure there are no rusted or rotted parts and look for loose screws or bolts, unstable parts, splinters, or frayed ropes. Immediately fix or replace any defects you come across in your equipment. Rake the ground-covering material frequently to keep the surface at an even depth.

Sports and Recreation

How we unwind and what we do for fun to a great extent defines who we are. Sporting and recreational activities give us diversions from the daily grind of weekday jobs. But what if these activities are dangerous? For many people, quitting an enjoyed sport is not an option even if it might cause injury. Of course, that is a person's right. After all, there is inherent risk in everything we do. But certain activities are very dangerous, and extra consideration should be given as to whether the risks are worth it, especially when the participants are children. Remember it is your child's life, health, and well-being we're talking about, not yours. Children are not old enough to make informed decisions about their own health, no matter how mature you believe them to be. Think about this the next time your child begs your permission to join other kids in an activity that you think could be dangerous.

Every year, nearly 4.5 million child injuries occur during athletic and recreational activities in the United States. Of course, the nature of these accidents change as children get older. Most of these injuries are relatively easy to predict and prevent. But it is important to know which injuries are most likely to occur so that precautions can be taken and proper safety equipment used. Fortunately, most sporting activities can safely be enjoyed by taking a few simple steps. This chapter will address the more popular sports and will highlight the necessary precautions to take when children are involved.

HEAD INJURIES

Head injuries account for most of the serious trauma associated with sports and recreation. Approximately sixty thousand head injuries occur in children each year on playground equipment, bicycles, skateboards, and roller skates, and in organized sports such as football. Most can be prevented by using protective headgear, while others can be avoided by practicing certain rules of safety that are discussed throughout this chapter.

BICYCLING

Bicycling is part of our society's fabric and is enjoyed by more than 100 million Americans every year. It is extremely fun and can provide exercise for the whole family. As your child gets older, his bike will become an integral part of his independence. It will probably be the primary mode of his transportation to and from the homes of nearby friends. But the hazards of bicycling must also be appreciated. Fortunately, most bicycle injuries do not jeopardize a child's health. Falls and minor collisions usually lead only to scrapes and bruises. Deeper cuts and broken bones occur less frequently. Serious injuries to the head and neck, however, are not uncommon. Approximately 1,300 bicycling deaths occur in the United States each year, and over 500,000 people are seen in emergency rooms every year for bicycling injuries. Children, as usual, are at greater risk of injury than adults. In fact, 50 percent of all bicycle-related fatalities involve children. Most likely to be injured are children between the ages of five and fifteen years.

Bicycles and Automobiles—A Deadly Mix

When it comes to serious bicycle injuries, one cause stands out—crashes with automobiles. In fact, 70 percent of bicycle-related fatalities result from collisions with automobiles. In 1997, 250 children were killed when the bicycles they were riding collided with motor vehicles; 97 percent of the fatally injured were not wearing helmets.

By limiting your youngster's biking to off-road locations, implementing early riding curfews, and having him wear a helmet, you will dramatically decrease his risk of suffering a serious injury. Keep in mind two important facts that relate to bicycle accidents.

- Most bicycle accidents involving an automobile occur when a child is exiting a driveway, crossing a street, or crossing an intersection.
- Most such accidents occur in the evening hours.

Bicycle Helmets

In 70 to 80 percent of bicycle-related fatalities, head injury is the cause of death. In 1996, 757 bicyclists were killed when struck by motor vehicles; 96 percent of those killed were not wearing helmets. Head injury also leads to other serious medical problems such as seizures, headaches, mental retardation, and chronic disability. Most of these deaths and disabilities can easily be prevented. Always be sure your child wears a standard bicycle helmet. There is no doubt about it—helmets have been proven to prevent bicycle-related head injuries. When properly worn, they can reduce the likelihood of death by at least 85 percent. But so far, the message has been slow in its public acceptance.

Certification. Can a child wear just any helmet when bicycling? The answer to this question is a resounding NO. Helmets designed for other sports, such as football or wrestling, do not provide the same type of protection for bicyclists and will not allow adequate visibility. Bicycle helmets have traditionally been certified by two nationally recognized organizations, the Snell Memorial Foundation and the American Society for Testing and Materials (ASTM). The U.S. Consumer Product Safety Commission (CPSC) has developed a new standard that went into effect in February 1999. Since then, all new helmets are required to be certified by the CPSC. Helmets not approved by the CPSC may be composed of material that does not provide adequate cushioning upon impact or may have design flaws. Be sure the new helmet your child wears is certified by the CPSC for bicycling safety.

Style. Bicycle helmets come in two basic styles, soft- and hard-shelled. The difference between the two is an additional tough plastic outer layer on hard-shelled helmets. This outer shell provides protection against penetrating injuries from sharp objects that might be encountered in an accident. Both types have an outer layer of polystyrene that encloses the hard foam material made to absorb the shock of an impact. Both hard- and soft-shelled helmets are safe and approved for use while bicycling.

Take your child with you when shopping for a helmet and let him choose the style. The look and feel of a bicycle helmet should be as important to you as it is to your child. If your child likes the helmet, he will be more inclined to wear it regularly. Just be sure the helmet color is bright so that others can easily spot him while he is bicycling.

Fitting a helmet. A helmet must also fit properly to be effective.

- Be sure the bicycle helmet on your child's head is snug, but not too tight, and does not block any part of the visual field.
- Be sure the helmet cannot easily be moved or pulled off when your child wears it.
- Position the helmet so it is straight atop your child's head, not at an angle, and fasten the chin strap and buckle to keep it in place.

A damaged helmet. A helmet is usually only good for one crash. After that, the foam may no longer provide adequate protection. If you have concern about a helmet's usefulness, send it to the manufacturer for inspection. Keep in mind, though, that it is probably cheaper and easier simply to throw away the helmet in question and purchase another.

Bicycle Size Is Very Important

The wide array of bicycle styles and colors can make any parent dizzy when searching for one that is just right. But take a step back and first consider the most important quality of your child's new bike—its size. Bring him along when shopping for a bicycle so you can see if the bike fits just right. The following are basic rules to help ensure that you choose the right bicycle:

- Have your child sit on the seat of the bicycle in a riding position while you hold it up. With your child's hands on the handlebars, his feet should sit squarely on the ground.
- When standing over the bicycle with your child's feet flat on the ground, his crotch should have at least a one-inch clearance from the center bar of the bicycle.
- If the bicycle has hand brakes, be sure your child can squeeze them with enough pressure to fully stop the bicycle. Children under ten years of age should always have coaster (foot) brakes to allow for easy stopping.

Manufacturing Standards

Bicycles must also be manufactured with specific safety features required by the CPSC. Reflectors are supposed to be present on the front and back of all bicycles sold in the United States, and on the wheels and pedals. Although they are not legally required, lights on a bicycle provide better visibility at night to the rider and recognizability for others. But as I've stated before, children have no business on the streets after dark.

Children as Bicycle Passengers

Your child will always be at greater risk of injury if placed on the back of a bicycle, no matter how slow and safe you are. The additional weight of your little one will change the center of gravity, making it difficult to balance and steer. I recommend that you avoid this activity altogether. But for those parents who must transport a child on a bicycle, the following rules apply:

- Place your child in an appropriate seat with a safety strap and make sure you equip him with a proper-fitting helmet. Secure your child's helmet before riding. (Helmets made for young children come with removable inner foam padding that can be replaced by thinner pads to maintain a nice fit as they grow.)
- Make sure the seat has a high back and is designed to prevent arms and legs from getting caught in the moving parts of the bicycle.

- Each time you ride, check the seat to be sure it is secured well to the bicycle.
- A sturdy shoulder harness and lap belt must be present in order to adequately restrain your child if an accident occurs.
- Bicycle seats are *only* available for child passengers between the ages of twelve months and four years. Infants cannot hold their heads upright, so until your child reaches one year of age, he should never ride in a bicycle seat as it will fail to provide him with the necessary head support.
- Ride only in parks or on designated bicycle paths; streets are too dangerous.
- Ride slowly to decrease the likelihood of an accident.
- Never bicycle with your child in a backpack or infant carrier; this would dramatically change your center of gravity, making an accident likely.

Teaching Your Child to Ride

A child's first bike will always be a cherished memory. The time you spend teaching your child to ride will provide wonderful memories for you as well. Don't be overzealous, though; it may take the fun and safety out of the whole experience. Ability varies and coordination develops at different speeds in each child. Typically, children begin to ride at about seven years of age. Toddlers can begin with training wheels as early as three, a wonderful way to make the learning process fun and safe.

- Always supervise young riders closely. Never take your eyes off your child.
- During the first few years of biking, be sure your child wears not only a helmet, but elbow and knee pads as well.
- Be sure your child is enthusiastic about bicycling before you begin giving lessons.

In time your child will be riding confidently and training wheels will become unnecessary. Still, leave them on until you are absolutely sure he is ready to go without them. And when the moment finally arrives, give lots of assistance as your child first tries to ride on his own. Support the bicycle with your hands and run alongside the bicycle. Expect some minor crashes and show plenty of support and care when they occur. As soon as your child begins to ride without help, he will want to hit the sidewalks and the streets. This is a dramatic transition, one in which the bicycle goes from being a toy in the yard to a vehicle. Be careful! Your child does not yet have the level of respect for safety that is necessary to ride alone. Supervise your child and allow riding only in the yard or in other safe, off-road locations until he is at least nine years old. Once he begins to bicycle in the street, supervision is necessary until he is at least twelve years old. Of course, there is nothing magic about these ages. Such guidelines will only give you a general idea of when your child is likely to demonstrate fully an understanding of bicycling rules and thus be ready to ride around the neighborhood without your presence. Each child will mature at a different rate and each will be ready to ride at a different age.

Basic Bicycle Safety

Begin teaching road safety as soon as possible. Every bicyclist who rides in the street must follow the traffic laws that apply. When is a child old enough to understand and follow these laws? Child psychologists believe that not until children reach nine or ten years of age do they have the mental capacity or quick decision-making ability that is necessary to follow basic traffic rules.

The following rules are a must for every bicyclist to know:

- Always wear a bicycle helmet.
- See and be seen. Always wear bright-colored clothes that allow maximum visibility to others, and equip the bike with reflectors.
- Be alert. Always look for traffic.
- Travel in the direction of traffic when possible.
- Always stop when entering an intersection, street, or parking lot and look in every direction before crossing, whether there is a stop sign or not.
- Always walk your bike across busy streets and intersections.
- Never bicycle after dark or in bad weather; call home for a ride if necessary.
- Never use headphones while riding. This can prevent hearing pedestrians, other bicyclists, or motor vehicles that might be approaching.
- Never ride close to parked cars—somebody could open a door. Hundreds of children are hurt every year when they ride into opening car doors.
- Obey all traffic signs and lights.

The sooner you begin enforcing these rules, the more likely they are to become a habit for your child. But simply teaching the rules of the road will not guarantee that they are followed. A little psychology up your sleeve is always necessary. Use lots of praise when he correctly follows your instructions; it will go a long way in reinforcing safe behavior. By the same token, use your authority temporarily to revoke bicycling privileges when safety rules are disobeyed. Encourage his friends to follow the same bicycle safety rules; this will set a neighborhood standard for all the kids to follow. Also, he will be more likely to ride safely if not standing out from friends while doing so.

Be a great role model. Remember, as a parent you are a role model for all children around you. Children are likely to follow the example you set for better or for worse. If you practice safe biking, they will follow your lead.

Safe Clothing When Bicycling

The clothes your child wears while riding are also very important. The two most important qualities are color and fit. First, be sure bright-colored clothing (especially a white top) is worn, so visibility to others will be the greatest. Second, be sure your child wears well-fitting clothing when bicycling. Loose or baggy clothing seems to be the fad for younger kids these days, but when bicycling, loose fabric can get caught in the moving parts of the bike and lead to an accident.

Community Safety Classes

Education outside the home can also be invaluable. Look for community organizations that teach child safety. Your child should take a safety class before bicycling in the street. If your community does not have such a program, ask for help in organizing one through your local police or fire department.

HOME EXERCISE EQUIPMENT

With the booming interest in health and fitness, exercise equipment finds its way into private homes now more than ever. The number of child injuries associated with exercise equipment has increased as well. In 1991, the National Electronic Injury Surveillance System (NEISS) reported over 25,000 emergency room visits for injuries associated with home exercise equipment. More important, half of those patients were less than fifteen years of age. Stationary bicycles, weight machines, and jump ropes alone were responsible for 85 percent of the injuries to children. Approximately 200 to 300 children, usually less than five years of age, annually suffer finger amputations due to exercise bicycles. Weight machines and other heavy equipment cause terrible crush injuries to the hands and feet of children. Infants and toddlers sometimes get tangled up and strangled in jump ropes. Keep children away from exercise equipment at all times.

ORGANIZED SPORTS

Each year millions of children enroll in organized sporting leagues and naturally injuries occur to some who participate. One recent study concluded that sports-related trauma is the leading cause of injury in older children who appear for treatment in Massachusetts emergency rooms. The popular sports that more frequently result in child injuries are basketball, football, boxing, soccer, baseball, and gymnastics. Fortunately, most of these injuries are minor and require little medical attention. Cuts, bruises, and broken bones are the sport-related injuries I usually see in the ER, but occasionally I treat a child with more serious problems.

Head Injuries

Although severe injury and death is rare, it does happen. Approximately thirty football-related deaths occur in young athletes every year. These injuries usually involve the head or neck. About six child deaths are associated with baseball each year. Serious baseball injuries usually occur when one player accidentally strikes the head of another with a swinging bat or a very hard hit ball. Most serious sport-related accidents involve head injury. The proper use of helmets will decrease the chances of this occurring.

Eye Injuries

Eye injuries during sporting activities are more likely to occur in older children. Eye guards, face guards, shields, or masks can be worn by children who participate in the following sports: baseball, football, and hockey. Some sports, such as racquetball and handball, now require eye guards to be worn during competition. Check with your local sporting goods store to obtain information on the proper eye guard equipment for your child's sport.

Heat-Related Injuries

Heat-related illnesses can occur in older children who are engaged in rigorous athletic events during warm weather. Physicians call it "heat exhaustion" when someone experiences the symptoms of extreme fatigue, nausea, vomiting, dizziness, and weakness. "Heatstroke" is the diagnosis given to those who suffer a decrease in level of consciousness as a result of overexposure to the heat. An example of heatstroke is a football player whose body temperature rises so high that it causes him to become delirious and pass out. Heatstroke is responsible for several deaths each year. Frequent water breaks should be allowed to all athletes when the temperature is above 70 degrees Fahrenheit and prolonged events curtailed if the temperature is above 85 degrees Fahrenheit.

Soccer Goals

The sport of soccer has a unique danger to children. Between the years of 1979 and 1994 there have been approximately 25 child deaths and 120 serious injuries associated with soccer goals tipping over. The goals that tip over are usually homemade, portable, unstable, and very heavy. A typical soccer goal weighs anywhere from 150 to 500 pounds. When bumped, an unstable goal can fall over and crush a child who might be under it. The Consumer Product Safety Commission has published specific guidelines for the safe use of soccer goals. For a copy of this booklet write: Guidelines for Movable Soccer Goal Safety, CPSC, Washington, DC 20207.

Rodeo and Equestrian Injuries

Rodeo and equestrian events are fraught with hazards and children are particularly vulnerable. Horseback riders are at risk of falling and sustaining serious head and neck injuries. It should come as no surprise that thousands of children are injured every year while horseback riding. I have also treated several young children who were kicked by horses. Helmets have been proven to decrease the risk of brain injury in horseback riders. Children should even wear helmets when grooming or just being near a horse. And if your child is involved with horses in any way, be sure she is knowledgeable as to all aspects of equine safety on the ground and in the saddle.

Bull riding is an extremely dangerous rodeo event. In fact, it is the most dangerous sport in the United States today. In the years 1992–1996, twenty-eight brain and spinal cord injuries occurred to bull riders in the state of Oklahoma. Forty percent of these victims were less than eighteen years of age. Three of the children were less than fourteen years of age and the youngest was nine. One fifteen-year-old boy was killed during a bull riding accident. None of the injured participants were wearing helmets. Anybody who rides horses, wild broncos, or bulls without protective headgear is in great danger of a serious head injury.

What Can You Do?

In the spirit of competition and with the emphasis that is so often placed on winning, child safety is sometimes forsaken in organized sporting activities. Here are several ways to encourage child safety when your child participates in organized sports:

- Take an active interest in your child's athletic activities. Get to know his coaches.
- Make time to attend practices and competition events.
- Be sure child safety is always given top priority by the coaches.
- Familiarize yourself with the proper safety equipment for your child's sport and ensure that it is used correctly.
- Finally, let other parents and coaches know your concern about safety. You may be surprised how much support and assistance you receive.

OUTDOOR SAFETY

Some of my favorite childhood memories are those from the many hunting and fishing trips I took with my dad. Millions of children enjoy the outdoors every year in the form of hunting, fishing, and camping, but outdoor leisure activities can be dangerous if safety is not given top priority. Fishermen can drown and shooting accidents can occur. Although deer hunters are at risk of being accidentally shot, they are most often injured when falling from tree stands. Duck hunters are at risk of drowning in icy water when a boat is capsized. Your child should be trained in gun safety and know how to stay safe in the outdoor activities in which he participates. And he should always be accompanied by you until he is an adolescent.

All-Terrain Vehicles

Three- and four-wheeled all-terrain vehicles (ATVs) have been associated with an extraordinary risk of serious injury to children. In 1987 a ban on the sale of three-wheelers went into effect. A ban on four-wheelers has recently been under consideration. Approximately 1,000 ATV-related deaths and 400,000 injuries to children have been recorded since 1982. Never let your child drive or ride as a passenger on any type of ATV—they are just too dangerous.

SWIMMING POOLS

(See also "Swimming" in "School-Age Children," page 172.)

There is no greater way to cool off on a hot afternoon than to jump into a refreshing pool. But the dangers of swimming pools cannot be overlooked. Every year over 350 children less than five years of age drown in swimming pools, while thousands more suffer near-drowning injuries. Approximately 90 percent of all child drownings involve swimming pools and 60 to 70 percent occur in ground-level residential pools. And it is not just your own pool that can be dangerous. About 50 percent of child drownings in private pools occur in the yards of neighbors, family members, or friends.

Should you even own a pool?

If you have an infant, toddler, or preschooler at home, a swimming pool can be extremely dangerous. It's not just in-ground pools that are hazardous. Although above-ground pools are much safer because access is easier to control, they are still dangerous to unsupervised children. If you're thinking about building a pool in your backyard, consider the risk to the young children around you. My recommendation: wait until your child is at least six years old and has taken formal swimming lessons. When she is older and if you still want a pool, go for it. Just be sure to learn the basic safety rules.

Fences

A fence around your pool is a critical factor in drowning prevention. Pools without fences are much more dangerous because access to unsupervised children cannot be controlled. Several features on your fence must be present to make it an effective barrier.

- First and foremost, surround your pool completely with a wooden fence at least five feet high.
- Have your fence built so the vertical slats are no greater than three and a half inches apart.
- Install a self-closing and self-latching gate. Be sure the latch is no less than fifty-four inches from the ground and faces the pool. This will prevent an exploring toddler from reaching up and disengaging it.
- Never allow the back of your house to serve as a barrier to the pool. I know one toddler who crawled through a pet door and nearly drowned in the backyard pool. Other possible points of exit from a house are the doors and windows. If your home leads directly to the pool area without a fence in between, keep doors and windows secure at all times to ensure that your exploring infant does not venture out when you aren't looking. And as soon as possible, construct a fence between your pool and house.

Pool Rules

Safety starts with parents. Your children are not the only ones who must follow rules of pool safety. You have some guidelines, too. The important safety rules for you to follow are listed below.

- Always, always, always supervise your child closely. Never leave an infant, toddler, or preschooler alone while in or near a pool. Some parents who know this rule forget it when the doorbell or telephone rings—this is precisely the moment that many child drownings occur. Remember, it takes less than thirty seconds for a child to drown.
- Keep a telephone and important telephone numbers at the poolside to decrease your likelihood of distraction.
- When your pool is not in use, put toys and other flotation devices up, so they will not attract young children to the water. Keep the pool grounds free of toys, tricycles, wagons, and debris when not being used—they can entice young children into the area.
- Keep the pool grounds well lit at night.
- Always close the latch and gate when coming onto and leaving the pool grounds.
- Keep the essential rescue items near the pool at all times (i.e., life preserver, buoy, and shepherd's hook).
- Take a CPR course and stay up-to-date on rescue techniques—so you'll always be prepared to save a young life from drowning.

Teaching safety. Whether you belong to a local swim club or have a pool in your backyard, your older child will probably be splashing away as soon as the summer heat arrives. Begin teaching basic water safety as early as possible, and remember, be patient and persistent. You'll no doubt recite the safety rules to her many times before they sink in. The important poolside safety rules to enforce are listed below.

- No swimming alone, even when your child is older.
- No running on the pool grounds.
- Restrict diving to the deep end of the pool—at least eight feet of water is necessary for safe diving. No diving from the side of your pool.
- No diving into above-ground pools.
- No roughhousing (i.e., dunking, pushing, or wrestling) on the pool grounds.
- No swimming at night or in a thunderstorm.

Pool Maintenance
Certain methods of maintaining and covering your pool can also be dangerous to children. Follow these tips for added child safety.

- Store all cleaning chemicals in a locked location. High concentrations of chlorine gas can be produced when these chemicals are mixed with water. If inhaled, chlorine gas can cause rapid damage to the lungs and airway of a child.
- Always keep children far away from the pool when adding chemicals.
- Place a sturdy cover over your pool in the off-season.
- Do not let water accumulate on the cover. A young toddler can drown in the small amount of water that collects on the soft cover.
- Be sure to secure the cover on all sides and corners so a child cannot slip beneath.

Baby pools. A baby pool can be a very safe alternative for your infant, but it is important to be aware of a few dangers. Baby pools are best suited for toddlers, and then only during very strict supervision.

- Never place a baby pool inside the fence of an adult pool. A young child playing in the baby pool could easily wander from there to the big pool during a lapse of supervision.
- Always empty your baby pool as soon as you are through using it.
- Store a baby pool upside down to dry. Just be aware that an unsupervised infant could crawl beneath and get trapped.

Public Pools and Water Parks

Many millions of children visit recreational swimming pools every year. Strict safety rules and skilled lifeguards generally keep kids safe. But don't take it for granted that your child is safe just because she's at the public pool or a water park. Here are a few rules to help you ensure a safe summer outing at your child's favorite swimming spot, whether it be a public pool, a lake, or a beach.

- Be sure certified lifeguards are always on duty in adequate numbers that allow them to monitor every child swimmer at every moment.
- Be sure your child takes periodic breaks from the sun and water to decrease the fatigue factor.
- Teach your child to always go feet first down a water slide.
- Teach your child to follow the pool rules in this section even when at a public facility.

Swimming Lessons—When to Start

At some point in your child's life, she must learn to swim. The ability to swim is important and will be the jumping-off point to a lifetime of fun in the water. Your local swimming pool or health club should offer lessons to children and personal instructors are probably available. But don't be overzealous. It is possible to start swimming lessons too early. The children should be least four years of age before taking formal swimming lessons. Until then, they tend not to have the physical strength or coordination to swim properly and will remember little of what is taught. You may even develop a false sense of security by thinking your child can swim when she really can't. Fortunately, most public pools don't allow children less than six years of age in the water without adult supervision.

But all is not lost for those children too young to swim. There are still wonderful activities your toddler can enjoy in the water. For instance, you can enroll her in a water class, which will acclimate her to the water and help her develop an early interest in swimming. As early as two years, toddlers can learn to hold their breath underwater for a few seconds, blow bubbles, and coordinate arm and leg movements. Just don't expect her to learn fully the techniques of swimming. And remember, young children require one-on-one attention and constant contact when in the water.

- Be sure your child is at least four years of age before you begin teaching her to swim.
- Never assume a toddler or preschooler knows how to swim, no matter what teaching method is used and no matter who the instructor is.
- Never enroll a kid under six years of age in a swimming class if there is not at least one instructor for each child.
- Be sure your child's instructor is well qualified to teach swimming lessons, is certified in CPR, and has passed a swimming instructor's course from either the YMCA or American Red Cross.
- If she has a fear of water, do not be discouraged. Be patient and give her time to accept the idea of swimming. And don't be overzealous; this may frighten her even more.

The Forced Submersion Technique. This method allows a youngster to briefly sink in the water when learning to swim. Some people believe this sink-or-swim approach teaches young children. But it can be dangerous. Children can swallow or choke on water when submerged. Never put your child in a swimming class that uses the technique of forced submersion.

Inflatable Swimming Aids

Flotation devices are not substitutes for close supervision. They can be dangerous to young children because they tend to give parents a false sense of security. Toddlers can also become overconfident if they wear flotation devices. I once treated a three-year-old boy named Jason who nearly drowned in a neighbor's pool after boldly jumping in. When I asked him what happened, he sadly replied, "I forgot to wear my floaties." Poor Jason not only suffered a life-threatening experience, he thought he was in trouble. Remember, there is usually nothing inherently bad about these toys—as long as they are never used in lieu of close supervision. Some flotation devices, however, may be dangerous in a more direct way. Recent reports have shown that certain products actually have a tendency to force a toddler's face into the water when not being held by an adult.

- Do not be lulled into thinking your child can swim unsupervised just because he is wearing a life jacket, water wings, or a water ring.
- When your child is in the water, be sure you are always within arm's reach, even if he is wearing an inflatable swimming aid.

HOT TUBS, SPAS, AND WHIRLPOOLS

Hot tubs, spas, and whirlpools can be dangerous to young children and should be treated with the same degree of caution as a swimming pool. The primary danger to children in hot tubs is drowning. Over two hundred children less than five years old have drowned in hot tubs, spas, and whirlpools. In addition, because children have a much greater surface-to-body ratio, they are vulnerable to heat-related injuries if exposed to hot water for too long. Relaxing in a hot tub while holding your baby may seem harmless, but the water in most hot tubs is far too warm for your baby's delicate skin. Pregnant women should also avoid excessive exposure to heated pools, as birth defects can result.

- Always place a locked, hard cover over your hot tub when not in use.
- Never allow children less than eight years to sit in a hot tub, spa, or whirlpool.
- If you are a pregnant female, never sit in a hot tub, spa, or whirlpool.

Drain Covers
Drains in hot tubs and some pools pose a unique danger. The sucking action of a drain can pull hair or clothing inward, causing it to become tangled and stuck. Several drownings to children have occurred when their heads were held underwater by the drain covers of suction fittings. Safe drain covers are now being manufactured, but they are not mandatory and are probably not present in your own pool or hot tub.

- Immediately replace your present cover with one that will prevent hair or clothing from getting stuck.
- Always supervise older children when sitting in a hot tub.
- Do not allow children to submerge their heads in a hot tub.

TRAMPOLINES

Bouncing high on trampolines has been a source of fun for children since the 1950s. Lately, the popularity of trampolines has skyrocketed. However, trampolines have long been recognized for their danger to children. In the last few years trampolines have come under international scrutiny because of the tremendous number of injuries associated with them. Injuries from trampolines have nearly tripled in the last six years. In 1990, 27,700 injuries were reported by the National Electronic Injury Surveillance System, while 58,400 injuries occurred in 1995. In 1996, over 83,000 child injuries were associated with trampolines. Most injuries occur on backyard equipment, where close supervision tends to be lacking. Approximately 70 percent of the injuries are limited to sprains and fractures, but many children have been killed or paralyzed on trampolines as a result of brain or spinal cord injuries. The safest place for a child to enjoy the fun of bouncing on a trampoline is at a school, and only when a highly trained supervisor is present. My recommendation: never allow your child to play on a backyard trampoline and be very cautious about how a trampoline is used at your child's school.

If you must own a trampoline at home, follow these safety rules:

- Keep children off trampolines until they are at least seven years old.
- Always supervise any child who jumps on the trampoline.
- Do not allow more than one child at a time to play on the trampoline.
- Forbid everyone from attempting backflips or somersaults on the trampoline.
- Never allow kids to jump from the trampoline to the ground or into a pool.
- Position the trampoline away from other structures such as pools, trees, and playground equipment.
- Place foam padding over the springs and frame to soften the blow if an impact occurs.
- Be sure no objects are nearby that could enable a toddler or preschooler to climb onto the trampoline.

HOT WEATHER SAFETY

(See also "Heat-Related Injuries" in "Sports and Recreation," page 78.)

During the summer, children spend more time outdoors than in any other season. Infants and toddlers will sit or run about the yard as parents visit with neighbors, work in the garden, or just relax on the porch. Young children swim, climb trees, and play all sorts of fun games with each other on hot afternoons, while older children often practice sports or work outdoors. Most warm-weather activities are safe, but overexposure to the sun and hot temperatures must be avoided. The hours between 11:00 A.M. and 3:00 P.M. are generally the hottest and brightest, so tailor your child's activities to keep him indoors, or at least in the shade, during these hours.

Infants
Babies are more likely to be harmed by hot weather and sunlight because of their small size. Dehydration and heatstroke can occur very quickly in hot weather. Their delicate, tender skin also puts them at risk of sunburn.

- Dress your baby in light-colored clothing and a wide-brimmed hat when he goes outdoors on sunny days, so the rays will be kept off his fragile skin.
- Be careful not to expose your baby to sunlight for more than a brief period.
- Until your baby is at least six months of age, his skin will be too delicate for sunscreen. He must rely on protective, light-colored clothing and shady hats and avoid direct sunlight as much as possible.

Toddlers

When your toddler or preschooler plays in the sun, a good-quality sunscreen (absorbs sunlight) or sunblock (deflects sunlight) with a sun protection factor of 30 or greater is definitely in order. The water-resistant sunblocks are best.

- Gently rub the sunscreen over your toddler's exposed areas about twenty to thirty minutes before going out. This allows enough time for the chemicals to bind to his skin.
- Most sunblocks, even the water-resistant types, need to be reapplied every one to two hours. Use these "sunblock moments" to ensure frequent breaks in the cool shade for rest and drinks.
- Dress your little one in light-colored clothing.

WINTER SAFETY

Snowmen and snowballs, sledding and skating would not be any fun without the little ones laughing and playing by our sides. These make for wonderful times, but specific winter dangers do exist. Because of their smaller body sizes, children are more vulnerable than adults to hypothermia and frostbite when exposed to cold weather. The younger your child, the greater the danger. Various types of injury can occur if a child has inadequate clothing and is overexposed to the cold. Frostbite is the diagnosis given when part of a person's body actually freezes. Frostbite usually involves the tips of fingers, toes, and ears. More severe injuries or even death can result from hypothermia, when a person's body temperature drops to a dangerous level.

Winter Clothing

Infants and toddlers generally do not belong outdoors when the temperature is less than 40 degrees Celsius. Always be sure your youngster is well dressed if brought into cold weather. Remember, infants won't be able to tell you when they get cold. Layering will allow you to add or take off clothing as needed throughout the day. The first layer should be a thin, close-fitting garment such as a pair of long johns that will keep moisture away from his skin. The second layer can be a long-sleeve, cotton turtleneck top and a pair of fleece pants. Warm bodysuits, parkas, hats, and gloves are ideal outer layers for young infants and toddlers in winter weather. Appropriate clothing is also imperative when your older child plays in cold weather. Body heat is lost primarily through the scalp and children have proportionally larger heads than adults, so a snug-fitting cap is a must if he is to stay cozy and warm. Of course, proper-fitting gloves and boots are necessary, as well.

Sledding

When the snow is standing high and school is canceled, children love nothing more than to climb that big hill in the neighborhood and race down it on a sled. A few basic rules of safety will help ensure an injury-free outing.

- Do not allow toddlers or preschoolers to sled without an adult.
- Be sure your child's sled is easy to steer.
- Teach your older child to avoid sledding in areas where obstructions such as trees, stumps, rocks, telephone poles, cars, or houses might cause a crash.
- Never let your child sled in the streets.
- Teach your child the proper way to sled—sitting up and facing forward with feet first. Head and neck injuries can occur if a child sleds stomach down and headfirst.
- Be sure your child wears protective headgear (such as a bike helmet) and pads to increase the likelihood of a safe outing when taking to the neighborhood slopes.
- Be sure your older child is always with at least one friend, and preferably several, when sledding. This way, if an injury occurs, help can be summoned by a friend.

Ice Skating and Skiing

Ice skating and skiing are two more exciting activities that children can safely enjoy during the winter season.

- Be sure your child wears skates that fit just right—not too big, not too small.
- Show your child how to lace her skates up correctly.
- Be sure your beginning skater wears a helmet, elbow pads, and knee pads for protection.
- Know the recommendations of local experts regarding frozen bodies of water in your area and their ability to support skaters. A local pond or creek can be an enticing place for children, but man-made ice rinks are the safest places to skate. Depending on the weather in your part of the country, a frozen body of water can be safe or very deadly. I recommend against allowing children to skate on natural bodies of water. Not only is there a danger of falling through a weak patch of ice, but the bumps, grooves, and other imperfections create a rough surface that makes skating more difficult. Your child should never be on the ice alone, no matter where he skates.

Toys

Toys are more than just a source of entertainment to children—they are a source of learning. Toys help children develop creative and interactive skills, and they help us educate and entertain children, adding enjoyment to all our lives. But if not made or used properly, toys can also hurt children. Be sure the toys with which your child plays are age appropriate. Most toys sold today are very safe; however, each year many are removed from store shelves because they are found to be harmful. In 1996, nearly 150,000 children were injured and 20 children were killed by dangerous toys; most were less than five years old.

SMALL TOYS AND PARTS

Choking deaths account for most of the serious toy-related injuries. Approximately fifteen to twenty deaths occur each year when children choke on small toys or pieces of toys. And five thousand children are treated every year in emergency rooms for nonfatal choking injuries caused by small toys or toy parts. Latex balloons account for the largest number of toy-related choking deaths in children.

Children's toys live very rough lives. They are often thrown and dragged about, kicked, hit, pulled, and slammed to the ground. As wear and tear occurs, each toy can become dangerous in different ways. Wooden toys splinter, metal toys develop sharp edges, small parts break off plastic toys, and stuffed animals come apart and spill stuffing that is a choking hazard to infants and toddlers. It is very important that you regularly inspect all of your child's toys. The following rules apply primarily to children less than six years old.

- Keep latex balloons away from your child.
- Keep small toys and parts away from your infant and toddler.
- Check your child's stuffed animals to be sure the eyes and noses are secure.
- Always be sure your child's toys are large and sturdy enough to withstand abusive play without breaking into small parts. In other words, choose only unbreakable toys.
- Fix or replace any toy that appears to be falling apart.
- Do not sell or give away a toy to another child if you think it might cause injury. Broken or worn-out toys should simply be thrown away.

AGE GRADINGS

Many toy manufacturers voluntarily label toys as being appropriate for children of specific ages. These age gradings do not guarantee that a particular child will enjoy the toy, only that it is safe to play with. When shopping for toys, carefully read the age gradings on each package and beware of any warnings or safety recommendations that are included. Having passed strict safety testing, many toys will also bear a label stating that ASTM standards have been met. Always read the instructions that come with your child's toys.

Toys sold in the United States must abide by the Federal Hazardous Substances Act. These regulations deal with such aspects as part sizes, electrical dangers, lead paint, choking hazards, and sharp edges or points. Toys must not be toxic to children in any way, and toys for young children must never have strings, cords, or elastic bands that could cause strangulation. Although this law helps keep our toys safe, many dangerous products fall through the cracks and still make their way into our homes.

AGE-APPROPRIATE TOYS AND ACTIVITIES

Understanding the physical and mental development of children will enable you to better choose toys and activities that are appropriate for your child. The following pages describe the basic characteristics of child development at each stage of growth. Lists of age-appropriate toys and activities that your child can safely enjoy are also included.

Baby Play

Your baby's play activities will change monthly during the earliest stages of life, characterized by rapid growth and development. Some toys will fail to please her and some will be just right. But most important, you must know which toys are appropriate for a developing infant. During the first three months of life, your baby will enjoy colorful toys and pictures. Watching the movement of toys and listening to soothing music will be two of her favorite activities at this stage. Although there are thousands of toys available in stores for infants, you needn't rely too much on toys. The best source of entertainment will be you. Human interaction and touch will not only be comforting to her, it is critical for psychological development.

Cheerful toys such as stuffed animals and pillows might seem a good way to brighten your baby's day. But never place these items in the crib—they can cause suffocation.

Safe Toys

One to three months old. The following toys or activities are best for this age group:

- rattles and musical toys
- soft squeeze toys and balls (balls should be at least one and three-quarter inches, or 44 millimeters, in diameter)
- unbreakable mirrors
- teethers
- bright pictures
- talking and singing to your infant
- pleasant facial expressions

Four to seven months old. From four to seven months of age, your baby will show an increasing interest in shaking, holding, touching, and mouthing objects. She will also start manipulating objects to produce movement and noise.

- rattles and musical toys
- soft squeeze toys and balls (balls should be at least one and three-quarter inches, or 44 millimeters, in diameter)
- unbreakable mirrors
- teethers
- bright pictures
- toys that have holes for easy gripping
- soft baby books made of vinyl or cloth
- interlocking plastic rings
- floor gyms
- a jumper in which your baby can bounce

Eight to twelve months old. By eight months, your infant will begin to take an interest in exploring the surrounding environment. Motor skills are developing rapidly, and soon she will learn to sit up, crawl about, stand, and eventually walk. Watch for her to start playing with objects—using them to shake, throw, poke, push, pull, and drop. Operating simple mechanisms such as pop-up boxes, musical toys, and push-pull toys will provide endless amusement and entertainment.

- musical toys
- soft squeeze toys and balls (balls should be at least one and three-quarter inches, or 44 millimeters, in diameter)

- unbreakable mirrors
- teethers
- baby books made of cardboard
- key rings
- sturdy cloth toys
- pop-up boxes
- containers to empty and fill, such as cups and small pails
- stackable toys in large sizes
- bath toys
- large stuffed animals
- push-pull toys

Toddler Toys

One to two years old. At one year, your toddler will partake in more active play that includes running, jumping, climbing, and exploring. Toys that can be used in these activities will be preferred. Also, toys for building basic structures will be enjoyed.

- big balls for throwing and kicking
- drawing and coloring books
- large picture books
- push-pull toys
- building blocks
- bath toys
- play clothing
- dolls
- make-believe toys (i.e., dinner sets and tools)
- peek-a-boo games
- wagons
- miniature lawn mowers, shopping carts, and baby strollers

Preschool Play

Three to five years old. From three to five years of age, your child will begin to enjoy more imaginative and creative play. Building recognizable structures and using smaller and more complex pieces will be preferred. Group play will become more important, too. As interactive and communication skills develop, she will begin to show more interest in toys that can be shared with other children.

- picture books
- basic musical instruments
- dolls and stuffed toys

- storybooks
- simple puzzles
- nontoxic arts and crafts
- construction toys
- card games
- sand and water toys
- toy telephones
- three- and four-wheel riding toys (with a helmet)
- roller skates (with a helmet)

School-Age Fun

Six to eight years old. During the early elementary school days, your child will be developing stronger muscles with improved coordination and dexterity. Social interaction will become more complex. At this age, she will develop some degree of competitiveness. Activities that involve these skills include sports, music, art, and outside play. Home activities such as reading, writing, and collecting also interest some children. Arts and crafts at home can be safely enjoyed by early-school-age children, as well. Watercolors are safe to use, as are blunt scissors and nontoxic white glue or paste.

- musical instruments and dancing
- books
- board games
- jigsaw puzzles
- riding toys, to include properly sized bicycles (with a helmet)
- sporting activities, to include gymnastics, swimming, baseball, softball, basketball, soccer, and football
- playgrounds

As you can see, the activities and toys that children enjoy become more diverse, varied, and complex as they grow older. An ever-increasing gray zone develops between what is safe and unsafe, so rely on your intuition and experience when deciding in which activities your older child can safely partake.

DANGEROUS TOYS FOR INFANTS AND TODDLERS

As you have already realized, children's toys are everywhere. You will find them in stores, fast-food restaurants, fairs, cereal boxes, and garage sales. You will receive them as gifts, prizes, and advertising gimmicks. But be very careful, because some of these toys can be very dangerous. The following pages contain descriptions of specific toy dangers that you might come across.

Hanging Crib Toys

Hanging crib toys, such as mobiles and gyms with long strings, can be very dangerous and have been implicated in strangulation deaths and injuries to infants. An infant may find the pretty colors and movements of a crib mobile irresistible and may reach and grab the tantalizing toy as it hangs above. If your little one can reach high enough to grab at a hanging crib mobile, it could get pulled down. A crib mobile can cause injury to a playful baby if it falls into a crib, because the long strings can get wrapped around a neck. If your baby can stand up, a crib mobile is too dangerous. The golden rules here: never buy a crib mobile if the strings are longer than four inches, and once your baby can push up on her hands and knees (or reaches five months of age—whichever comes first), remove all hanging crib toys.

Broken Toys and Small Parts

Toys such as rattles and teethers can cause choking if small parts break off. Other toys might simply be composed of dangerous pieces that are meant to come apart. If a toy is broken or seems capable of breaking into small pieces or comes apart, throw it away.

Until your child reaches six years of age, only unbreakable toys that can withstand abusive play should be allowed. Balls or marbles less than one and three-quarter inches in diameter are choking hazards. A useful tool for gauging the size of a toy or toy part is the inner cardboard tube of a toilet paper roll. The tube has a diameter of one and a half inches. If a toy or a removable piece can fit through the cylinder, it is too small for children less than six years. The Consumer Products Safety Commission (CPSC) has developed a similar device called a truncated cylinder test tube, which serves the same purpose. Children should not play with toys that have small removable pieces or parts. Also, beware of pieces that might fall off as wear and tear occurs, such as the eyes and noses of stuffed animals.

Cleaning Up

In order to keep your home neat, clean, and safe, put away your child's toys when not being used. By allowing toys to clutter the floor you increase the chances of somebody tripping and falling. This also helps to preserve the toys. Teach your older child to put her toys in a designated place when she is finished with them. If you have only one child, it will be relatively easy to keep dangerous toys put up, but if you have two or three or more children in the home, keeping track of and cleaning up your child's toys can become a monumental task. Nonetheless, it must be done. Your infant can be injured by the toys of her older siblings. Examples of toys that can be safe for older children yet deadly to an infant include board games, Lego pieces, puzzles, and marbles.

DANGEROUS TOYS FOR OLDER CHILDREN (FOUR YEARS AND UP)

Sports and Recreation

Older children often get hurt while playing, but the toys themselves are not as important as the activity that leads up to the accident. For instance, a ten-year-old child is more likely to be injured while climbing a tree or jumping a fence. Activities such as bicycling, skateboarding, basketball, and football are also associated with more play-related injuries in older children. Keep in mind that only you will know when your child is old enough and responsible enough to play with certain types of toys or participate in specific activities. Use these age limits merely as guidelines and apply your own good judgment.

Children between four and eight years of age have fewer toy restrictions than toddlers, but some basic rules must still be followed.

- Avoid toys with sharp or jagged parts. Wooden toys may develop splinters and metal toys may develop rusty edges.
- Use ear protection when necessary. Some toys are very loud and may damage your child's hearing.
- Avoid toys that are dangerous to the eyes. Eye injuries can result from toys that fly through the air or fire projectiles. Examples of such toys include darts, BB guns, bows and arrows, and slingshots.
- Never allow a child less than nine years of age to operate an electrical toy. These toys can cause burn injuries when used improperly.
- Battery-operated toys are okay for older children, but the batteries themselves can be toxic if leakage occurs, so keep them away from small children.
- Chemistry sets can produce heat, so do not let a child less than twelve years old play with one.

MISCELLANEOUS TOY-RELATED INJURIES

Riding Toys

Nonmotorized riding toys and tricycles are wonderful fun for young children. Beginning at about three years of age, your child will begin to take an interest in tricycles, wagons, battery-powered vehicles, and other similar toys as motor skills and coordination are rapidly developed. Riding toys have many positive aspects about them; however, there are potential pitfalls. Each year, riding toys are associated with over twenty thousand injuries to children that require trips to the emergency room. Tricycles alone account for about twelve thousand of these injuries.

How do such injuries happen? Minor injuries occur when little hands and feet get caught in the moving parts of the toy. Your child could also strike the ground if a toy falls over or your child falls off. Tricycles do not have brakes, and young children are often not yet able to determine when to slow down or turn. Serious crashes occur when children ride without close direction and supervision, and are usually the result of being hit by automobiles, rolling into swimming pools, or falling down flights of stairs.

Riding toys are most appropriate for children between the ages of two and five years. Follow these rules and your young traveler will be playing it safe.

- When shopping for a safe riding toy, look for wide-based wheels and a low seat. These features keep the center of gravity as low as possible, thereby decreasing the likelihood of a rollover.
- Be sure your child is able to plant her feet firmly on the ground while sitting in the seat of a tricycle.
- Always have your child use a safety helmet. Consistent use of a helmet at an early age will also begin a habit of safety that will carry her into adulthood.
- Most important, always closely supervise your hot-roddin' toddler—it is the absolute best injury-prevention measure you can take.

Toy Chests

A nice toy chest can add a touch of charm to any child's bedroom, but they can be hazardous. If a chest lid is heavy and falls easily, it can injure little fingers. Serious injuries can also result from a falling toy chest lid. A heavy lid that closes onto a poorly ventilated toy chest can quickly suffocate a child who gets trapped inside. Since the early 1970s, approximately forty-five children have been killed when toy chest lids either fell on them or entrapped them. Hundreds more have suffered nonfatal head, neck, or extremity injuries the same way. Most of these children were less than two years old. New toy chests in the United States are built with spring-loaded lid-support devices to prevent sudden closing; however, many thousands of toy chests were built before these design changes were made, and most are still out there.

- Install a lid-support device on your toy chest so it remains fixed in an open position and will require some force to close. To purchase a lid-support device, contact Carlson Capitol Manufacturing Co. at P.O. Box 6165, Rockford, IL 61125, or by telephone at 815-398-3110. Have the measurements of your toy chest lid when you call so the salesperson can order the correct size.
- Be sure your toy chest also has adequate ventilation.
- Never let your child play inside a toy chest.

Simply removing the lid can make your child's toy chest safer, but low-set toy shelves are the safest system for storing and organizing her toys. Also, large wicker baskets or laundry baskets without lids make excellent storage places.

PART II

Age-Related Injuries

Infants
(0–12 Months)

The first sight of your new baby will stir up feelings of excitement, joy, and pride. Some of the most incredible moments of your life will take place during the next twelve months! It's also true that you are about to take on a huge responsibility. At times caring for such a precious little person will seem overwhelming and frightening. Don't worry, though; it is perfectly normal to be nervous and even scared at the outset of parenthood. You can alleviate this anxiety by educating yourself and working to create a safe environment for your new baby.

Creating a safety-conscious attitude in your family begins with you. But a child-safe environment is not created by just a single family member. It's important for everyone to work toward this common goal. Explain to your friends and family that safety is an important issue for you and try to set a positive example for everyone around you.

Infancy is the most important time in your child's life, because that's when a child's attitude about safety is shaped. Actions performed now will instill a lifetime of safety habits. By the time your little one becomes a toddler, certain steps, such as being fastened into a car seat, will have become habits not only for your child but for you, too. For example, one day you may find that your child refuses to ride in a car unless secured in a safety seat. Kids who learn their safety lessons early will be more inclined to follow your safety rules (i.e., wearing a seat belt or a bicycle helmet, or looking both ways when crossing a street, as they grow older). Many of her future decisions in life will be based on your practices during these first twelve months. So be consistent and emphatic about your baby's safety from the very beginning.

DEVELOPMENTAL MILESTONES

One of the great paradoxes in life is how the developmental milestones of a child can strike both pride and terror into a parent's heart. On one hand, you think, "Look what he can do!" and on the other, "Look what trouble she can get into!" Understanding the developmental stages of your baby is fundamental to predicting the most likely accidents and preventing them from occurring.

The First Months

During the first weeks of life, your baby's activities will be limited to sleeping, sucking, crying, and moving her arms and legs. Most of her movements will be reflexive and have little purpose.

By the age of one month, a baby begins to move her arms and legs more actively. Squirming, wiggling, and rolling are a few of the movements a baby can capably perform by three months of age. Gradually, infants begin to grasp objects, reach toward you, and are able to raise their heads up to look around. By three to four months of age your baby will also enjoy placing her fingers and objects in her mouth. The dangers to your baby at this age are usually found in those objects that are nearby, such as pillows, blankets, crib toys, clothing, and food. If your baby is exposed to any danger in the first four months it will be because somebody inadvertently placed a dangerous object near her or placed her in a dangerous situation. Your baby will be very dependent on *you* to keep potentially harmful objects away from her.

The first few months of life are spent lying fairly still. But, by four or five months your infant will be in constant motion and difficult to protect. At this age accidents are likely to occur simply because you might not be expecting the performance of a new physical skill. I have talked with numerous parents who were horrified when their baby suddenly learned how to roll and went right off the changing table, bed, counter, or chair upon which they'd been placed. Remember, your infant will develop fast, sometimes overnight, and you need to be prepared for these changes and new skills. **If you haven't done so already, now is the time to childproof your home.**

From Six Months On

By six months of age your infant will be sitting up with support, rolling over, squirming across the room, and transferring objects from one hand to another. The later months of infancy will be full of excitement and pride as your baby begins to crawl, stand, and eventually walk. By twelve months your baby will probably be standing and taking a few steps with assistance—ready to set out and experience the world. The desire to see, touch, taste, and smell will lead her to explore all corners of your home. And although this is a joyous and special time, your level of supervision and concern for safety must increase with your baby's newfound mobility, because babies are fearless and their appreciation for danger is as yet nonexistent. At this age many infants crawl into dangerous situations and become burned or poisoned. Falls from tables, countertops, and beds are also common. Other injuries occur because infants have not yet fully developed the skills of coordination and dexterity that enable them to escape dangerous situations.

SUPERVISION

Careful supervision is the absolute best measure you can take when it comes to the safety of your baby. So if you follow only one piece of advice in this book, let it be this one—**never let your baby out of your sight for a single second.** The only exception to this rule is when she is safely in her crib. Although your home is meant to be a safe and comfortable haven for all members of the family, it is full of potential child traps. In fact, home is where most infants are injured.

COMMON CAUSES OF INFANT INJURY AND HOW TO PREVENT THEM

Now let's discuss the common causes of specific infant injuries and how they can be prevented.

Next is the following information has been organized alphabetically into two categories: "General Hazards" and "Object-Specific Hazards." This format will enable you to first consider the broader issues of safety and the necessary steps for global injury prevention. Then you can turn to the product-specific information that is necessary before purchasing child care products.

GENERAL HAZARDS

BURNS/FIRES

(See also "Home Fires," page 47.)

Nearly 125 infants die each year in the United States from fires and burns. Thousands more suffer nonfatal burn injuries. Home fires account for over 80 percent of these deaths, while other specific causes include electrical burns, scalds, outdoor flames, and child abuse. Many of these injuries can be avoided by following some basic rules.

Clothing
(See also "Clothing," in "Toddlers and Preschoolers," page 141.)

Infant clothing made of flame-retardant material is a must. The material is not fireproof, but it is slow to catch fire and stops burning once removed from a flame. It can be a lifesaver if your infant is ever exposed to fire. Check the manufacturer's fabric content label to verify a garment's safety.

Electrical Burns

(See also "Electrical Burns" in "Toddlers and Preschoolers," page 144.)

Keep your baby away from all electrical cords. Electrical cords may not seem dangerous at first, but remember how your baby likes to put things in his mouth and chew them. He could be severely burned on the lips and tongue if he chews through a cord.

Cigarettes

A lit cigarette or cigar is a common cause of minor burn injuries to infants. If you smoke, never pick up a child when a lit cigarette is in your mouth or hand. And never smoke in bed—a house fire could result.

Other Causes of Burns

One type of burn injury I occasionally see in the emergency room is caused by furnaces that are built into the floors of older houses. An infant crawling around such a home can easily be burned by a floor furnace if a safety cover is not present. Of course, space heaters, radiators, fireplaces, and wood-burning stoves are also dangerous to unsupervised little ones. Outdoor grills also pose a temptation to exploring infants and must never be left unattended during use.

- Cover all floor furnaces.
- Block access to rooms that have these hazards by using strategically placed safety gates.
- Use a playpen to hold your baby during backyard cookouts.

The Most Dangerous Room

(See also "Kitchens" in "Toddlers and Preschoolers," page 143.)

Can you guess which room in your home is the most dangerous to your baby? If you said the kitchen, you're right. The kitchen is a treacherous place for infants, and the potential for burn injuries is the primary reason why. Stoves cause the greatest number of burns in kitchens. Aside from the dangers posed by burners and ovens, pots of boiling water and hot grease can be pulled from the stove by a curious infant who grabs the handles.

Making the kitchen off-limits to your baby. Although the following suggestions are very helpful and should be followed in every home, my best recommendation is to keep your baby out of the kitchen as much as possible. It is easy to forget the potential hazards that surround you, so just try to avoid feeding your baby in the kitchen. While working in the kitchen, put him in a playpen just outside the kitchen area, yet still within your view.

Hot foods. Remember, foods or drinks heated in the microwave can feel cool on the outside yet be simmering hot on the inside.

- Do not use a microwave oven to heat your baby's food unless absolutely necessary. If you must use a microwave, always check to see how hot your baby's food is before it goes into his mouth. By mixing or stirring the food after cooking you will eliminate hot pockets, giving a more accurate temperature.
- Never attempt to hold or consume a hot drink while also holding your infant; it could spill and scald him.

The Bathroom
(See also "The Scalding Dangers of Residential Water" in "Toddlers and Preschoolers," page 142.)

An infant's skin is softer and more delicate than an older child's or adult's and can be burned far more easily. About 10 to 20 percent of scald injuries occur when infants are placed in bathwater that is too hot. What may feel like a comfortable, soothing tub of hot water to you might scald an infant in a single second. To prevent this from happening, preset the thermostat on your hot water heater to 50 degrees Celsius (122 Fahrenheit) so the water is less likely to become dangerously hot when you run bathwater. Just remember, water at this temperature is still way too hot and must be from 27 to 38 degrees Celsius (80 to 100 Fahrenheit) to be comfortable for your baby. Antiscald devices can also be placed on your bathtub faucets, to keep the bathwater below a preset temperature. Although they can be helpful, don't rely on thermometers, thermostats, or antiscald devices alone to tell you that the water temperature is within a safe range. Always use your inner forearm to be sure the water is warm, but not so hot that it is uncomfortable. First learn what water at the right temperature feels like against your skin. This comes with practice and repeated testing with a good thermometer.

CHOKING

(See also "Choking" in "Toddlers and Preschoolers," page 145.)

Household Choking Dangers
Imagine my surprise one day when I looked into the mouth of a coughing four-month-old boy and found an open safety pin stuck in the back of his throat! When his parents brought him to the emergency room for cold symptoms, they had no idea that something like this was the cause of his recent coughing. He ended up doing fine, but it sure made an impression on everybody in the ER that night.

Your baby's natural desire to place small objects in her mouth makes her prone to choking. The most common causes of choking in infants are the following everyday items:

- balloons
- button batteries
- buttons
- coins
- jewelry
- marbles
- nails
- paper clips
- plastic bags
- rubber bands
- safety pins
- screws
- stickpins and needles
- toothpicks

- Always be sure to put small items in a safe place. Search your pockets at the end of each day for any small objects you might have acquired.
- Check beneath chairs and sofa cushions for small objects that may have fallen from adult pockets.
- Be sure desk drawers are either locked or do not contain possible choking hazards.

Pacifiers and bottle nipples. These can break or be bitten into small pieces, causing an infant to choke, so check them before each use for wear and tear. Some pacifiers are poorly designed and more likely than others to be dangerous. Several types of defective pacifiers are currently on the Consumer Product Safety Commission recall list and are in the product recall section of this book (see page 210).

- Purchase only those pacifiers with one-piece construction.
- Be sure the mouth guard is wider than your baby's mouth.
- Be sure your baby's pacifier has ventilation holes in the shield that would allow breathing to continue if it ever becomes lodged in or pressed against her mouth.
- Immediately discard your baby's pacifier if it begins to show signs of breakage.
- Never place a string or necklace around a neck. A pacifier tied to a string and hung from a baby's neck may at first seem handy, but it can be a cause of strangulation.

Foods. Infants don't chew well and therefore are at a risk for choking on food. Stick to baby foods at this age and never give your baby the following foods:

- apples
- beans
- biscuits
- carrots
- chewing gum
- cookies
- cubes of cheese
- dried cereal
- grapes
- hard candy
- hot dogs
- macaroni
- nuts
- pieces of hard vegetable
- pieces of meat
- peanut butter
- popcorn
- raisins
- seeds
- shrimp

- Always be sure to monitor what your infant eats and keep a close eye on her when she is eating.
- Teach older children not to share these forbidden food items. Infants often get food from the plate of an older sibling, so supervise your older children during mealtime, too.
- Know what to do in case a child begins choking; enroll in a CPR course.

Clothing. Be aware that decorative items such as buttons or bows on infant clothing can loosen and fall off and become a choking hazard. Avoid clothing with such features. Check your baby's clothing after each wash and before dressing him to be sure that no snaps or threads have loosened.

DROWNING

Bathrooms
(See also "Bathrooms" in "Toddlers and Preschoolers," page 148.)

An infant can drown in as little as two inches of water. Bathtubs and toilets represent a great danger to infants and children less than four years of age. Remember, it takes less than one minute of submersion for such a tragedy to occur. Typical reasons that a parent might leave an infant briefly unattended in a bathroom include answering the telephone or doorbell or checking on dinner in the oven. If you must leave the bathroom while bathing your baby, take him with you even though you may think, "I'll only be gone a minute." The extra time spent bundling up your baby and taking him along could save his life.

Safe bathing. Bath time for your baby can be a fun time if you follow certain rules of safety. Don't worry, it's okay to be nervous when just getting started. Safe baby bathing is a skill that you must learn. Have an experienced family member or friend who can teach you. A good teacher can be very helpful in alleviating the initial anxiety that comes with a new baby.

During your baby's first few weeks of life it is best to gently sponge-bathe him with warm water, a washcloth, and soap. This can be done on a changing table. After a few weeks, a baby bathtub can be used.

- Never use the sink to bathe your baby—it's too easy for him to fall out onto the floor.
- Keep a close eye on your baby during bath time. You'll be surprised how quickly he can move from one position to another while in the tub.
- When holding or picking up your baby after a bath, be very careful to place your hands beneath her bottom so you don't drop her. A little soap and water will make her slick as a frog!
- Be sure your baby's bathtub has a slip-resistant seat that is situated at a comfortable angle. Always place a towel beneath your infant while he's in the tub to prevent him from slipping.
- Before bathing your infant, place no more than two to three inches of warm water into the bottom of the tub.
- When you first begin bathing your infant, also test the water with a thermometer to confirm that it is less than 38 degrees Celsius (100 degrees Fahrenheit). Test the water against the skin of your inner forearm to ensure that it is not too hot. You'll soon be accustomed to what your baby's bathwater should feel like, but at the beginning it's important to always double-check.
- Never allow a child to stand up in the tub, as he could easily slip and fall.

Bathtub rings and seats. A common misconception is that bathtub rings and seats protect infants from drowning. They don't. In fact, these rings can actually increase a child's risk of drowning because parents who use these products might be more likely to leave their baby unattended in a bathtub. Don't let these flotation devices give you a false sense of security—never leave your baby unsupervised in a bathtub. In the last twenty-five years over forty-five infant deaths have been associated with bathtub rings. In most cases the infant either flipped the bath ring over or fell from the ring into the water. The average time these injured infants were left unattended in the bathtub was six minutes. Remember, nearly every bathroom-related drowning involving an infant is associated with a brief lapse of supervision.

Buckets

The five-gallon plastic bucket you use to wash the car or mop the kitchen floor poses a real danger to infants. These buckets are approximately fourteen inches high. When buckets of this size are filled with water they are difficult to topple over. If an infant falls in head first, he can get stuck and drown. The U.S. Consumer Product Safety Commission estimates that about 230 infants and toddlers have drowned in such buckets during the last ten years. Most of these victims are between the ages of eight and fourteen months. Currently, the CPSC now estimates that at least one child drowns in a bucket each week.

- Never leave a bucket of water unattended.
- When working with a bucket (with or without a lid) of water, always empty it before leaving the area, even if you're leaving for just a minute!
- When you've finished your chores, always empty large buckets and place them well out of your infant's reach.
- Keep your little one away from ice chests (even if they have lids) filled with liquid.
- Never leave a trash can or diaper pail holding water.

Other Bodies of Water

(See also "Ponds, Troughs, and Wells" in "Toddlers and Preschoolers," page 148.)

Be sure your little one does not have access to creeks, ditches, wells, and other potential drowning hazards near your home. Infants and toddlers are at great risk when structures such as these are close by.

FALLS

(See also "Seats" in "Infants," page 128; "Walkers" in "Infants," page 131; and "Falls" in "Toddlers and Preschoolers," page 148.)

One simple and very basic way that infants get hurt is by falling from elevated surfaces they were placed upon. Never place a baby on an elevated surface without one hand on him at all times.

Tyler's Story

I recently treated a six-month-old boy named Tyler for injuries that occurred when he fell from a pool table at home. His parents were getting ready to go out and planned to take Tyler along. His father placed him on the table while putting on his own coat. In the few seconds he took, Tyler crawled off the table and fell to the floor, landing on his head. Fortunately, the little fellow suffered nothing more than a mild concussion, but he could have been seriously injured.

MOTOR VEHICLE ACCIDENTS

The bad news: Sadly, motor vehicle accidents (MVAs) result in thousands of infant injuries and deaths each year. When infants are involved, the injuries can be particularly severe because of their small sizes. Infants are more easily tossed about on impact and the disproportionate weight of their heads to their bodies puts them at even greater risk for brain injury. At 30 miles per hour, a 10-pound infant can become a projectile, hitting the dashboard with an estimated force of 300 pounds. Even a slow-speed collision can cause an unrestrained infant to be thrown across the car or through a windshield.

The good news: Infant and child safety seats can save the lives of our little ones even in the most serious car crashes.

Buckle Your Baby

(See also "Restraint Devices—Never Let Your Child Ride without One" in "Automobiles," page 15; and "Motor Vehicle Accidents" in "Toddlers and Preschoolers," page 150.)

In all fifty states, parents are now required by law to place infants and young children in safety seats while traveling on the road. Despite this, I frequently see children in cars without any protection whatsoever, and I'm sure you do, too.

A properly used infant seat will decrease the risk of injury to your baby in an MVA by 55 to 75 percent. When on duty in the emergency room, I breathe a sigh of relief when an infant from an MVA arrives in a safety seat, because I know the chances of that infant having been injured are extremely small. In fact, I have never seen a serious injury to an infant who was properly restrained in a car safety seat. By restraining your baby in a vehicle you not only protect him, but you set a good example for others in the community. Remember, most MVAs occur only a mile or two from home, so don't forget that even on these short trips your baby is at risk. Always buckle your baby in his safety seat even if you are only taking him on a brief trip down the road.

Two basic types of seats. There are two types of infant seats available for babies: "infant-only" and "convertible." Infant-only seats are for children between birth and twelve months of age, or up to the time a child reaches eighteen to twenty pounds in weight. Infant-only seats are smaller and lighter and can also be used as infant carriers. Always position an infant-only car seat in the backseat of your car facing backward.

A convertible seat requires a little more training because it can be used in both directions. It can serve as an infant seat by facing it backward in a reclining position, or as a toddler seat by facing it forward in an upright position. When your child is one year old, reposition the seat to face forward with the shoulder straps threaded through the higher slots. Convertible seats may not offer the same degree of support for infants as infant-only seats, but because your child can use it up to the age of four years, a convertible seat can be more economical.

In addition to these two basic seats, there is also a "car bed" that lies sideways in the backseat with the infant's head toward the center of the seat. This style of restraint device is specifically made for those babies weighing less than seven pounds.

Positioning your baby's seat. It is vital that your baby sit in the *backseat* of the vehicle. This provides him with the greatest protection if an accident occurs. By placing him in the *middle of the backseat* you will further decrease his chances of injury by keeping him away from a front seat that could be shoved backward during an accident. Facing your baby backward will help prevent his neck from being injured by a whiplash injury and will protect his delicate abdomen and chest from an impact. If your automobile has a front passenger seat air bag it is critical that your baby sit in the backseat. Many infants have been injured or killed by deploying air bags while sitting in the front seats of automobiles.

When transporting your baby in a vehicle, place him in a reclining position (angled no higher than 45 degrees). You may need to place a tightly rolled bath towel beneath the front edge of the safety seat in order to get the proper angle for your baby. Young infants do not have the strength to hold their heads up on their own. This is even more true for those born premature by three weeks or more. The same holds true for infants with breathing disorders such as apnea or asthma. These infants are even more likely to have difficulty breathing if placed in an upright position.

Abe's story. To be effective, a safety seat must be secured and properly used. One night in the ER I examined a baby boy named Abe who was involved in an MVA. He was properly strapped into a safety seat, but the seat was not secured into the car by the seat belts. This was a huge mistake. When the accident occurred, both infant and seat were ejected together through the van windshield. They traveled twenty feet down the road before coming to a stop. Abe was secure in his safety seat the whole time. Remarkably, he sustained only superficial abrasions and went home with his family later that night. The poor police officer who picked him up from the road was still visibly shaking in the emergency room hours later. Obviously, this outcome would have been much worse if Abe had not been in a safety seat at all, but not securing the seat in the car could have been a deadly mistake. Remember, a child not secured inside a vehicle will become a missile during an accident.

Top safety seat mistakes. A recent survey by the National Safe Kids Campaign found that approximately 85 percent of car seats are misused. The most common mistakes made are:

- seat belt not secure—63 percent
- harness straps over child's chest loose—33 percent
- harness straps placed through wrong slots—20 percent
- harness retainer clip not positioned at armpit level—19 percent
- locking clip misused—17 percent
- seat belt not locked—11 percent
- children placed in the forward-facing direction too early—11 percent
- the car seat being used had been recalled—9 percent

There are several types of seats available. When learning the ins and outs of your baby's new seat, follow both the vehicle's owner's manual and the instructions that come with your safety seat. Several general rules apply to all models:

- Be sure you purchase only a safety seat that bears a sticker that reads, "Meets Federal Safety Standards 213."
- When installing a safety seat, be sure it is snug against the seat of your car. Use your knee to keep the seat in place while adjusting and tightening the seat belts.
- Always buckle the car's seat belt after threading it through the safety seat.
- Remember to use only a firmly fixed lap belt when securing a safety seat. Shoulder belts do not work for this purpose.
- Never bundle your baby in a blanket before placing him in a car seat; this will prevent a snug fit. If you must use a blanket, put it over your baby *after* he is firmly fastened in his seat.
- If necessary, place a cloth roll between the seat buckle and your infant's crotch to keep her in a reclining position. Otherwise, never use padding between your infant and the straps, as this can affect their restraining ability.
- Fit the harness straps firmly yet comfortably over the shoulders and thighs of your baby.
- Always be sure your baby's back and bottom are firmly against the seat. He shouldn't be able to slump forward.
- Periodically check your baby's seat to be sure the seat belt has not loosened.
- Because your infant is growing, at times you will need to adjust the harness in his car seat to keep a comfortable fit.
- Before using a child safety seat, install it in your automobile to be sure it fits and is easy to use. A seat that is difficult to secure is more likely to be used improperly or not at all.
- Be sure to have your infant "test-drive" a seat before making the purchase. A seat that is not comfortable will cause him to be fussy when he travels.
- Whenever possible, try to have an adult (other than the driver) attend to your baby while in the car.

- In hot weather, remember that car seats can scorch a baby's skin. Before placing your baby in the seat, allow it to cool down so he does not get burned.

Community programs. In Oklahoma, where it is estimated that only 50 percent of infants are properly secured in automobile safety seats at any given time on the highway, the Oklahoma Safe Kids Coalition has started a program called Please Be Seated. This program allows any citizen who sees an unprotected child in a moving vehicle to anonymously send in the license plate number of that car. The coalition then sends a friendly reminder to the owner emphasizing the importance of child safety seats and describing how they can obtain a reasonably priced seat. Programs like this help encourage safe travel for infants, and it is my hope they will soon exist in all fifty states.

POISONING

(See also "Poisoning" in "Toddlers and Preschoolers," page 154.)

Unfortunately, approximately 175 infants each year are killed when they ingest poisonous substances. Certain cleaning formulas, especially pipe and drain cleaners, are very damaging to human tissue and can lead to immediate burns of the mouth and throat when taken in small amounts. They can also cause swelling in the throat that can lead to airway blockage and suffocation. Severe burns can also occur to the stomach if a drain cleaner is swallowed completely. Furniture polishes, which often contain pine oil, can be very dangerous to lungs, and certain insecticides can kill when ingested in small amounts, too. Any type of fuel, particularly gasoline, lamp oil, and kerosene, can also be deadly when swallowed. Be sure to store dangerous products well out of your child's reach.

If your home is like most others, you have a variety of harmful substances stored in closets, cabinets, and the garage. And if your infant is like every other, she would just love to get at them for a taste! Fortunately, your baby cannot take large swallows and tends to avoid things that taste bad, so her risk of serious injury after tasting a medicine or other toxic substance is low. But the danger does exist and will only become greater as she enters the toddler years. Although it does help to know which substances are poisonous, the only true prevention measure is to keep all potential poisons such as cleaning solutions, chemicals, medicines, insecticides, and gasoline and other fuels out of your baby's reach. Also, be sure to discard any toxic substances not being used.

STRANGULATION AND SUFFOCATION

Nearly 350 infants die and thousands more are injured from strangulation or suffocation each year in the United States, representing approximately 19 percent of all injury deaths to infants.

It goes without saying that you would never want to give your child something that could hurt him. But this is exactly what thousands of parents inadvertently do each year. Your infant's breathing can be compromised very quickly and quietly by seemingly innocent items such as drapery cords, crib gyms, and plastic garbage bags. To help reinforce this point, I have included some descriptions of ways in which these injuries occur. These are sometimes graphic and can be unpleasant to consider. I don't intend to scare you, but every parent needs to know how such terrible accidents happen.

Strangulation
(See also "Does Your Crib Measure Up?" in "Infants," page 119; and "Strollers" in "Infants," page 129.)

Infant strangulation occurs in three ways: wedging, constriction, and suspension. A brief inspection of your home will probably turn up many ordinary, innocent-looking household items and locations that can cause strangulation to an infant.

1. An infant's neck could become wedged between two firm objects placed close to each other, such as a mattress and bed board, crib and wall, dresser and wall, or sleeping person and wall.
2. An infant's neck could get constricted by tight material, such as a jacket, shirt, necklace, or bib, which can get caught on something, or by the straps from a baby chair or a car seat.
3. An infant's head could get caught and his body suspended between two mattresses, a hole in a mattress, space between an adult bed and a dresser, crib and dresser, mattress and bunk bed guardrail, crib bars, or any other such pieces or parts of furniture.

Cord, rope, string, elastic bands, and wire are just a few examples of materials that can strangle infants by constriction. Specific examples of such dangerous items include drapery cords, jump ropes, electric cords, fishing line, and kite string. Watch out for any similar items in which your infant could become tangled. An infant could also be strangled by strings or ribbons if tied around his neck to hold a pacifier or toy. A bib or necklace can catch on baby crib corners or stairway railings. Balloons usually come with strings or ribbons attached, which can also be dangerous to your infant. This makes them doubly dangerous, because when popped, balloons are also a choking hazard.

- Always keep strings, wires, and other strangulation hazards away from your baby.
- Never tie a necklace, ribbon, or string around your baby's neck.
- Always remove a bib immediately after your baby is finished eating.
- Never let your baby in the same room with a balloon, whether it has a string attached or not.

Drawstrings.

(See also "Drawstrings," page 157, and "Escalators," page 161, in "Toddlers and Preschoolers.")

Your baby's clothing can also be hazardous. Drawstrings on shirts, jackets and hoods have caused numerous infant strangulations. They can get caught on a crib part or other catch points in the home such as those found on chairs, sofas, and bed frames. Most manufacturers have stopped producing child clothing with neck and hood drawstrings, but be aware that dangerous garments are still out there. Drawstrings can get caught on a crib part or other catch point. Consequently, clothing strings should never be longer than three inches. What may appear to be a harmless short string can become a longer string when pulled from your infant's garment. One solution to this problem is to cut the string into two short pieces and sew each into the fabric of the clothing so they can still be used. Elastic can then be sewn into the clothing to give your child the same comfortable fit. A better way to eliminate the hazards of clothing drawstrings is to simply remove them completely and use Velcro, snaps, or buttons instead. But you can also just sew the center part of the drawstring into the garment.

Window-covering pull cords. In the last fifteen years over 150 infant strangulations have been attributed to window-covering pull cords. Often, these infants were sitting next to a window that had a drapery, miniblind, or vertical blind cord hanging to the floor. Sometimes a crib is placed close enough to a window so that the pull cord can be reached by a playful infant. The safest and most effective way to prevent these types of strangulation injuries is to shorten pull cords until they are well out of the reach of your infant. Several alteration techniques for various types of pull cords are available. For further information and free window cord tie-down devices, call the Window Covering Safety Council at 800-506-4636.

Loose threads and long hairs. Although they don't cause strangulation, loose threads also pose a danger to infants. They can cause injury by being wrapped tightly around a finger, toe, or penis. This can cause the circulation to be cut off, leading to amputation. Periodically check your infant's clothing for such loose threads. A long hair can also cause this type of injury, so if you or your baby's caregiver has long hair, be on the lookout for loose strands.

Suffocation
(See also "Playpens" in "Infants," page 127; "Strangulation and Suffocation" in "Toddlers and Preschoolers," page 157; and "Garage Doors" in "Toddlers and Preschoolers," page 162.)

To better predict and prevent suffocation injuries, it is important to understand how they can occur. To that end, I have classified such injuries into three basic types: constricting, smothering, and trapping.

1. An infant's chest could become constricted in material such as a hammock or the mesh siding of a playpen.
2. An infant's face could be smothered by airtight material, such as:

- plastic mattress covers
- plastic dry-cleaning bags
- thick blankets
- bags
- pillowcases
- trash bags
- grocery bags
- newspaper covers

3. An infant could become trapped in a poorly ventilated or nonventilated space, such as a toy chest, an unused freezer, or a large safe.

Be certain to eliminate the above hazards. For example, take your dry-cleaning bags and mattress packaging and immediately tie them into knots and discard them. Remove the doors from unused appliances and place spring-loaded hinges on the toy chest lid to prevent sudden closing.

SUDDEN INFANT DEATH SYNDROME

Few phrases strike greater fear into the hearts of loving parents more than sudden infant death syndrome (SIDS). First identified in 1969, SIDS is now believed to be responsible for the deaths of approximately ten thousand infants every year in the United States. It is the leading cause of infant death and is most common between the ages of one month and one year. SIDS is not considered an accident or injury—it is a tragic disease with an unknown cause. Although several factors have been associated with the occurrence of SIDS, researchers have yet to conclude what actually causes it. We do know that infants are at greater risk of dying from SIDS if they are born at a low birth weight or if born into a family with a history of SIDS. Also, babies whose mothers smoke are at an increased risk of SIDS.

Position Your Baby

We now know that infants who sleep facedown are at greater risk of dying from SIDS than those who sleep on their backs. Consequently, in 1992 the American Academy of Pediatrics recommended that infants not sleep facedown. In 1994 the National Institute of Child Health and Human Development at the National Institutes of Health launched the Back to Sleep campaign, urging parents to place sleeping infants on their backs.

Since then SIDS deaths have decreased by over 30 percent. Be sure your baby sleeps on her back until she is at least twelve months old.

What do you do if your baby simply won't sleep on her back? The truth is that at least 20 percent of all infants prefer sleeping on their tummies. If your baby has trouble sleeping on her back, try any one of a number of products that gently props babies on their sides while sleeping. It should be mentioned, however, that such products have not been proven to prevent SIDS.

One product that shows more promise in the prevention of SIDS is the Halo Sleep System. This specially designed mattress has a built-in fan that continuously recirculates the air. Early evidence suggests that it may reduce the likelihood of a baby rebreathing carbon dioxide, thus decreasing the risk of SIDS. The Halo Sleep System can be ordered on the Internet at *www.onestepahead.com* or by calling (800) 274-8440.

Near-Miss SIDS

Infants sometimes experience near-miss SIDS episodes in which breathing stops but resumes spontaneously or when the infant is wakened. If your baby ever experiences such an event, she may be at risk of SIDS. Bring this to the attention of your pediatric, emergency, or family physician immediately.

Not All Sleeping Deaths Are SIDS—Avoid Soft Bedding

Many infant deaths previously attributed to SIDS are actually due to a soft mattress, pillow, blanket, comforter, cushion, or stuffed animal. These items can cause suffocation if the material molds around an infant's mouth and nose, forming hollows of exhaled air while sleeping. Suffocation injuries that occur to infants while sleeping are not the same as SIDS.

Should Your Baby Sleep in Bed with You?

An infant should absolutely and positively NEVER sleep in an adult bed, with or without an adult. Here are the reasons why.

- Infants are prone to suffocation when placed on, near, or beneath adult bedding, such as comforters, bedspreads, pillows, and blankets. The material tends to conform to a baby's face and leads to the rebreathing of exhaled air. This can cause a gradual decrease in consciousness until breathing stops and death occurs. Many cases previously labeled SIDS deaths were in fact a result of this mechanism.
- An infant can, in fact, suffocate if an adult in the bed rolls onto her or pushes bedding material over or against her face.
- Infants are also at risk of strangulation because they can roll off an adult bed and become wedged between the mattress and bed board or footboard.

Please do not think for a second that these injuries are rare. Every year in the United States alone, approximately two thousand babies suffocate because they were placed to sleep on or near a cushion, quilt, pillow, or comforter.

Baby Monitors

When you are not in your baby's room, baby monitors with speakers can be set up in your bedroom or living room for reassurance. These monitors can be connected to an infant who is at risk for SIDS and will sound an alarm in the event that breathing stops. Speak to your pediatrician if you feel that your baby may need a monitor.

OBJECT-SPECIFIC HAZARDS

In most cases, there is no inherent danger in a particular object itself—danger only exists if it is poorly made or misused. Certain products, of course, carry a greater risk of injury to an infant than others. In this section I discuss many products that can be harmful to infants if used improperly or do not meet safety standards.

ADULT FURNITURE

(See also "Should Your Baby Sleep in Bed with You?" in "Infants," page 115; and "Dangerous Furniture" in "Toddlers and Preschoolers," page 159.)

It is dangerous to put your baby on any type of adult furniture, especially when sleeping. Cots and lawn chairs can easily collapse onto infants, and some chairs and sofas have soft cushions that can cause suffocation. Beanbag chairs are dangerous because infants can suffocate in the soft material, and they might choke on the contents if the fabric of the chair is torn. Adult beds (including regular mattresses, water beds, futons, etc.) are also off-limits to your sleeping baby. Soft pillows and blankets pose suffocation hazards, and bed boards can trap an infant against the mattress who crawls over the edge. Smothering can also occur if a sleeping adult rolls onto an infant.

- Never leave your baby unattended on a piece of adult furniture.
- Never sleep with your baby on an adult bed, couch, or other furniture.

BASSINETS, CRADLES, AND CARRY-COTS

Three other types of baby furniture that parents often purchase are bassinets, cradles, and carry-cots. These items are smaller than cribs and require less floor space. They are also portable and can be carried easily from room to room, often being used in the parents' bedroom for close monitoring of a sleeping infant. Federal guidelines for the manufacturing of bassinets, cradles, and carry-cots are lacking, so it is incumbent upon you to search out the safest one for your baby.

Bassinets

Most bassinets are quite small and are on wheels, so they are easy to push from room to room. These features also make it easier for them to be accidentally pushed across a room or knocked over by you or an older child.

Bassinets have one other major drawback. Because they are so small, they will be outgrown and obsolete by the time your baby is only a few months old. Bassinets can be quite dangerous to older infants who are likely to climb out. A bassinet can even be tipped over by an active infant inside.

- If older children are in the home, do not use a bassinet for your baby.
- Always use a bassinet with great caution, and avoid placing your baby in one without close supervision.
- When shopping for a bassinet, look for one with a wide, sturdy base that will be the least likely to get knocked over.
- Do not place your infant in a bassinet once she has reached three months of age.
- Since bassinets rarely have the required safety features of cribs, do not substitute a bassinet for a good-quality crib.
- Some bassinets are made to fold at the legs. Be careful to check the leg locks on this type. You want locks that are reliable and will prevent the bassinet from collapsing with your baby inside.

Additionally, the mattress pads of bassinets tend to be softer than crib mattresses. Studies show that approximately fifteen to twenty infants each year die while sleeping facedown in bassinets. Many of these are probably SIDS deaths, but there is some suspicion that the softer mattresses could be partly to blame.

Rocking Cradles

Did you know that rocking cribs or cradles can be deadly? In Australia and New Zealand, where rocking cradles are popular, numerous infant deaths have been attributed to them. Injury occurs when a baby rolls so far to one side that the cradle fails to rock back in the other direction. If the cradle becomes angled to a degree that prevents an infant from moving off the railings, pressure against her chest can become great enough to prevent breathing. While most cradles have a safety pin that prevents them from angling too far to either side, danger exists if this pin breaks or falls out. Never place your infant inside a rocking cradle unattended.

Carry-cots

A carry-cot is a small infant bed with a handle that can be used to transport a sleeping infant. Two basic types of carry-cots exist—those made of woven wicker and those made of fabric. The wicker models are less comfortable to carry and more prone to wear and tear.

- Use a carry-cot for short naps only, and never substitute one for a crib.
- Be sure your carry-cot has a wide base and remains very stable when your baby is in it.
- Be sure the handles are firmly attached and widely spaced.
- As with cribs, avoid placing pillows, blankets, soft cushions, or stuffed animals in a carry-cot.
- Never let your carry-cot serve as a substitute for a car safety seat.

CHANGING TABLES

Changing your baby's diapers will soon become a well-rehearsed ballet. And since repeated bending can cause backaches and stiffness, you will naturally seek ways to accomplish this work more efficiently and comfortably. A changing table is one option that provides both an elevated surface on which to work and a handy way to keep all your necessary changing aids nearby. But approximately 1,500 babies annually are treated for injuries after falling from changing tables. It's important to know the specific safety considerations when buying and using a changing table.

- Always follow the most important rules: Never leave your baby unattended even for a second. And when your baby is on a changing table, always keep one hand in contact with her.
- Be sure the base of the table is wide enough to keep it stable when bumped.
- Be sure a guardrail is present around each side of the table. The higher these rails, the better.
- Use the safety belt that comes with your table to secure your infant every time you place her on the table.
- Stop using a changing table once your child reaches four to five months of age, because she will then be more likely to roll or crawl off.

Everything at Arm's Reach

Many of the accidents associated with changing tables occur when a parent reaches for a baby product, leaving the little one alone just long enough to roll off. Develop a routine that includes first gathering all the necessary items, such as powder, diapers, washcloths, clean diapers, and clothing, and then placing them within reach of the table. Always do this before placing your infant on the table and you will eliminate the temptation to step away for something.

- Be sure to keep ointments, pins, and other hazardous materials out of baby's reach.
- Be sure to keep powders away from your baby's face, as they can damage little lungs if inhaled.

Alternative Tables

Changing tables that fold up for easy storage are also available and can be used safely by following the manufacturer's instructions. I do not recommend adapter tables that fit onto dressers. Most dressers are not made for this purpose and may fall over if an infant is not centered correctly.

CRIBS

Your baby's crib should be a haven of safety and comfort. He will certainly spend many hours here, both at play and at sleep. A good crib, you will find, is a place where you can keep your baby safe while sleeping or taking some time for yourself.

Government manufacturing standards set in 1973 have greatly improved crib safety, so most new cribs sold in the United States are very safe. Despite this, cribs continue to be associated with the highest child injury rates of any nursery item. Approximately fifty infants each year are killed and another nine thousand are injured in crib-related accidents in the United States.

Safety, Safety, Safety!

When shopping for your baby's crib, the three top features to consider are: safety, safety, and then safety. Once you have found several safe cribs to choose from, then—and only then—should you consider shape, style, and color.

Does Your Crib Measure Up?

Regulations established by the Consumer Product Safety Commission ensure crib safety. Before you purchase a crib, make sure the following safety standards have been met:

- The vertical bars or slats must be no farther apart than two and three-eighths inches (or 60 millimeters) to prevent infants from slipping through or becoming stuck between them. An infant's head is relatively larger than the rest of his body and could become stuck between bars that are too far apart if his body slips through.
- Any openings at the end walls of your crib, such as decorative cutouts, must not exceed two and three-eighths inches, because they might also allow an infant's body to slip through.
- If a vertical bar on a crib side is broken off, the gap between the remaining bars will likely be dangerous to an infant inside. Be sure the crib bars are sturdy and intact.

- Injury can also occur if an infant crawls or climbs over the side of a crib. Be sure the top of each crib side is not less than nine inches at its lowest position and twenty-six inches when raised.

Secondhand Cribs

Sometimes baby furniture, such as cribs and dressers, get passed down from grandparents to parents or sold in antique stores, garage sales, and used-furniture stores. Beware of secondhand cribs—over 25 million unsafe cribs are still out there! Some were made long before crib safety was considered important, while others were just made without regard to recent safety standards. Older cribs very likely will not have the safety features required of cribs manufactured today. Although you will pay more, a new crib is well worth having solely for the reason that it is up-to-date on safety standards.

Corner Posts

Cribs with high corner posts (greater than a sixteenth inch, or one and a half millimeters) can catch an infant's clothing and cause strangulation. Many such cribs are still being passed around to family members and friends or sold in garage sales and used-furniture stores. Manufacturers have voluntarily stopped designing cribs with elevated, decorative corner posts because of this danger. If your infant's crib has elevated corner posts and you prefer not to purchase another, saw them off and sand the edges down. If you cannot correct the defects, destroy such a crib rather than sell it.

Cribs on Rollers

Cribs on rollers can be dangerous if older children are in the home. Playful siblings, who might be inclined to push a crib around, could tip it over or push it down a flight of stairs. Also, by leaning against a wheeled crib you might inadvertently shove it away from you. Hardwood floors allow for easy rolling with such cribs, so be extra careful here, too. Look for a crib with casters that can lock the wheels and prevent rolling, or better yet, get a crib with no wheels at all. Obviously, such a crib is the safest way to go.

Crib Mattresses and Mattress Covers

The two most important qualities in a crib mattress are firmness and fit. A firm mattress is necessary in order to minimize the risk of suffocation. If a mattress is too soft it can allow an infant's mouth and nose to be engulfed in the fabric. An infant could then be at risk for rebreathing his own exhaled air, which is high in carbon dioxide and low in oxygen, leading to extreme drowsiness, coma, or even death. Soft mattresses have been responsible for some deaths that were initially attributed to SIDS. This is part of the reason your baby should not sleep facedown. Always place your infant faceup when he sleeps.

Mattress size. A mattress should fit snugly against each side of the crib. A mattress that does not properly fit the crib can pose a risk to an infant who might crawl beneath it. If you can fit two side-by-side fingers between the side of the crib and the mattress, the mattress is too small. The standard mattress size is $51\frac{5}{8} \times 27\frac{1}{4}$. Be sure your baby's mattress fits his crib.

Mattress hangers. Mattress hangers support the floor of the crib and can be used to lower or raise the mattress to a desired height. As your infant grows taller, you will need to lower the floor of the crib to prevent him from climbing out. Be sure each hanger is always securely fastened to the corners of the crib.

Bumper pads. Mattress bumper pads are soft cushions that fit around the inside of a crib and help prevent your baby from hitting his head against the crib bars. Secure all bumper pads to the crib and cut the strings as short as possible after being tied. This will eliminate the danger of strangulation. Once your infant can pull himself up, remove all pads and crib toys to keep him from standing on them while attempting to climb from the crib.

Mattress covers. Mattress covers have also been associated with suffocation injuries. Be sure the mattress cover in your crib is made of a tough material that cannot be torn or punctured. This will prevent your infant from crawling beneath it. Never use plastic garbage bags as mattress covers. They are much too weak. Several suffocation deaths have also been caused by wrapping material that was left lying around. Tie into knots and discard any plastic wrapping material that came with your new crib.

Crib Cushions, Quilts, and Comforters

Crib accessories such as cushions, quilts, and comforters, with their bright colors and designs, can certainly beautify any room. They may seem harmless at first, but the dangers they pose to infants are very real. Nearly two thousand infant suffocations each year are caused by cushions, quilts, and comforters. Recently, the Consumer Product Safety Commission placed a manufacturing and sales can on crib cushions, crib pillows, and crib comforters. Never place cushions, quilts, and comforters in your baby's crib.

So, what can you put in your infant's crib? Limit what you put in your baby's crib to small, age-appropriate toys, a crib bumper that is properly secured, and a pacifier. If you dress him in a cozy, warm bodysuit you will only need a lightweight cotton blanket to keep him warm. Such blankets are porous and present the least risk of smothering a baby. When using a light blanket, tuck it around the mattress at the foot of the bed, allowing it only to cover your baby up to his chest. The safest bet, however, is to use sleepwear rather than a blanket. (*See also "Age-Appropriate Toys and Activities" in "Toys," page 89.*)

Using Your Crib Correctly

No matter how sturdy and well-built, a crib is only as safe as the parents who use it. Keep crib safety in mind and remember a few basic rules.

- Always raise the crib sides to full height and lock them when your infant is inside.
- If a drop side does not have a locking, hand-operated latch, replace it.
- Once your infant is able to sit unassisted, adjust the floor of the crib to a lower position. And when he can stand, put the crib floor in its lowest position to prevent him from climbing out.
- Avoid placing large toys and pillows in your baby's crib. They just might enable him to climb out.
- When your child reaches a height of thirty-two to thirty-five inches (usually about two years of age), he should no longer sleep in a crib, because it may no longer hold him. Your toddler could outgrow a crib due to his size or activity level well before reaching this height, so pay attention to his physical abilities and look for signs that he may be learning to escape. For instance, if he can pull himself up off the crib floor by grabbing the crib sides or if he can climb up the sides, he is too big and strong for a crib. When this occurs, he should then begin sleeping in a toddler bed.

Crib Location

(See also "Window-Covering Pull Cords" in "Infants," page 113.)

The location of your baby's crib is of extreme importance. It is tempting to move the crib next to a large piece of furniture so diapers, clothing, and other accessories are close by. However, placing a crib up against a dresser or other piece of furniture puts your infant at risk of getting wedged in between the two pieces of furniture if he climbs out. This same type of injury can also occur if a crib is placed against a wall. Another dangerous location for a crib is next to a long drapery cord. Strangulation injury can occur when a crib is situated too close to any type of window-covering pull cord.

- Pull your crib at least one foot away from all furniture and walls.
- Never place your baby's crib next to a drapery or window-blind cord.

Crib Maintenance

Frequent inspections of your baby's crib will help you identify wear and tear before an injury occurs.

- Periodically check the slats and end boards to be sure they are not loose and check all nuts and bolts, tightening them when necessary.
- Be sure no screws or nails are protruding from the wood, as they can catch your baby's clothing or scratch his skin.

- If your crib has defects that cannot be fixed, dismantle it and throw it away. This will prevent it from being used by another family. Never sell a bad crib. The few dollars you gain will not be worth the injury that may be caused to somebody else's baby.

Portable Cribs

Portable cribs are very convenient to have when visiting a friend or relative. During vacations it can be tempting to use a portable crib at night for your baby. But a portable crib is not a substitute for a full-size crib. Significant differences exist that could place your infant at risk. In fact, safety standards don't even exist for portable cribs. Most manufacturers simply adhere to the regulations for playpens.

- When using a portable crib, check the top rails and be sure they are locked before your baby is placed inside. The fabric sides of portable cribs are comparable to playpens and can cause suffocation if a wall collapses or is left down.
- Look for holes in the sides that could cause your infant to become stuck and strangled.
- The greatest difference between standard cribs and portable cribs is the level of supervision required. Just like a playpen, never leave your infant unattended while he is in a portable crib.
- Follow the safety rules and tips that apply to playpens.

GATES

(See also "Stairs" in "Toddlers and Preschoolers," page 164.)

No matter how hard you work to make your home child safe, there will always be places that should be off-limits to your baby. You may have clothes piled high in the washroom one day and marbles on the floor in a sibling's bedroom the next day. Baby gates can help you prevent your baby from entering places that are off-limits. If used improperly, though, gates can be dangerous. One of the biggest problems is the false sense of security that parents develop when using one. A gate should never be used in place of close adult supervision.

Gate Types

Three gates are currently used in many homes: the accordion, the pressure-bar, and the installed gate.

Accordion gates. The collapsible accordion gate is very dangerous—it is too easy for a child to stick her head, arm, leg, or finger through one of the many openings in this type of gate. Also, a child might attempt to crawl over a collapsible gate. Many infant injuries and some deaths have occurred when such gates collapsed onto an infant or toddler. The Consumer Product Safety Commission has placed a manufacturing and selling ban on these gates, but it is estimated that 15 million such gates are still in use today. Never use an accordion style gate around your infant.

Pressure-bar gates. The type of gate made to expand by using a pressure bar is one of the safest and most popular type in use today. Be sure the pressure bar is placed on the side opposite your infant so she cannot disengage it. Be sure the gate does not have holes large enough to allow your infant's head or hand to pass through. Pressure gates are only considered reliable for use with children less than twenty-four months of age.

- Use a gate only when you are in the same room as your infant. Your close supervision is still critical. Infants often find ways to get around or over them.
- Vertical slats are preferred over horizontal because they do not allow a child to get a foothold when trying to climb over. The slats should be no more than two and three-eighths inches apart.

Installed gates. Although portable gates can serve a valuable role in your home, never trust one to restrict your baby's access into a dangerous area, such as a pool or stairway: they are simply not that reliable. To keep your baby away from dangerous areas, install a properly mounted swinging doorway gate. Should you decide that a mounted gate is not to your liking, install a half-door instead.

HIGH CHAIRS

If you are like most parents, your high chair is a treasured piece of furniture. A high chair can make the difference between a pleasant family meal and an out-of-control food fight. But don't develop a false sense of security with this wonderful piece of furniture. High chairs are associated with nearly nine thousand injuries to infants and toddlers and at least a few deaths every year.

- Never place your child's high chair next to a counter, a wall, or a table.
- Always keep a close watch on your child whenever he sits in his high chair. Accidents usually occur during a brief lapse of supervision.

Four common ways that infants get injured in a high chair:

1. Crawling out and falling to the floor
2. Slipping below the tray and becoming entangled in the safety straps
3. Falling out when the tray disengages
4. Tipping the high chair over by kicking off with his feet when the high chair is placed too close to a counter, wall, or table

Older High Chairs

In 1975 high chair manufacturers began to follow a voluntary industry safety standard. Several features of high chairs on the market today owe their existence to these standards, and may not be present in older high chairs. Be on guard when shopping at garage sales and antique shops or if somebody offers to give you a high chair.

Restraining Straps

Two restraining straps with working buckles should be present on your high chair. One goes around your baby's waist and the other between his legs. Buckle each strap immediately after placing your infant in the high chair.

Other Safety Features

Wide-set legs ensure stability and tray locks should be reliable and strong. A tray that comes off or loosens while your infant is in the chair could enable him to slide forward and onto the floor. If the high chair itself is poorly made, it can even collapse while your infant is sitting in it. Be sure your baby's high chair has wide-set legs, strong tray locks, and sturdy construction.

Booster Seats

Booster seats are available for young children who are too large for a high chair yet too small for a dining room chair. This type of seat is secured to the chair with a safety belt. A small child can then be secured into the seat with a seat belt. Be sure the booster seat is adjusted to your child's height so he will be less tempted to move around. Booster seats are generally very safe, but a child can wiggle out and get hurt, so close supervision is a must.

Hook-on Chairs

Hook-on chairs can be temporarily secured to your dinner table. While they are generally safe, accidents do happen. Also, lightweight tables can topple over if the weight of a hook-on chair is too great. Although hook-on chairs are convenient, high chairs are preferable.

- Avoid using a hook-on chair if your baby weights more than thirty pounds or if he is active. If your baby cannot sit still for very long, he might shake the chair from the table.
- Always be sure your baby's hook-on chair is well secured to the table with a clamp or lock.
- Never use your hook-on chair on anything but a sturdy dinner table.

INFANT CARRIERS

The day-to-day activities of parenthood often require that you bring your baby along when running errands, going to and from work, or just visiting a friend. Since carrying a little one in your arms everywhere you go is simply unrealistic, an infant carrier is a must-have item. The use of soft carriers and backpacks to tote infants dates back to ancient times. You will no doubt find many opportunities to use modern-day infant carriers while raising your baby.

Infant carriers are capable of supporting children up to thirty to thirty-five pounds in weight. However, some parents find that carrying an infant of even lesser weight causes them to suffer shoulder and back pains. You may be too small to safely perform the task of carrying a ten- to fifteen-pound baby on your back or over your chest. There are no guidelines to help you make this decision—it is simply for you to determine. So, before purchasing a carrier, consider your own ability and strength. Do not use a carrier if it is uncomfortable.

Two Types of Carriers

Today there are two basic types of infant carriers—those with frames and those without. Soft carriers, worn across your chest, are designed to provide support for your infant's head. In a framed backpack, he may experience difficulty breathing if his head falls to one side. Use a framed backpack only after your infant has begun holding his head up, at about four to five months of age.

Choosing a Carrier

When shopping for a carrier, be sure to bring your infant along for a "test drive" and look for the following features:

- a safety strap and buckle, so your infant can be comfortably secured
- leg openings that are small enough to prevent your infant from slipping through, yet large enough to prevent chafing
- soft padding at the top of a backpack, where your infant's face will rest
- no pinch points anywhere on a framed pack
- a wide base, to decrease the chances that the pack tips over while you are putting it on

Proper Technique

You will probably need assistance when learning to place a backpack on yourself, and you may prefer to have an assistant help you each time. This is certainly okay, as accidents are most likely to occur during the process of putting on a backpack. Many infant injuries have also occurred when a pack was placed on an elevated structure and left unattended, sometimes for only a second or two.

- When placing the pack on, always bend from the knees. Bending from the waist may cause your baby to fall out. This technique is also easier on your back.
- If you have a framed pack with a built-in stand, never stand the pack up with your infant inside unless someone is holding it with both hands.
- Always secure your baby into an infant carrier so she can't wiggle or pull herself out.

Growing Out of a Carrier

As your infant grows older, his activity level and strength will increase, making him more likely to squirm from a backpack. If you notice your baby becoming restless, take him out of the carrier.

- Once he reaches twenty pounds (six months), do not place him in a carrier or backpack for more than an hour at a time. At this age he will tend to grow restless very quickly.
- Once your infant reaches thirty pounds, it is no longer safe for him to be in a carrier for any period of time.

PLAYPENS

A playpen, or play yard, is a small pen enclosed by mesh walls that allows your baby to play or nap nearby while you perform other jobs at hand. Do not develop a false sense of security with playpens, however; they are no substitute for close supervision. Moreover, playpens are not without their dangers. Over three thousand infants are injured annually in playpens. The biggest mistake parents make with playpens is using them with older toddlers. Do not place your child in a playpen once she has reached 35 inches (about 2 years) or becomes persistent in her efforts to get out.

Playpen Walls
(See also "Cribs and Playpens" in "Product Recalls," page 202.)

Each year three or four infant deaths are caused by the collapsible walls of playpens. These injuries happen in one of two ways. First, a single wall can fall down if the locking mechanism is not engaged or is defective. Suffocation or strangulation occurs when an infant gets trapped in the mesh material of a collapsed wall. Even if an infant is outside the playpen, injury can occur if she crawls back inside and gets tangled in the material. Second, some playpens sold in the past had accordion-type walls (just like the gates) with diamond-shaped openings. These walls can collapse, causing the diamond-shaped openings to crush any part of an infant that is caught inside.

The material of playpen walls should be woven tightly enough to prevent buttons or fingers from becoming stuck in the holes. Large holes should not be present either, as an arm, leg, or even a head might get caught. Vinyl or other soft fabrics are not good material for use in playpens, as they can be torn or bitten into small pieces on which a child might choke.

- Never leave a playpen wall down.
- Never use the type of playpen that has collapsible, accordion-type walls.
- Be sure the material of your baby's playpen walls is sturdy and tightly woven. The mesh sides should have openings that are no larger than one-quarter inch. If vertical slats are present, they should be no more than two and three-eighths inches apart.

Dangers with a Playpen

As with cribs, comforters, pillows, cushions, and quilts can cause suffocation if placed in your baby's playpen. Since large stuffed animals might give her enough height to crawl over the side, keep these out of her playpen as well.

Standards

Playpens are usually manufactured according to the voluntary safety standards put forth by the American Society for Testing and Materials (ASTM) and tested by the Juvenile Products Manufacturers Association (JPMA). If you intend to purchase a playpen, look for a label stating that these standards have been met.

SEATS

Infant seats are a great way for your child to be near you even when you cannot hold him. They are also handy for feeding. It's generally safe for your baby to nap in a seat, but only when supervised. Whereas carry-cots have no safety straps for sleeping infants, your infant seat will have a built-in restraining system to prevent your baby from crawling or falling out. Most seats sold today have safety belts that fit around the crotch and waist of an infant. Be sure to use this restraining system on your baby's seat according to the manufacturer's instructions. And always fasten them immediately after placing your baby in his seat.

What to Look For

When shopping for an infant seat, be sure the base stand is sturdy and wide, so the risk of toppling over is minimized. Also, look for a seat with a skid-resistant base to prevent sliding. Your baby's seat will come with age and weight restrictions—follow them.

Elevated-Surface Falls

As with other infant products, infant seats can be dangerous if used improperly. Nearly four thousand injuries are associated with infant seats each year in the United States. The most serious injuries occur when a baby falls from an elevated surface. Two big mistakes are usually responsible for this type of accident. First, an infant seat is placed on a platform at a dangerous elevation. And second, an infant is not closely attended to. If he squirms in a seat, he might move the seat just enough to cause it to fall. Another common mistake is not knowing when a baby is too big for a seat. Your infant will be too large and active for a seat when he reaches about four or five months of age.

- Never place your infant on an elevated surface without keeping one hand on him at all times.
- Do not place your infant in a seat after he reaches four months of age.
- Finally, remember that your seat is not an automobile safety seat, and never use it as such. It will offer no protection to your infant in a motor vehicle accident.

STROLLERS

A walk in the park or down the street of your neighborhood can be a relaxing and enjoyable activity for the whole family. A stroller allows you to bring your baby along. But it is important to understand the potential dangers that exist. About fifteen thousand children are injured annually in stroller-related accidents in the United States. Once again, a common mistake is not knowing when a child is too old for a stroller. When your infant reaches thirty-six pounds or three years of age, she will be too large and too active to ride in a stroller.

Manufacturing Standards

Strollers come in many styles and degrees of quality. The Juvenile Product Manufacturers Association enacted specific safety requirements for strollers in 1983, greatly improving their quality. These standards are now followed by most manufacturers. Models that meet the federal standards as tested by the American Society for Testing and Materials will bear a label stating that the stroller is in compliance with the ASTM F-833 safety standard.

The general characteristics that must be present in a certified stroller are:

- stability
- durability
- adequate braking ability
- protection against a child slipping through a leg opening
- no sharp or jagged edges or protruding screws
- adequate child-restraining system
- locking mechanism to prevent the stroller from spontaneously folding
- labeling to remind adults to always secure and supervise the child while in the stroller
- proper instructions for assembly of the stroller

Dangerous Leg Openings

Numerous strangulation deaths have occurred in strollers during the last several years. These accidents usually occur when an infant wiggles through and strangles in a leg opening. Ideally, a stroller should not have leg openings at all, though many still do. When shopping for a stroller, be sure you find one with the smallest possible leg openings, so small that your infant's body cannot slip through.

Seat Belts

Seat belts should also be integrated with your stroller. Don't let stroller seat belts give you a false sense of security. Watch your infant closely as she gets older, especially when she enters the toddler years, because she will begin to figure out ways to escape the seat belts. Use your stroller restraints every time you place your baby in her stroller—no exceptions!

Brakes

Reliable stroller brakes are also very important for the safety of your baby. Be sure your stroller brakes allow for a brisk yet smooth stop when applied.

Hanging Baskets

Hanging baskets or other items off the back of the stroller can be dangerous because they may cause the stroller to flip backward. If a basket is attached to the back of the stroller, place it low on the stroller to maintain the lowest possible center of gravity.

Locking Mechanisms

Strollers are usually made to fold up for easy storage and transportation. Thoroughly check the locking mechanism on any stroller you are considering. You want it to be strong enough to prevent the stroller from collapsing when your child is in it. Don't hesitate to have the store's sales associate demonstrate how the locks work, so you are completely satisfied that the stroller is safe.

Choose a Safe Route

For safe strolling, pick a path that is used primarily by pedestrians, not bicyclists or motorized vehicles. Avoid busy streets, escalators, stairways, rocky paths, and secluded areas. Be particularly cautious near a busy street or a body of water. An active child might be able to escape if your attention is briefly lost.

Carriages

Carriages differ from strollers in that they are flat inside, allowing a baby to ride supine.

- Place your baby in a stroller or carriage that allows her to recline fully, until she is old enough to hold her head up. In an upright position, her head will fall to one side, making it difficult for her to breathe.

- When she can hold her head upright for more than a few minutes (this occurs at about four or five months of age), it is safe to put her in an upright position.
- Do not place your baby in a carriage after she demonstrates the ability to pull herself up. Once she can do this it becomes possible to climb from or topple the carriage.

SWINGS

Babies love to be rocked. A baby swing with a smooth, rhythmic motion can provide great entertainment for both you and your baby. During irritable times, it can also serve to pacify him, giving you much-needed rest. But don't relax too much. National safety standards do not yet exist for baby swings. Once again, you must be the safety advocate for your baby.

Two basic types of swings are available: those that are battery-powered and those that wind up. Neither one is safer than the other.

- Never take your eyes off your baby when he is in a swing.
- Never put him in a swing for longer than twenty minutes at a time.
- Use only a wide-based, freestanding swing. Those that are suspended from furniture or door frames can be dangerous.
- Once your baby exceeds the manufacturer's weight limit, he should not be placed in a swing. Infant weight limits vary from one swing to another, but are generally in the seventeen- to twenty-pound range.
- Always use the restraining system that comes with the swing to prevent a fall.
- Once again, close and constant supervision is mandatory with swings.
- Read the manufacturer's instructions carefully before using your swing.

Your Loving Arms Are Better Than Any Swing
Remember, your baby loves being held by you, and his most preferred rocking will always be in your arms. So use a swing judiciously, and only to the extent that it provides you with that brief, yet much-needed, break. Any more and your infant may grow restless, and attempt a dangerous escape. Do not use a swing for more than thirty minutes at a time and no more than about two to three times each day.

WALKERS

The sheer enjoyment of watching your baby take her first steps will leave you speechless and proud. Most parents look forward to this developmental milestone almost as much as hearing their baby's first spoken words. A walker enables your baby to move about as if she were actually walking before she could do it on her own. But this product allows her to perform a physical action that far exceeds her understanding of movement and danger.

Walkers Are Very Dangerous

Walkers are one of the most popular child products sold in the United States today. They are also one of the most dangerous. Parents often fail to appreciate the hazards associated with walkers. An estimated twenty-eight thousand infant injuries are associated with walkers every year in the United States. Since 1973, walkers have been associated with the deaths of thirty-four infants. These accidents can be as minor as pinched toes and fingers or as serious as burns, suffocations, and drownings. In fact, nearly 30 percent of all head injuries to infants in the United States occur as a result of walker-related accidents. Can you guess how most infants are seriously injured? Seventy-five percent of walker-related accidents occur when an infant rolls into and falls down a stairway.

In Canada, infant walkers have been banned from stores. Consumer groups in the United States have stated publicly that infant walkers are too dangerous and must be banned from our stores as well. In 1995, the American Academy of Pediatrics also called for a U.S. ban. Infant walkers are inherently dangerous—it is best to not purchase one for your infant.

Manufacturing Standards

Should you decide to purchase a walker anyway, several facts are worth knowing. Voluntary safety standards are followed by some manufacturers. These standards are set by the American Society for Testing and Materials and are tested by the Juvenile Products Manufacturers Association. These walkers are built with many features of quality and bear a label stating compliance to ASTM guideline F-977. Compliance with these standards does not, however, safeguard your infant from rolling into dangerous situations, which is the greatest pitfall of walkers.

- Never allow your infant to play in a walker without your constant supervision. Only direct supervision can prevent an injury from happening.
- Never allow her to use a walker near a swimming pool, a stairway, a fireplace, a driveway, or any other dangerous place, even with your supervision.

A Safe Alternative to Walkers

If you do like the concept of a walker but don't want the danger that comes with one, there is a safe alternative that has recently been introduced—stationary activity centers. The Evenflo Exersaucer, as one example, allows your infant to perform the same movements and experience similar sensations but remains stationary, so the risks of injury are minimal.

CONCLUSION

Excellent work! You have completed a very important chapter of reading. Although you may not realize it, you have already become very knowledgeable about infant injury prevention. You understand the basic development and behavior issues of infancy and how these can lead to different types of injury as your baby grows, and you have learned about the types of hazards that commonly injure babies. Finally, you learned how to eliminate these hazards from your baby's environment. I know that confronting these unpleasant and scary issues is not easy to do, but now you can begin to put this new-found knowledge to work in your daily life. As you are beginning to see, injury prevention is vital to your child's health and has far-reaching consequences in determining his future.

Nothing in life is black-and-white, and the stages of childhood are no exception. Some children develop faster and some slower. Precisely when a child becomes a toddler is more a matter of individual growth and development than of age. Your infant may be at a very different behavioral and developmental level than his peers when he reaches his first birthday. I point this out to stress the importance of continuing to read into the next chapter. The years of toddlerhood will soon approach, if they have not already done so, and the next chapter is packed with crucial information about your toddler. In fact, much of the information in the toddler chapter is also pertinent to infants, especially older infants. In short, the chapters "Infants" and "Toddler and Preschoolers" should be read together and as soon as possible if you already have an infant at home. The chapter after that can wait a little while—you have time. But for now, keep reading.

Toddlers and Preschoolers (1–5 Years)

Congratulations. You and baby have safely enjoyed the first twelve months. Give yourself a pat on the back for a job well done. But don't celebrate too long; the first year of your baby's life was just a warm-up for what's ahead. During infancy it was relatively easy to supervise and protect your baby. You focused on making his environment safe, and when you needed a break, his crib was always standing by. In a bittersweet sense, those days of your baby lying about and shaking a rattle are long gone. Yes, the rules of the game are changing. His physical abilities and desire to explore will be the greatest factors that change how you must now approach the issue of safety. He'll scoot about here, there, and everywhere looking for interesting things to do and see. By twelve to sixteen months of age he will be toddling, and by two years he will be running. Prepare to enter a world where your little one develops rocketlike speed and amazing endurance. You must not only keep up with him, you must stay ahead of him, teach him, feed him, clothe him, and keep him safe—no small job indeed!

Your toddler will be attracted to all sorts of objects with new sounds and movements, and when something interests him he will go after it with zeal. His hand-eye coordination will enable him to better explore the environment and discover all that is possible. If there is a dangerous item or situation to be found, he will find it. You might say your toddler is self-destructive. Childproofing your entire home and yard now becomes a crucial aspect of maintaining a child-safe environment.

Bumps, scrapes, and bruises will naturally occur as your child learns to walk, run, jump, and skip about his wonderful new world. Most toddlers get by with just minor scrapes and bruises, and sometimes stitches are needed for deeper cuts. More serious injuries do occur, though. In fact, trauma accounts for 45 percent of all deaths in toddlers. Once again, these injuries are very predictable. Most accidents take place in or around the home or in motor vehicle collisions.

If you are nervous about the approaching years, don't worry. Anxiety and even fear is normal and healthy. Remember how nervous you were when your baby was born? Continue to believe in yourself and you will do just fine.

Many of the same types of injuries to infants also occur to toddlers. If you haven't already done so, read the infant chapter first to prepare you for some of the important hazards to toddlers not mentioned in this chapter. Your toddler is also vulnerable to being injured in new ways that will be discussed in the following pages.

TODDLER DEVELOPMENT

One to Two Years
Somewhere between the ages of one and two years, your child will begin to walk and run. At first his walking will be very unsteady and wobbly. We call this "toddling." During this phase he will fall frequently. But soon he will be steady on his feet and moving about. With his newfound mobility, your toddler's primary interest will be to explore the surrounding environment (i.e., your home and yard).

By the age of one year, your toddler will be holding, feeling, and touching whatever he can get his tiny little hands on, enabling him to experiment and learn. He will begin using his thumb and forefinger to grab and play with objects. He will use his hands to carry away objects that he likes. Pulling, tugging, pushing, and knocking things over will be some of his greatest pleasures. Toddlers have a tendency to place things in their mouths as they use the newfound senses of taste and touch to further investigate objects. "Mine" and "give me" will be commonly used phrases as your toddler grows more possessive. Gradually, she will develop more advanced play interests that involve sharing and giving, but until then expect her to be very self-oriented.

Two to Three Years
As your youngster reaches two years of age, his activity and energy levels will skyrocket. Expect more running, jumping, climbing, and tumbling. Because of this, he will now be at greater risk of injury.

By the age of three years, your child's motor skills will be well-developed. He will use his hands and fingers with greater dexterity. Constructive projects, such as building and creating things, will be enjoyed. With his curiosity and keen imagination, your toddler might also be tempted to play with dangerous items such as:

• machines and appliances
• sharp instruments such as scissors, knives, and other household tools

- poisons such as cleaning solutions, alcohol, fuels, and medicines
- firearms

Remember, close supervision at all times is the rule especially during the toddler years.

Because he is better able to manipulate his surroundings and escape uncomfortable situations, your toddler is less likely to be involved in a suffocation or strangulation accident. Drowning, however, continues to be a great danger because toddlers are rarely afraid of pools, bathtubs, hot tubs, or other bodies of water. Burn injuries are also very common during the preschool years. House fires, hot bathwater, and kitchen mishaps are the top three reasons toddlers suffer burn injuries. Toddlers sometimes play near streets. Consequently, auto-pedestrian accidents are more likely to occur. Despite all these possible ways of being injured, the greatest danger your little one will face is when he rides in an automobile. If your child is going to be injured, it will most likely occur while traveling in the family car, truck, or minivan. Toddler safety may seem like an overwhelming job, but it really isn't. In fact, as you will see, the rules are rather simple and straightforward. Just follow the basic tips in this chapter and you will dramatically decrease his risk of serious injury.

TODDLER-PROOFING YOUR HOME

Your child's primary environment is still his home. He will spend more time here than anywhere else. It is no surprise, then, that so many toddler injuries occur in homes. In fact, over 25 million children are injured each year in home accidents. Begin toddler-proofing your home as soon as possible to give you plenty of time for preparation.

Have a System

Try as you might, you will not be able to keep track of your toddler's comings and goings every second of every day. It is just not physically possible. For those brief moments when he does escape your watch, child-proofing is essential.

- Systematically go through each room searching for and eliminating specific child dangers. For example, identify and secure unstable furniture throughout your house, and when this is done move to the next job, such as replacing electrical outlet covers with ones that are child safe.
- Try looking at the world through your toddler's eyes. Get down on your hands and knees and crawl beneath tables, couches, beds, and desks looking for dangling electrical cords, small objects, unstable furniture, and sharp surfaces. Open cabinet doors in search of poisons.
- At least once a day, make a quick run-through looking for small objects on the floor or other new dangers that may have just arisen.

An Everyday Job

Not to be pessimistic, but childproofing is a job you will truly never complete. You can keep up with it, though. Maintaining a child-safe home requires continued diligence at fixing some things and discarding others as wear and tear occurs to furniture, toys, clothing, and so on. Simply put, child safety is a job that will remain a work in progress as long as you have children in the home.

- Keep a well-organized and clean home. Coins and other small items can choke young children and house dust might contain lead.
- Don't try to toddler-proof your home in one day. This is not a job to be done all at once. Make it a part of your daily routine.
- Tackle one project at a time. For instance, focus on burn injuries one day and go from room to room making a list of potential hazards as you go. The next day, shop for and install the necessary safety devices and equipment that will enable you to eliminate the identified dangers.

YOUR PRESCHOOLER

Preschool is that time just before your child begins grade school—ages four to five years. By now she is no longer toddling. In fact, she's probably faster than you are, as she darts about the home and yard with lightning speed. Her appreciation for danger, however, has yet to develop. The types of hazards she faces are generally the same as during the toddler years, but there are some notable differences.

Child safety takes planning and preparation. Hopefully you are reading this section before your child has reached the preschool years. But if not, keep reading—there's no time to waste.

Preschooler Development

By now your preschooler is capable of doing many more things than ever before. She can instinctively avoid some of the injury pitfalls to infancy and toddlerhood. But new and unique dangers are just around the corner. As your child grows up, the focus of child injury prevention will gradually shift from inside your home to the yard and then to the community. Her exposure to the adult world is much greater now as she travels more and interacts with people outside the family. Consider the dangers that exist in parks, playgrounds, automobiles, pools, yards, and other homes. Education also begins to play a role in the prevention of injury. As she understands more of what is said, start teaching her about safety. On the other hand, as she gets smarter she will occasionally try to manipulate you to get what she wants. At times her attention span will be poor or her motivation lacking. Expect these situations and prepare to deal appropriately with them, rather than just react with frustration and anger.

Teaching Safety to Your Preschooler

Repeat, repeat, repeat. Your preschooler is fully capable of learning basic safety rules. So start the education process early. Be persistent and patient; your hard work will eventually pay off. Keep things fun and interesting and don't be too lengthy or formal—at this age she is not yet ready for classroom-style lectures. Remember, the key to learning is repetition. Repeat, repeat, and repeat what you want her to learn, and before you know it, she'll be telling you and the rest of the world all about her rules of safety.

Be a good example. As your little one enters the preschool years, don't forget to set a good example. You are the center of her world, and she will be watching and listening to everything you say and do. Her behavior and actions will be molded by the examples you set. Be sure to always follow the safety rules you teach.

Setting limits for the sake of safety. The psychological tactics of rule making, positive rewards, and discipline become ever so important during the preschool years. Setting well-defined boundaries will not only let your child know what is expected of her, it will help keep her safe.

- Consistently enforce your rules of safety and set reasonable limits to teach your toddler self-discipline.
- When she follows your safety rules, provide her with rewards like hugs, kisses, praise, and smiles.
- When she steps out of line and acts in an unsafe manner, immediately let her know you disapprove.
- Firmness in your rule making will set the stage for a respectful relationship between the two of you and will go a long way in creating a child-safe environment in your home.
- Do not punish your child by screaming at, slapping, or hitting her. This can do much more harm than good. Use techniques such as time-out periods and taking toys away as negative reinforcement for toddlers and preschoolers.

Don't give up, don't give in. As she struggles to establish independence from you, your toddler will occasionally throw fits and defy the rules you set. At times, her natural attempts to separate from you will be marked by assertiveness and hyperactivity. This period can be hectic and exhausting. Whining or complaining are to be expected. At times you may feel like throwing in the towel and letting the little tyrant have her way. But be patient and persistent and your efforts will be rewarded. During these periods of disobedience and tantrums, you may find yourself getting frustrated or even angry. Be careful not to let your anger lead to physical abuse.

- Never strike your child.
- Try to maintain a cool disposition during these trying times; it will go a long way in preserving your sanity and your child's safety.
- Never allow the stressful periods to distract you from your priorities. Safety must always come first.

Don't worry—child safety can be fun. There are many safety concerns of which you must be aware when raising a youngster in today's world. Stay upbeat and approach the issue of injury prevention with diligence. By the same token, don't get wrapped up in child safety so much that your toddler is prevented from enjoying life to its fullest. Childhood is meant to be a time of innocence, joy, and learning. The freedom to explore and play is very necessary for child growth. Fortunately, you need only look around to see how many wonderful, yet safe, family adventures do exist.

GENERAL HAZARDS

AUTO-PEDESTRIAN ACCIDENTS

(See also "Halloween" in "Holidays," page 54; and "Auto-Pedestrian Accidents" in "School-Age Children," page 167.)

It is no secret that toddlers do love to run, and at times yours will run simply for the sake of running. Whether she travels in tight circles around the living room or shoots straight across your lawn, you can bet she will be impulsive and unpredictable. One moment she can be playing in your backyard, and in the next darting across the street. Although your toddler's physical skills will allow her to move about quickly, her cognitive skills will take a while to catch up. To make matters even more difficult, she will have very poor judgment and little understanding of danger. In her mind, a moving automobile is as harmless as her own tricycle. And she will be unable to recognize boundaries such as property lines, sidewalks, driveways, or streets. Combine all this with the fact that she is so small and barely visible to drivers, and you can see why supervision near a street is always a must. Most auto-pedestrian tragedies do, in fact, occur close to home—either on the driveway or in front of the house. Also, they occur with some frequency near schools and bus stops.

Indeed, auto-pedestrian accidents account for some staggering statistics. Roughly 35 percent of all auto-pedestrian accident victims are toddlers. And over five hundred children in this age group are killed in this way every year. National estimates reveal that the majority of toddlers in the one-to-two-year age range who are struck by automobiles were hit when a vehicle was being backed down a driveway. Older toddlers, on the other hand, were usually playing near their homes without supervision and were hit by automobiles driving down the street.

The Three Outs

Several common factors are typically associated with auto-pedestrian accidents that involve toddlers. Be aware of these scenarios and avoid them at all costs.

Dart-outs. Most important is the "dart-out" move, which is when a child darts from between or behind parked cars into the street. Often the driver of an oncoming vehicle has little warning when this occurs. Dart-outs account for nearly 70 percent of auto-pedestrian accidents involving young children. What prompts a young child to dart out into a street? Sometimes a preschooler is chasing a ball or another toy, and at other times is running after an adult, another child, or a pet.

- Move all cars from both sides of your street to decrease the chances of a dart-out.
- Never allow your toddler to play in the front yard.
- Always keep a close eye on her when she is near a street.

Back-outs. Your toddler can also be injured if she happens to get behind a car as it is being backed down a driveway. Always take the time to fully walk around and to look beneath your vehicle before getting in.

Afternoon outs. What time of day do you think auto-pedestrian accidents involving toddlers and preschoolers are most likely to occur? Once again, this type of injury is very predictable. Most kids are struck by moving vehicles after they have been released from school or day care but before dinner—between the hours of 3:00 and 7:00 P.M. During this time, many people are driving home from work. Keep your child away from streets, especially between these hours.

What to Teach Your Child

Educating your tyke on pedestrian safety is one of the most important protective actions you can take. She will carry this knowledge for the rest of her life. Teach her the following rules during the preschool years:

- Always hold the hand of a familiar adult when crossing a street or intersection.
- Never play in a street—this includes riding a toy, throwing a ball, or talking with other children.
- Never chase a ball or a toy that rolls into the street.
- Never play on a driveway or in a parking lot without an adult.
- Never go in between or beneath a parked car.

Wheels Beneath Your Child

Tricycles and other riding toys are immensely entertaining to toddlers and preschoolers and there is nothing inherently wrong with them. Just be very choosy about where your child is allowed to ride. The safest place for her to ride is a fenced backyard. An auto-pedestrian accident is much more likely to occur if she rides on the driveway or a street. If she must ride on your driveway, be sure to block the entrance. Remember, most riding toys for toddlers have no brakes, so a barrier from traffic is very important. If your driveway is sloped toward the street, a barrier probably isn't enough to keep her safe. Some neighborhood streets are not busy. They can give parents and drivers a false sense of security. So, even if you live on a quiet street, follow the rules in this section.

- Closely supervise your child whenever you let her cruise up and down a sidewalk or a blocked-off driveway.
- Never let her ride in or near a street.

BURNS/FIRES

(See also "Home Fires," page 47; "Fourth of July" in "Holidays," page 52; "Burns/Fires" in "Infants," page 101; and "Burns/Fires" in "School-Age Children," page 171.)

Burns are the third-leading cause of accidental death in toddlers. Nearly 1,000 toddlers and preschoolers die each year in the United States from various types of burns. Home fires cause over 80 percent of these deaths. Another two thousand young kids are permanently disabled and many thousands more are physically scarred every year. Fireplaces and wood-burning stoves are responsible for about three thousand serious burns to toddlers each year, and thousands more suffer mild injuries that require only minor treatment. Clothing fires, scald injuries, and assault are other common causes of burns in young children.

Clothing
(See also "Clothing" in "Infants," page 101.)

Each year more than 300 children suffer burn injuries when household flames catch flammable clothing on fire. Common causes of a child's clothing catching fire are candles, stovetops, cigarette lighters, and fireplaces, not to mention house fires.

As your child grows into toddlerhood, she can begin wearing regular clothing during the daytime, but when she goes to bed, her pajamas should be flame-retardant. A quick check of the manufacturer's content label will verify a garment's safety.

In addition, infant and toddler pajamas should be snug fitting rather than loose and baggy. Large T-shirts and gowns are out. Any space between a child's skin and her clothing provides additional oxygen that can serve to fuel a nearby flame.

What to Teach Your Child
The earlier you start teaching your toddler about fire safety the less likely he is to get burned. You will be surprised how early a child can understand the meaning of H-O-T.

By showing him a cooking appliance such as a crockpot, for example, and saying the word *hot* with a big frown on your face, you can teach him not to touch it. He may forget sometimes what you've taught him, but by repeating such lessons over and over he will soon be telling you what things are hot, as he exhibits his own version of a frowning face.

Playing with Fire

As your child grows older, the dangers he faces will change. Older children are at greater risk of being burned by gasoline, kerosene, and gunpowder, because they tend to experiment with flammable materials and fire. But toddlers and preschoolers can also be at risk when tagging along with a big brother or sister. Never let your child play with another youngster who experiments with fire.

The Scalding Dangers of Residential Water

Scalding is another way toddlers get burned. Over fifteen thousand children are treated in ERs for scald injuries each year in the United States, and most are toddlers. Your toddler is at greatest risk of being scalded when he is one to two years of age and just learning to walk, climb, and grab. Hot tap water is a common way toddlers are scalded. Ten to 15 percent of scald injuries in young children occur while entering a tub of hot water. Sometimes a child is placed into a bath by a parent not expecting the water to be so hot.

Residential water can reach very high temperatures, as high as 71 degrees Celsius (160 degrees Fahrenheit). This is way too hot! At 71 degrees Celsius the full thickness of a young child's skin can be burned (third degree) in less than one second. At 60 degrees Celsius (140 degrees Fahrenheit), the same burn will occur within five seconds. Antiscald devices are currently being marketed. They will shut off hot-water delivery at the faucet if a specified temperature is exceeded. Faucet handle covers that prevent children from running water into a tub or sink can also be purchased. Although these devices make excellent preventive tools, supervision of your toddler is still critical.

- Set the dial on your family's hot water thermostat to 50 degrees Celsius (122 degrees Fahrenheit). This gives you hot water for washing clothes and dishes, yet decreases the likelihood of scald injuries. But don't trust a thermostat alone; there have been reports of inaccurate readings. Use a thermometer to directly verify your water temperature at its highest.
- Use an antiscald device to prevent your toddler's bathwater from ever getting too hot.
- Become familiar with what a safe temperature feels like, and always test it against your inner forearm skin before placing your child in the tub.
- Never leave your toddler unsupervised while in or near a bathtub. Not only can he get burned, but the risk of drowning is present.
- Place a sliding bolt high on the outside of your bathroom door, to control your toddler's access.

Jimmy's story. In the emergency room I treated a thirteen-month-old toddler named Jimmy whose four-year-old brother had dropped him into a bathtub of very hot water. Jimmy was scalded over 40 percent of his body. The older boy later said with tears streaming down his honest face, "I was just helping out with the baby." This injured toddler spent several days in the hospital, but did well and will fortunately suffer no permanent scars. Going back to the very basics of injury prevention, strict supervision by an adult could have prevented this near disaster. Never leave the responsibility of supervising your toddler to another child.

Kitchens

(See also "The Most Dangerous Room" in "Infants," page 102.)

Of all the rooms in your home, the most dangerous to your toddler is the kitchen. Burns are the primary reason why. Boiling water and hot grease can cause extensive burns to a young child who pulls a pot down off the stove. And don't forget, the kitchen is also the most likely place that a home fire will start. Keep these facts in mind when cooking.

- Turn the handles of your pots and pans toward the back of the stove when cooking to decrease the likelihood that your toddler grabs one.
- Avoid using the front burners on your stove.
- Remove the control knobs to the front burners, so you will be less inclined to use them.
- Be sure your stove and oven are always turned off when not in use.
- Always close the oven door when it is not in use. Infants and toddlers have been killed because they leaned or crawled onto an open oven door and caused the stove to crash down upon them.
- Keep step stools, chairs, and similar items out of the kitchen so your infant can't crawl up to the table or stove.
- Keep a fire extinguisher in the kitchen at all times.

Watch Out for Dangling Dangers. One frequently overlooked danger in the kitchen is the dangling appliance cord, which can be used by a toddler to pull down a hot coffeepot, waffle iron, or other such item. A tablecloth that hangs too far over the edge can also enable your toddler to pull hot drinks or dishes down.

- Never leave appliance cords out where a toddler might reach them.
- Leave as little tablecloth as possible hanging off the edge of your dinner table. One trick is to tuck the corners underneath so they don't hang too far down. Of course, you can also alter your tablecloths so they fit the dinner table just right.

Electrical Burns

The two most common ways that youngsters get electrocuted are by jabbing something (i.e., electrical plug, hairpin, key, knife, letter opener, paper clip, etc.) into a wall socket or by playing with a worn-out electrical cord. One effective way to prevent this type of injury is by using a ground-fault circuit interrupter (GFCI).

- For information on how to have your home wall sockets updated with GFCIs, send a postcard to Ground-Fault Circuit Interrupters, Washington, DC 20207, and a copy will be sent to you.

Severe burns to the lips can result if a toddler chews through the insulation of a cord. Electrocution can also occur if an appliance such as a radio, telephone, curling iron, or blow dryer is pulled into a bathtub or sink full of water.

- Never leave an electrical cord lying out in the open where your toddler might find it.
- Keep all appliances out of the bathroom when he is bathing.

Electrical outlets. Outlets are responsible for over five thousand fires and forty deaths each year in the United States. An electrical outlet that becomes worn or damaged may spark and cause a fire. Outlets also are dangerous to exploring toddlers who might get shocked. Outlet covers are the best way to prevent electrical burns. The best electrical socket covers are those that can be mounted to the wall and locked. Some covers will flip up or slide back and forth, springing into place when let go; these are also useful and safe. The rule of thumb here is to choose a cover that requires two separate actions to remove, making it nearly impossible for a toddler to figure out. Plugs and caps are not sufficient to keep toddlers from getting into a socket. When pulled out, these small covers can also cause a toddler to choke.

- Place safety covers over all electrical outlets in your home.
- Never use removable plugs; instead, use the type of safety covers that are mounted to the wall.
- Thoroughly inspect your home for deteriorating receptacles and have a licensed electrician replace any that are damaged.

Curling Irons

A major cause of facial burns to young children is the hair curling iron. Children five years and under suffer over six thousand curling iron burn injuries every year. Sometimes burns to the eyes cause blindness. Beware of hot curling irons left lying in a bathroom or bedroom, especially when toddlers and preschoolers are roaming the house.

Irons and Ironing Boards

Ironing boards and the irons that sit atop them are a hazard to children who might topple the board. Even when unplugged an iron can cause serious cuts and bruises if it falls onto a child. Never leave an iron—plugged or unplugged—sitting on an ironing board when young children are in the room.

Radiators

Nearly a thousand infants and toddlers are burned by radiators each year in the United States. These injuries can be severe if a little one becomes wedged between a radiator and a piece of furniture after rolling off a bed or chair. Be sure to place a safety cover over any radiator with which your child might come into contact. Move all furniture away from radiators to prevent your child from getting stuck between the two.

Chemicals

Caustic chemicals such as battery acid, turpentine, and drain cleaner can also cause burns to children. Keep chemicals far out of reach of children, preferably outside the home where your flammable materials are stored.

CHOKING

Balloons and Plastic Bags

Toddlers are very much at risk of choking on small objects and foods. Items such as latex balloons, plastic bags, rubber bands, rubber gloves, coins, buttons, marbles, button batteries, jewelry, safety pins, paper clips, nails, screws, and even pins or needles are dangerous to young children.

Would you believe that balloons cause more choking deaths in young children than any other small object? It's true—toddlers who have a tendency to put small things in their mouths are at risk of choking when they chew on a balloon or a piece of balloon. Tragedies sometimes result during birthday parties and other celebrations. Even health professionals need a little education in this department. A common yet dangerous mistake that nurses and doctors make is to blow up hospital gloves (like balloons) and hand them to infants and toddlers.

• Keep balloons (inflated or deflated) away from toddlers at all times.
• Keep plastic wrappers and plastic bags out of reach; they can also be wadded up to fit in a toddler's mouth.

Food Dangers
(See also "Choking" in "Infants," page 103.)

Look to your refrigerator for many of the common items that choke infants and toddlers. Foods such as hot dog pieces, nuts, raisins, carrots, grapes, corn and potato chips, popcorn, hard candies, and chunks of meat are all choking hazards. Chewing gum is another hazard that has been linked to the choking deaths of toddlers. Any of these items can easily become lodged in the airway of a toddler and cause serious injury or death.

- Never give the above-mentioned foods to children younger than five years of age, and cut all food into very small pieces for easy swallowing.
- Remove small magnets on the door of your refrigerator. These can easily be choked on by young children.
- Never give chewing gum to a child less than six years old.

Jennifer's story. One afternoon a four-year-old preschooler named Jennifer was eating hard candy at the kitchen table. Suddenly she began acting agitated and grabbed the arm of her ten-year-old sister Lisa. Within seconds Jennifer's skin had turned blue. Lisa concluded that her little sister was suffocating. Using the skills she learned in a Girl Scouts CPR class, Lisa immediately performed the Heimlich maneuver and saved Jennifer's life. The outcome would certainly have been tragic had Lisa not known what to do. But the whole incident could have been prevented if Jennifer had never been given hard candy to eat.

Coins

Of all the small objects that toddlers swallow, coins most frequently get stuck in the esophagus (the passageway between the mouth and stomach). If your toddler swallows a coin, she should immediately have an X ray taken so your doctor can tell where it is. A coin that gets stuck in the esophagus will need to be removed by a specialist, but one that reaches the stomach should pass through the digestive tract without causing any discomfort or complications. Coins can get stuck in the airway, too, and sometimes this results in suffocation. Never leave coins lying around where your toddler can reach them.

Button Batteries

Every year six hundred button batteries are swallowed by young children. When swallowed, button batteries can leak toxic acid into the esophagus, stomach, or intestines and cause life-threatening internal injury. Surgery is sometimes necessary in these situations. Never leave a button battery where your toddler might find it. If you ever suspect that your toddler has swallowed a button battery, immediately bring her to your local emergency room.

Doorstops

The spring action of most doorstops often catches the attention of curious toddlers. The danger to these stops is in the little plastic tips that can sometimes be removed and choked on by little children. The best remedy for this danger is to replace the stops near the floor with ones near the top of the door. Solid, one-piece doorstops made of polyethylene are also available in most hardware stores.

Ear and Nose Dangers

Small objects tend to get stuffed into nostrils and ears by curious young children. Keep such items away from your toddler. Fortunately, most are easy to remove with the proper equipment when they do get lodged. In one ER we collected all the items found in the noses and ears of toddlers and kept them in a jar. Our collection included candy, peas, nuts, glass, pebbles, and necklace beads. Though these little mishaps usually get a laugh or two from doctors and nurses, they can cause serious problems. Sometimes a child's eardrum is injured during removal of the object. Also, a child might require sedation in order to remove the object, and this involves certain risks, as well.

DROWNING

(See also "Fourth of July" in "Holidays," page 52; "Swimming Pools" in "Sports and Recreation," page 80; and "Drowning" in "Infants," page 105.)

Drowning is the third-leading cause of death in toddlers. Between six hundred and seven hundred children in the one-to-four-year age group drown every year in the United States. Another three thousand toddlers are treated in emergency rooms for near-drowning injuries. In some states, such as Florida, California, and Arizona, drowning is the single most common cause of deaths in young children. Reasons for the higher incidence of drowning in these states include a longer swimming season and more pools and beaches.

Children do not fear water until they reach four or five years of age. Any body of water, no matter how shallow, is therefore a huge danger to toddlers and preschoolers. Children in the one-to-three-year age range are at greatest risk because they do not understand the dangers of water and have little ability to swim. Your child might even have a natural attraction to a pool, a pond, a creek, or a hot tub. Don't be surprised if one day he tries to toddle right on up to the edge of a swimming pool or other body of water. As far as he knows, water can be walked on—and if you don't stop him, he just might try it.

Supervision Is Key

Children can drown very quickly. Many of the children I have treated were submerged for less than five minutes. Some drownings can occur in just seconds. Despite all the dangers described in this section, the most common reason a child drowns is a brief lapse in supervision. Always keep little ones safe by your side when near a body of water.

Bathrooms

(See also "Bathrooms" in "Infants," page 105.)

Bathtubs and toilets are also dangerous to children under five years of age. In the last five years, over thirty toddlers have drowned in toilets when they fell in and became stuck upside down. Gerber and Fisher Price both have lid locks on the market that can help you prevent access to the toilet by your exploring toddler. Young children also drown in bathtubs and basins. Close supervision is the only sure way to prevent such accidents, but by adding a lock (such as a sliding bolt) to the outside of the bathroom door you can better restrict your child's access to all bathroom hazards. As your preschooler becomes older and more responsible, the dangers to a bathroom will diminish, and he will eventually be able to use it independently.

- Put a lock on your toilet lid so your toddler cannot open the lid. Replace the lock after each use.
- Always drain your own bathwater immediately after bathing if a little one is running about.
- Use a sliding bolt lock on the outside of your bathroom door to keep your toddler from entering by himself.

Buckets

(See also "Buckets" in "Infants," page 107.)

Another danger is that large bucket you use for housecleaning or mopping. Five-gallon buckets have been associated with numerous infant and toddler drownings.

Ponds, Troughs, and Wells

Any body of water to which a toddler has access is dangerous. Ponds, troughs, and wells are sometimes overlooked until a tragedy takes place. I know of one toddler who made it through the strands of a barbed-wire fence and drowned in a cattle trough. Toddlers will go over, under, through, and around inadequate barriers to find trouble—remember, they are self-destructive. A wooden fence like the one described in "Swimming Pools" in "Sports and Recreation" (see page 80) is ideal for keeping a toddler away from an outdoor body of water.

- Eliminate all water hazards around your home.
- Construct a toddler-proof barrier around any body of water that cannot be removed.

FALLS

As your toddler learns to stand, walk, jump, and run, she will experience many falls. Fortunately, she is more durable than you probably realize. In fact, your child's soft, flexible bones and joints allow her to tolerate falls much better than we adults. When a toddler or preschooler falls, the injury is usually minor. But falls from elevations greater than one or two feet can result in greater injury. Falls result in seventy-five toddler deaths each year, and thousands more are nonfatally injured. Toddlers usually crawl into these situations during a brief lapse of supervision. One reason toddlers fall so frequently is that they have yet to develop the cognitive ability to recognize the danger of height. Another reason is that sometimes young children get placed on elevated surfaces. Your toddler can move very quickly, and in a single moment she can fall to the floor if placed on an elevated surface. Don't give in to the temptation of leaving your toddler on a table or countertop thinking you can watch her closely while she is there.

Furniture, steps, and bathtubs are typical places from which toddlers fall. Place chairs and sofas up against the wall so your child can't climb over the back. And teach your little one never to climb, stand, or jump on furniture.

Windows

Serious injuries or death can occur if a child falls from a window. Most children involved in this type of accident are between the ages of one and four years, but older children are still at risk. Often, a piece of furniture is used by an active toddler or preschooler to reach the window, so never place a chair or other piece of furniture beneath a window that can be opened. Check all windows in your home to be sure they are all closed and unable to be opened by your child. Usually the windows involved have no screens and are left wide open, although five inches of space is all it takes for a child to slip through. And don't rely on window screens—children have been known to fall right through them. I know of one child who crawled from her bed to an open window and fell through the screen to the outside. Sturdy window guards can prevent most of these injuries. Look for a window guard that does not allow your window to be opened more then three and a half inches. Just be careful not to place a window guard over a window that is a designated emergency exit. Your best bet is to find a window guard that has a quick-release mechanism that allows an easy escape in the event of a fire. Window guards cost from $8 to $30, depending on the size and design you buy, and in many urban apartments they are installed free of charge. Check with your landlord or local housing administration about the requirements.

Slipping, Tripping, or Stumbling

Just like adults, young children can slip, trip, or stumble. Injuries that result can be serious, especially if a child falls into another piece of furniture or onto a sharp object such as a knife or pencil. Fireplace hearths and coffee tables are two common objects upon which toddlers hurt themselves. Throw rugs that can slide or bunch up can also cause young children to fall at home. The bathroom and kitchen are the most common areas inside the home in which children slip and fall. Moisture on the floor is usually responsible for a slippery surface. Slip-resistant strips or bathtub mats can decrease the likelihood of tub and shower falls, too.

Cushioning the impact. A product called Toddler Shield is now on the market. This foam device will fit onto the edge of your table, cushioning the blow if your child falls into it. A similar foam shield can be placed around the edges of your fireplace hearth.

- Tack down your small rugs so they cannot slide out from under your child.
- Always mop up water that finds its way onto your floors.
- Use slide-resistant rugs and place stick-ons in the bathtub in your child's bathroom.
- Toys and other tripping hazards can lead to injury, too, so always keep your floors free of such dangers, and teach your child to do so as well.

Winter Falls

The ice and snow on outdoor sidewalks and stairs is responsible for hundreds of slipping injuries each winter. These falls can lead to cuts and bruises, but can cause broken bones. Be sure you keep outside surfaces free of winter's slippery dangers.

MOTOR VEHICLE ACCIDENTS

(See also "Automobiles," page 11; and "Motor Vehicle Accidents" in "Infants," page 108.)

Our little ones spend considerable time riding in automobiles. If your toddler or preschooler is like most, on average he will spend one to two hours each day traveling to and from the day care center or just running errands with you. This puts him at risk of being injured in a motor vehicle accident (MVA). In fact, for the next thirty or forty years the greatest threat to his health and life will be an MVA. About five hundred toddlers are killed in MVAs each year in the United States, while another fifty to sixty thousand are injured and require treatment in hospital emergency rooms. Most of these injuries and deaths can be prevented if the simple rules in this chapter are followed.

Child Seats

By now your toddler has outgrown his infant seat and must ride in a forward-facing child seat. Be sure he always rides in a child seat until he reaches four years of age or weighs forty pounds. Child seats come in several designs and styles. Those with a five-point harness system (two straps for the shoulders, two for the waist, and one for the crotch) are the best. The seats using the padded T-shaped shield attached to the shoulder straps are not to be used with infants. If you used a convertible seat for your baby, you may now turn it around (facing forward and sitting upright) and use it for your toddler.

Integrated Safety Seats

The simplest solution to obtaining and positioning a car seat is to have one already built into the automobile you purchase. Most vehicles, however, do not possess integrated safety seats for toddlers. The following is a list of recent models that do. Just remember, though, integrated safety seats are not for infants.

Buick	1997 Century
Chevrolet	1994–96 Lumina van 1996–97 Astro, Lumina Sedan 1997 Camaro, Venture
Chrysler	1993–96 Concord 1994–97 Town & Country 1995–97 Cirrus
Dodge	1992–97 Caravan, Grand Caravan 1993–96 Intrepid 1995–97 Neon, Stratus
Eagle	1993–96 Vision
Ford	1993–97 Aerostar 1994–97 Escort 1995–97 Explorer, Windstar
Geo	1997–97 Prizm
GMC	1996–97 Safari
Jeep	1996 Grand Cherokee
Mercury	1994–97 Tracer 1996–97 Villager 1997 Mountaineer, Sable Wagon
Mitsubishi	1997 Diamante
Nissan	1997 Quest
Oldsmobile	1994–97 Silhouette

Plymouth	1992–97 Voyager, Grand Voyager
	1995–97 Neon
	1996–97 Breeze
Pontiac	1994–97 Trans Sport
Saab	1997 All models
Toyota	1997 Corolla
Volvo	1997 All models

In 1997 parents reported difficulty with the latch mechanism of the integrated seats in the following automobiles:

Chrysler Town and Country
Dodge Caravan
Grand Caravan
Plymouth Voyager

These latch mechanisms, if not cleaned properly, can become difficult to release after a child is buckled in. In some circumstances these straps can even tighten around an infant as attempts are made to open the latch. No injuries have been reported yet. If you own one of these minivans and have an integrated child seat, contact the manufacturer for recall information.

Booster Seats

So, at what age can a kid begin to ride without a safety seat? Definitely not yet! During the preschool years, your child will be making the important transition from safety seat to seat belt. Children can be vulnerable at this time if their parents don't know what to do next. At about the age of four years or at forty pounds, a child becomes too big for a safety seat. But is he tall enough to use a regular seat belt? Probably not. That's where booster seats come in. Booster seats were developed for children in the four-to-six-year age range. They allow children to sit high enough to fit a standard seat belt. Use a booster during the preschool years, and by age six a seat belt should be just right.

There are two basic types of booster seats currently on the market: the front-shielded boosters and the high-back boosters. Until recently, both were considered safe for children between thirty and sixty pounds, but recent crash tests by Consumer's Union have shown that front-shielded booster seats could be dangerous to children weighing more than forty pounds if secured only by a lap belt. In these seats, a child's head and torso might not be restrained well enough in an accident to protect against injuries. If used with a lap and shoulder belt and with the shield removed, this type of booster should be okay.

The high-backed models seem to offer the best protection for a child's head and neck. A kid over forty pounds in this seat must be secured by the car's shoulder and lap belts, while a smaller child must use the harness system that comes with the booster seat.

Older cars and boosters. For cars built before 1988, there is disagreement about where to place a booster seat. Most older cars do not have backseat shoulder belts, and booster seats require both a shoulder and lap belt. If your vehicle does not have shoulder belts in the backseat, be sure your child sits up front in his booster seat, where it can be used properly.

Positioning for Safety

The safest place in a car for a young child is the middle of the backseat. The middle position keeps your busy toddler away from the doors and windows so he does not get his fingers slammed and where he cannot unlock the doors. This position also gives you easy access to him in the event of an emergency, and it decreases the likelihood of injury by keeping him away from the front seats, which can be shoved backward during an accident.

The front seat can be very dangerous to a child if a passenger-side air bag is present. Many deaths and severe injuries have occurred to children sitting in the front of a car when a passenger-side air bag deployed.

(For more specific information on air bag safety, see "Air Bags" in "Automobiles," page 16.)

Window and Door Locks

Toddlers are more likely than other children to fall from moving vehicles, because they have a tendency to fiddle with door and window handles and control buttons. New cars are equipped with buttons that can prevent windows and doors from being opened by children. To prevent children from opening a door or rolling down a window, be sure window and door locks are present in the back of your family vehicle.

Chaos in the Car

During the toddler years, your kid will be quite active and more likely than ever to leave his seat while the car is in motion. He might also try to move around the car. Be consistent and firm when enforcing the rules of car safety. Do not tolerate unruly behavior, but do not discipline your child while driving. I have treated several children from accidents caused by parents who were yelling at or trying to grab a misbehaving child while driving. If your child needs immediate attention, pull the car off the road and then address the problem. Be sure to look for a parking lot or rest stop where you will not likely be hit by another vehicle.

POISONING

Over 1 million children are poisoned each year in the United States, and 90 percent of these cases occur in the home. Some poisonous substances taste good and are, therefore, more likely to be ingested in large amounts.

Most ingestions by infants do not result in significant harm because the amount swallowed is too small. Have you sat lately and watched your toddler eat? By now, she is a very active eater and drinker. Because of her growing appetite and desire to taste things, she is also more likely to swallow large amounts of toxic substances if she comes upon them. In fact, toddlers are at greater risk of severe poisoning than children of any other age.

Proper Containers

It is not uncommon for children to drink poisons that are stored in glass jars or drinking glasses. Placing a poison in a jar, glass, or cup can also give a kid the impression that it is a food or a drink. Another disadvantage with secondary containers is that the label is no longer available. Too often, physicians are confronted with a child who has swallowed a potential poison, but because the poison cannot be identified, specific treatment cannot be rendered. Keep all potential poisons in their original containers. This allows quick and easy access to the proper instructions if an ingestion occurs.

Proper Storage of Toxic Substances

The most important step a parent can take in preventing a child from being poisoned is to store toxic substances in a safe location. If possible, put them in an outdoor shed that remains locked at all times when not in use. A secure garage is the next best place to store hazardous substances. Whether in a shed or garage, keep ALL personal hygiene items, cleaners, insecticides, pesticides, herbicides, and fuels out of your child's reach. And properly dispose of those substances no longer being used.

Super Glue

Youngsters can also get into trouble with Super Glue. Fingers can be stuck together and eyelids glued shut in a matter of seconds. Always keep glue away from your young child.

Plants

Many plants can be toxic to young children. Keep all plants out of your toddler's reach to avoid this source of potential poisoning.

Medicines

Your kid will naturally be curious about medications. Many elixirs have unique and even pleasant tastes. The bright colors of pills, capsules, and tablets can be enticing. The fact that these medications sometimes resemble candy just adds to the danger. I have treated toddlers who swallowed over a month's supply of medicine in a single sitting. Clean out your medicine cabinet frequently and throw away all unnecessary and out-of-date medications.

Some prescription medications are particularly dangerous to infants and young children. For example, a single pill of clonidine (a blood-pressure medication) can kill an infant who eats it. Medications that come in the form of patches have unusually high concentrations. A single patch of nitroglycerin (a heart medication), fentanyl (a narcotic pain medication), or nicotine can be deadly if swallowed by your infant. Over-the-counter medications can be just as deadly to infants. Acetaminophen and aspirin are two such examples. Child-resistant caps on medication bottles help prevent such accidents, but they are not always effective—the reason they are not called childproof. Be sure to keep all medicines (prescription and over-the-counter) in their proper containers and store them in a locked cabinet.

Grandma's purse. Grandparents, as grandchildren quickly learn, often carry gifts and tasty candy. Your child will come to believe that nothing but good things come from grandma's purse. Of course, we know that dangerous medications can be present. Indeed, children are often poisoned by their grandparent's medications. One study showed that over 35 percent of prescription drug overdoses by children involve a grandparent's medication. This makes sense when you think about it. Today's elderly are often on multiple medicines and, because of frequent dosing schedules, have no choice but to carry pill bottles with them. And some elderly cannot use child-resistant packages due to arthritis or weakness. Don't forget that a purse or coat lying on a kitchen table or chair can also harbor bottles of medication. When relatives and friends arrive for a visit, immediately put coats and purses out of your toddler's reach. Although you might worry about hurting the feelings of others, it is important to ask everybody who enters your home about the potential dangers they might be carrying.

Vitamins and iron. Vitamins are not generally dangerous. But many vitamin preparations are fortified with iron, and iron can be deadly if taken in large doses. In fact, child vitamins are one of the most frequently implicated products in toddler poisoning. Approximately 30 percent of all toddler poisoning deaths are a result of iron. Iron can also be found in prenatal vitamins and over-the-counter tablets and pills labeled ferrous gluconate, ferrous sulfate, and ferrous fumerate. Some vitamins and over-the-counter herbal preparations are also dangerous to young children if taken in large amounts. Your local poison control center can help you determine whether or not a specific herbal medicine is poisonous to your child.

Acetaminophen. When taken in the recommended doses, acetaminophen (usually known as Tylenol) is very safe, but in larger amounts it can be deadly. Even one and a half times the recommended dose given every four to six hours for a couple of days can cause liver damage. The symptoms are often delayed by two to three days. Fortunately, there is a very effective antidote that, if given early, can prevent liver damage from occurring. If you ever suspect that your child has overdosed on acetaminophen (or any other medicine), bring her immediately to the ER.

Acetaminophen comes in two basic nonadult preparations: a children's formula and an infant's formula. The infant's formula is much more concentrated than the children's formula and is dosed in drops rather than teaspoons. If a child accidentally receives the infant's formula in the volume directed on the children's formula label, she will have received a large overdose of acetaminophen. Dozens of toddler deaths have been caused by this mix-up. Do not confuse the infant's formula of acetaminophen with the children's formula; the concentrations are very different.

Aspirin. Another common over-the-counter medicine that can be deadly in large amounts is aspirin. Be aware that other products such as oil of wintergreen, Pepto-Bismol, and topical analgesics such as Ben-Gay contain very concentrated forms of aspirin that can kill a toddler who swallows even a small amount.

Child-resistant packaging. Use child-resistant containers and packages to store all medicines in your home. Manufacturers of prescription drugs and many over-the-counter medications are now required by the Consumer Product Safety Commission (CPSC) to use child-resistant packaging. Since the advent of child-resistant caps and other packaging safety measures, there has been a dramatic drop in the incidence of child poisonings. The CPSC estimates that over seven hundred children have been saved by child-resistant aspirin bottles. Many more lives are believed to have been saved by child-resistant containers used with other types of medicine as well. Still, each year over fifty children die from accidental poisoning. The lesson here is not to rely on child-resistant packages alone. Sometimes little ones find ways to get around these barriers, and sometimes a medication bottle is left open. As usual, your close supervision is necessary.

Your behavior counts. Parents resort to various tricks when dispensing medicine to their children. One such method is to call medicine "candy." Watch out—these tricks can give your child the wrong impression. If she believes that medicine *is* candy she might eat it as if it were. Young children learn behavior by modeling after their parents. When you take medicine in front of your child, she might later try to mimic your actions when you are not looking. So, be discreet here as well.

Alcohol and Tobacco

Remember that dinner party you put on last month for a few friends? It was late when company departed, so your dishes were left in the sink and several half-full glasses of mixed drinks remained on the coffee table. You may not think of alcohol as a poison, but to your toddler a single swallow can be fatal. Alcohol can cause rapid and severe hypoglycemia (low blood sugar) in a small child. Many over-the-counter medications such as mouthwashes and cold preparations also contain alcohol and are just as dangerous. And don't forget about tobacco. Just a few cigarettes or used butts contain enough nicotine to harm your toddler if she swallows them. The same is true for cigars, chewing tobacco, and snuff. Never leave alcohol or tobacco within reach of children.

Illegal Drugs

Children who are unfortunate enough to live in a home where illegal drugs are used by parents or older siblings can be poisoned by a small taste of cocaine, amphetamine, or heroin left lying around the house. This is not only a thoughtless and careless act by those who should know better—it is illegal and considered child neglect. If you know of a child who is exposed to illegal drugs, contact your local health and human services department or police department immediately. Remember, you are legally obligated to report such cases and may do so anonymously.

STRANGULATION AND SUFFOCATION

(See also "Playgrounds," page 65; "Strangulation and Suffocation" in "Infants," page 111; "Strollers" in "Infants," page 129; "Garage Doors" in "Toddlers and Preschoolers," page 162; and "Hammocks" in "Toddlers and Preschoolers," page 163.)

By now your little one is learning to open closets, cabinets, and drawers. His hands are busy pulling and grabbing at all sorts of things. Fortunately, if something hurts or doesn't feel right, he is likely to escape the situation. This is why toddlers and preschoolers are less at risk than infants to suffer suffocation and strangulation injuries. The possibility of these types of injuries, however, is still present. About a hundred toddlers are killed this way each year. I will not discuss the same mechanisms covered in the infant chapter (this should be reviewed again by you), but don't forget that cords, ropes, wires, and strings must still be kept out of your toddler's reach.

Drawstrings

(See also "Drawstrings in Infants," page 113, and "Escalators" in "Toddlers and Preschoolers," page 161.)

Drawstrings on your toddler's clothing can be dangerous. If a clothing drawstring catches on a piece of metal or an exposed screw, it can be pulled tight around a child's neck. At least seventeen child deaths and more than fifty other injuries have been reported in recent years. Most of these mishaps are associated with shirt, jacket, or hood strings. Playground slides seem to be the most common outdoor site for the most serious drawstring injuries, while chairs, sofas, and bed frames serve as indoor catch points. Current recommendations from the Consumer Product Safety Commission (CPSC) state that drawstrings should never be present on the hoods or around the necks of shirts or jackets. Also, if present elsewhere on a garment, they should not be longer than three inches when maximally stretched.

Be aware that a short drawstring can be made dangerously long if stretched or pulled. One solution to this problem is to cut the string into two short pieces and sew each into the fabric of the clothing so they can still be used. Elastic can then be sewn into the clothing to give your child the same comfortable fit. A better way to eliminate the hazards of clothing drawstrings is to simply remove them completely and use Velcro, snaps or buttons instead. You can also just sew the center part of the drawstring into the garment. Your best bet, however, will be to simply avoid children's clothing with drawstrings.

Appliances

As your toddler or preschooler begins to play and explore outside the home, keep a close eye on him. He can find himself in great danger if not properly supervised. Young children love to play hide-and-seek. Discarded appliances such as refrigerators, freezers, washing machines, dryers, ice boxes in campers, and even picnic coolers pose a tremendous hazard to toddlers and preschoolers because they are a tempting place to hide and put children at risk of being trapped. If a kid crawls inside an appliance and the door is shut, he might not be able to get out. Such containers are often air- and soundproof, causing a helpless child to quickly and quietly succumb to a lack of oxygen. These types of accidents are usually associated with abandoned equipment, but working appliances in the kitchen or garage such as washers and dryers have also been implicated. For more information on how to safeguard your refrigerator or freezer, write to the Association of Home Appliance Manufacturers (AHAM), 20 North Wacker Drive, Chicago, IL 60606.

Car trunks. Don't forget that a car trunk is just as dangerous to young children as a discarded appliance. Last year nearly twenty children were killed when they were inadvertently trapped in car trunks. Some major American carmakers are now selling dealer-installed kits that enable anyone trapped inside a trunk to escape. These kits will only fit newer models. A recent panel of experts recommended that the National Highway Traffic Safety Administration (NHTSA) require automakers to have handles or latches in the trunks of new cars so children can escape if locked inside.

• Rid your yard and home of all unused appliances.
• Remove the doors on all unused appliances if you cannot remove the appliance itself.

- As a last resort, lock up appliances with a chain and padlock. Just remember, the danger will still be present. Sooner or later a young child will figure out a way to look inside.
- Never let children play in or around a discarded appliance or an open automobile trunk.
- Always supervise your child; it is the only safe way to prevent suffocation injuries.

OBJECT-SPECIFIC HAZARDS

CLUTTER

Eliminate all clutter from your home and garage to keep your toddler safe. Cluttered closets and storage shelves also present dangers to the little ones in your family. In a closet or garage, place heavy and sharp items on the floor, rather than balance them on mountains of junk or on shelves. I treated a two-year-old boy named Eli who was injured when playing in the family garage. He tugged on an electrical cord that was dangling from a shelf above. A full bucket of paint that was sitting on the cord fell from six feet above and struck him on the head. Eli did fine after having his scalp wounds sewn up, but we all learned a lesson from that incident.

DANGEROUS FURNITURE

(See also "Bunk Beds," page 20.)

Youngsters have a natural tendency to view furniture the same way they do toys on a playground. Your kid's instinct will be to climb, jump, and crawl all over your living room. This natural desire to play can lead to accidents. In 1986 over thirty-three thousand children were injured when they fell from home furniture.

Bed Safety
Once your child gets to be two years old, she will be too old for a crib. A children's bed will be your next purchase. A few safety rules are in order here, too.

- Put the mattress as close to the floor as possible, or even on the floor.
- Install bed rails to prevent your child from rolling off in her sleep.
- Enforce a strict policy of no playing or jumping on beds.

Recliners (and Other Collapsible Furniture)
Recliners are dangerous to children for many reasons. Young children have been killed and seriously injured when recliners collapsed on them. Lawn and patio chairs have also been implicated in child injuries when they collapsed unexpectedly. Until your

child is old enough to understand the dangers of recliners and lawn furniture and can properly use them, these pieces of furniture should not be accessible to her.

Miscellaneous

End tables and coffee tables cause a large number of furniture-related injuries to young-sters when they fall or jump from nearby sofas or chairs. Usually these injuries are lim-ited to lacerations on the head or face.

- Move your coffee table at least four feet away from all other furniture in the room, especially the sofa.
- Do not allow jumping from furniture or running in the house.
- Keep your child's bedroom furniture at least four feet away from her bed.
- Check all pieces of furniture to be sure they are void of protrusions (nails, screws), splinters, or loose knobs.

Glass Tabletops

Youngsters often jump on or pound on tabletops. Severe lacerations to a child's arms and legs can occur if a glass tabletop shatters. Children have even been killed when they fell through glass tabletops. Avoid glass tabletops.

Unstable Furniture

Sometimes it isn't the child falling from or onto the furniture but the furniture falling onto a child that leads to injury. Remember, toddlers are constantly pulling and tugging at whatever interests them—and everything interests them. Examples of unstable fur-niture that are most likely to fall onto young children include bookcases, entertainment centers, television sets, dressers, grandfather clocks, vase stands, lamps, sculptures, and baker's racks. Chairs can also be unstable and may topple when an active toddler is climbing about. Aquariums are frequently placed on flimsy stands and can be brought down quite easily if pushed, pulled, or rocked. Your best bet is to secure all unstable furniture to the wall. If this cannot be done, be sure your toddler is not able to get into a room in which dangerous furniture sits. Just remember, this method is rarely suc-cessful because toddlers are extremely persistent. The best way to ensure against this type of injury? Store your unstable furniture outside the home for a few years or get rid of it altogether.

- Secure your tall furniture to the walls with brackets.
- Eliminate all unnecessary top-heavy furniture from your home.

Dresser drawers. Just like the living and dining rooms in your home, your child's bedroom should be void of tall or unstable furniture. However, there is one piece of fur-niture that is hard to do without. Dressers are a necessary yet potentially dangerous item found in the bedrooms of most children. If a young child crawls over or onto an open drawer, the whole dresser can tumble over. Believe it or not, this scenario kills several children every year in the United States. You can prevent dresser accidents by securing your child's dresser to the wall with brackets.

ESCALATORS

With the excitement of shopping in a crowded mall, it is easy to forget that children can get hurt. Escalators are a danger that must never be overlooked. Each year two thousand children are treated in U.S. emergency rooms for injuries sustained on escalators. Half of these accidents result from falls, while 40 percent occur when a youngster's hand or foot gets caught in the moving stairs.

Safe Clothing
(See also "Drawstrings" in "Toddlers and Preschoolers," page 157.)

Close supervision is definitely important when your child is on an escalator, but the other key to preventing this type of injury is the proper clothing. Accidents occur when shoestrings, drawstrings, clothing, or extremities get caught in the moving parts of an escalator. Long or tea-length dresses or skirts can easily catch on the moving stairs of an escalator and be pulled downward. Sandals that allow little toes to stick out can lead to pinching injuries on escalators.

- Remember, it is generally safest to take stairs rather than the escalator when shopping with your toddler.
- Before getting onto an escalator, be sure your child's clothing has no loose strings or material.
- Be sure all toddler clothing is greater than two inches off the ground.
- Buy shoes that have Velcro straps or buckles instead of laces.

FIREARMS

(See also "Firearms," page 45; and "Firearms" in "School-Age Children," page 180.)

A young child is in danger anytime a gun is in the home, whether loaded or unloaded, locked up or left out. Handguns are more dangerous than any other type of weapon because kids are more likely to pick them up and handle them. Preschoolers in particular are likely to play with a handgun found lying around the home. And don't think your four-year-old can't pull back the hammer and squeeze the trigger of your handgun. Trust me, he can. One situation that often leads to serious injury in toddlers and preschoolers is when an older child plays with a loaded gun around a younger child. Often the curious toddler or preschooler is just tagging along when an older child accidentally fires the gun. The fact is, a handgun in your home is fifty times more likely to be involved in the inadvertent shooting death of a child than used in self-defense.

So when you bring a gun home, just think about whose little hands might find it. And when you load a gun, think about whose little heartbeat could be stopped by that bullet. Simply placing your gun on the top shelf of a closet or in a drawer does not prevent an injury. Children find ways to access those things they are curious about—and most children are curious about guns. Trigger locks provide additional safety, but they are no substitute for a locked cabinet or safe.

- Always unload your weapon before bringing it into the home, and lock it in a cabinet or safe that is inaccessible to your toddler or preschooler.
- Be sure to keep ammunition locked in a separate location from your weapon. This makes it twice as difficult for your child to handle a loaded gun.
- Finally, ask yourself how important a gun in your home is to your family. The only way to really play it safe when raising a child is not to own a gun at all.

Guns in Other Homes

Unfortunately, many tragedies occur to children while visiting other homes. Approximately 40 percent of all accidental handgun shootings that involve kids take place in the homes of friends and relatives. Always inquire about guns before allowing your child to play at somebody else's home—and if you have any doubt, keep your child away.

GARAGE DOORS

Each year in the United States about five children are trapped and killed beneath automatic garage doors, while many more are critically injured. Automatic garage door manufacturers are now required to install devices that cause the door to reverse when an object is beneath it. The reverse mechanisms of older models require that an object or child be struck before the door will reverse. These products, however, sometimes fail and lead to the injury of a child. If your home has one of these older models, it should be periodically tested. Place a soft object such as a paper towel roll beneath the door just before closing it. The door should reverse immediately after contacting the object and should not significantly depress it.

Newer models of garage door openers are equipped with electronic-eye sensors that cause door reversal even before contact is made. These sensors can loosen or become misaligned, however, causing the reversal function to fail. Test your garage door's auto-reverse mechanism by rolling a small object such as a basketball in its path while closing it. Regardless of which type garage door opener you have, test it every thirty days.

- Position the wall switch at least six feet off the floor to minimize your child's access.
- Keep your remote-control device out of your kid's reach.
- Teach your child why an automatic garage door is hazardous.

GLASS DOORS

Accidents can also happen when a child runs into or through a sliding glass door. If a glass door is clean and poorly visible, the doorway may seem open to a toddler who is blazing by. Severe lacerations to the neck, face, and scalp can result. Place safety stickers at the eye level of your toddler on such doors to alert him that the door is closed.

HAMMOCKS

In general, hammocks are not safe for toddlers and some can even be deadly. When a hammock is *not* held open at each end by a spreader bar it can be a death trap to children. A toddler who crawls into a hammock without a spreader bar might get hurt if it rolls over and twists around her. Suffocation can result if the material of the hammock tightens around a child's neck or chest. Since the 1970s, hammocks have been responsible for the strangulation injuries of several young children. Many recalls have been made and are listed in the "Product Recalls" chapter of this book. If you own a hammock without spreader bars, return it to the store from which it was purchased or discard it.

NURSEMAID'S ELBOW

As you will soon discover, toddlers can be very determined when trying to get what they want. Retreating beneath tables, grabbing onto furniture, and screaming are not beneath most tykes in the battle against authority. You might find one day that your toddler decides to sit on the ground and refuse to take another step, or she might insist on going in the opposite direction without you. Remember, she is in the process of trying to establish independence from you and will misbehave at times just to let you know she is an individual. Be calm and patient, and don't make the common mistake of pulling up on her arms in the attempt to get her standing. This common maneuver can cause her fragile elbow to become partially dislocated, a condition called nursemaid's elbow. When this happens a child will refuse to use that arm, holding it close to her body in pain. If you ever think your child has suffered a nursemaid's elbow, bring her straight to the ER. Nursemaid's elbow can usually be treated by a trained physician in just a few seconds. Because this condition is usually caused by parents with good intention, it is not considered abusive. But it can be prevented by not pulling children up by their arms.

SHOPPING CARTS

There will be times when you take your toddler or preschooler along when grocery shopping. The shopping cart is an effective way to keep him close to you and out of harm's way while walking the aisles. But shopping carts are not without their disadvantages. Young children commonly fall from shopping carts and suffer head injuries. Approximately twenty-one thousand children less than five years of age visit emergency rooms each year for head injuries related to shopping cart falls. The incidence of youngsters falling from shopping carts is on the rise, too. Since 1985, the number of injured children has increased by 30 percent. Although fatalities are rare, several children have died in the last fifteen years. Broken bones, cuts, and bruises also commonly occur. Some stores now outfit their shopping carts with infant and toddler seats that are safe to use and comfortable. Instead of seats, some shopping carts have safety straps that allow your child to sit up front. Both products are believed to be effective in preventing falls.

In fact, avoid shopping carts that do not have a seat with a safety strap. Never allow your child to stand up in a shopping cart. If your grocery store does not have child-safe shopping carts, ask the manager if they can be made available to customers. If the manager refuses, shop at a store that values your child's safety more than a few extra dollars. If that is not possible, you can purchase your own Baby Comfort Strap, which is a portable safety belt made for shopping carts. Call 800-546-1996 for a store near you. Finally, don't let a safety belt give you a false sense of security—never turn your back on a curious toddler sitting quietly in a shopping cart.

STAIRS

(See also "Gates" in "Infants," page 123.)

Your toddler is just beginning to walk. His balance and coordination have yet to develop fully, so stairways present an obvious danger. His ability to negotiate a stairway at first will be very poor. Although safety gates can help control your child's access to a stairway, they cannot be relied upon. Toddlers are particularly skilled at getting around or over safety gates. For the upstairs entry, a mounted gate or half-door is the best option. Supervision, of course, is the only sure way to prevent your toddler from entering a stairway. In fact, as soon as your baby can scoot (at about six months), be on guard if you have stairs.

• Until he is at least two years old, never let your toddler crawl up or down stairs, and block both entries to the stairway with gates.
• To prevent tripping, keep the stairs and hallway free of clutter and pick up any clothes and toys left lying on or around the stairs.

- Check for loose steps or railings on your stairway and repair them immediately when damaged or worn.
- To prevent your child from squeezing through and falling, be sure the banister posts on your stairway are no more than three and a half inches apart. This will prevent your toddler from slipping through. If the posts are too far apart, have the banister remodeled or fitted with a guard. A sheet of Plexiglas attached to the banister can also solve this problem.
- Be sure handrails are present along every step, so your child can steady himself.
- If you have noncarpeted stairs, place non-skid strips or individual mats to prevent slipping. You can use Velcro to secure the mats.
- Avoid placing loose mats anywhere near your stairway.

CONCLUSION

We have now covered the most common ways that infants, toddlers, and preschoolers get hurt, and you have learned how to prevent all of these injuries. You've read up on everything from auto-pedestrian accidents, motor vehicle accidents, falls, and drownings to choking and poisoning injuries. As you have discovered, the toddler years are the most hair-raising and hectic of all. An enormous amount of time and energy will go into being a safe parent. When you find yourself getting frazzled and worn out by your energetic, self-destructive toddler, just stop for a moment, take a deep breath or two, look at that darling little child, and consider what a wonderful job you've done so far. There is a lot of information to digest in this book, so don't be frustrated if you find yourself having to reread some chapters or sections in order to remember all that is covered. Just like children, we adults learn best by repetition.

As your child begins elementary school, the focus of injury prevention will change from those dangers that exist at home or in day care to those at school or other areas of the community. He will gradually be integrated into society as he interacts with teachers, coaches, and other children. You are about to discover the dangers your youngster will face during the school years are quite new and different from those of earlier years.

School-Age Children
(6–13 years)

Three cheers for having safely guided your child through infancy, toddlerhood, and the preschool years. A milestone has been reached—your child is about to start school. This can be a bittersweet time, though. Yes, your child is growing up, and yes, you will soon regain some of your personal freedom. But she is becoming more self-reliant and will gradually spend more and more time away from home as she gets older. As she becomes more independent, the primary focus of injury prevention will shift from home to your child's activities in the community.

A TIME TO TEACH

Early in your child's life, close supervision was the golden rule of injury prevention. Though supervision with certain activities is still necessary, now that your child is older, you will not always be there to protect her. The best thing you can do now is teach her to protect herself. Your role is gradually becoming more like that of a teacher than a guardian. As early as first grade you can begin educating her on the issues of safety. She can learn most of the information in this chapter, if you take the time to teach her.

Be a Great Teacher
How you teach is just as important as what you teach. In order to capture and keep your child's interest at this age, make safety education fun. Establish an open, honest dialogue with her during the school years and frequently discuss your thoughts and feelings about safety. Avoid long and boring lectures—keep it informal and interesting. And don't expect your child to learn on the first go-round—repetition is still the key.

- Always practice what you preach. Teaching by example is the most important way to show your commitment to injury prevention.
- Use positive reinforcement for following safety rules; it will go a long way in molding your child's behavior. Kids are more inclined to develop a safety-conscious attitude about life if rewards are given for following your rules.
- Immediately correct your child in a firm yet loving manner when she fails to follow your safety rules. Don't get frustrated or angry when mistakes are made. Instead take advantage of these opportunities to teach proper behavior.
- Finally, don't be overzealous about the rules of safety. A child should know it is okay to explore and learn about the world without every move being critiqued and corrected. Remember, minor bumps and scrapes are as much a part of a child's life as eating, drinking, and sleeping.

Individualize your approach. Children mature at different speeds, and each will develop a unique personality. Your child may be more active and strong-willed or she may be shy and forgetful. So, individualize your approach to teaching safety. You know her better than anybody else. Your judgement and instinct will guide you in deciding which approach works best.

GENERAL HAZARDS

The types of injuries most likely to occur in your little one reflect his changing abilities. His muscles are now much stronger and larger. He has greater strength and speed. And his agility and coordination allow him to participate in sports and other activities that involve new dangers. Your child may try activities that are potentially dangerous, such as roller skating, bicycling, neighborhood games, and climbing. Curiosity and advancing intelligence lead kids to explore areas that were previously inaccessible. For instance, that locked gun cabinet in the garage will no longer be secure once he learns how to use a key. Guns, knives, power tools, exercise equipment, and kitchen devices are all dangerous to school-age children. Matches, lighters, and other flammable materials frequently entice young children into playing with fire, so be on guard here, too.

AUTO-PEDESTRIAN ACCIDENTS

(See also "Halloween" in "Holidays," page 54, and "Auto-Pedestrian Accidents" in "Toddlers and Preschoolers," page 139.)

The early school days are a time of great excitement and joy for children. Friends are being made and a whole new world outside the home is being discovered. As he enters school and begins to interact with other children in the neighborhood, your youngster is more likely to find himself in and around neighborhood roads as he goes to and from school. Many children at this age are expected to negotiate walking routes that involve busy intersections and heavy traffic, while others play in the street outside their home. The truth is that most children less than ten years old are not ready to deal with traffic unless directly supervised by an adult. Younger kids usually do not have the capability to gauge the speed and distance of approaching cars. Unfortunately, we adults often fail to teach our children about the dangers of traffic. Some children receive no formal education on pedestrian safety at all. Even when street safety is taught, children might not fully grasp the concept of pedestrian danger because they do not grasp the meaning of death or injury.

How They Occur

Indeed, your school-age child is at risk of being injured in an auto-pedestrian accident. Among five- to thirteen-year-olds, approximately five hundred are killed every year in auto-pedestrian accidents, making this one of the most common causes of traumatic death in school-age children. As with most injury mechanisms in children, the circumstances surrounding auto-pedestrian accidents are very predictable.

Dart-outs. Over 50 percent of auto-pedestrian accidents occur when a kid darts out from behind or between cars into the path of an oncoming vehicle. If you remember what I said in the previous chapter, this is how most toddlers and preschoolers are hit by automobiles, too. Most such accidents occur in residential streets or near schools or playgrounds. Move all parked cars from the sides of your street. And teach your child never to run into a street.

Play areas. Playgrounds, parks, and outdoor sports facilities adjacent to busy streets are very dangerous for children, because this is where they are most likely to mingle with traffic. Most fatal auto-pedestrian accidents take place on busier streets. Be sure there is an adequate fence around any area in which children play.

Wheels. Auto-pedestrian accidents are more likely to occur when children ride bicycles, skateboards, roller skates, and nonmotorized go-carts. These toys enable children to travel at great speeds through neighborhood streets, making it more likely that an oncoming car won't see them in time. Although most older schoolchildren do have the physical capacity to manage these toys with some degree of precision, they do not have the necessary mental skills required to manage unexpected encounters with automobiles.

• Enforce strict rules of behavior when your child gets her first set of wheels.
• Never let kids ride after dark.
• Never let kids play in a busy street or where drivers are known to speed.

- Be sure all kids always wears a protective helmet when riding any type of toy with wheels.

Motorized Go-carts

Motorized go-carts pose a unique danger to children. The speed achieved with these vehicles requires either a road or mini raceway on which to ride. All too often a parent chooses to let a child ride in a neighborhood street or country side road, and all too often this decision leads to tragedy. Kids simply do not have the skills required to handle a motorized vehicle on a street. Never let yourself fall into the trap of believing that your child is different from the rest.

The Story of Nathan and Danielle

One summer while working in the ER, I took care of a brother and sister who were involved in a tragic accident. Nathan (eight) and Danielle (ten) were riding a motorized go-cart down their neighborhood street in the late evening. The kids never slowed down as they approached a stop sign at the end of the street, and a car ran them over at the intersection. Both were severely injured and required life support when they arrived in the ER. Both were taken to the operating room to repair chest and abdominal injuries. Danielle went on to a full recovery, but unfortunately Nathan sustained brain damage and has frequent seizures.

This tragedy has more points from which to learn:

- Never let your child ride in a street with a motorized vehicle.
- Never let your child ride a motorized go-cart without a sturdy helmet.
- Never let your child ride any type of wheels after dark.

School Bus Stops

Did you know that schoolkids are twice as likely to be injured in an auto-pedestrian accident at a bus stop than in a bus accident? Over three hundred schoolchildren have been killed in bus stop tragedies since 1985. Nearly 70 percent of all children who are injured at a bus stop are struck by a school bus, while the rest are struck by passing vehicles. Fifty percent of these tragedies involved children from five to seven years old. Auto-pedestrian accidents at school bus stops are most likely to occur when a child is boarding, exiting, or waiting for the bus. These accidents almost invariably occur inside the "danger zone." This is the area within ten feet of the bus in all directions. Any child in the danger zone is less visible to passing motorists as well as the bus driver.

- When talking with your child about bus stop safety, always stress the danger of other automobiles that are passing by.
- Always have your child arrive at the bus stop five to ten minutes early to prevent a last-second mad dash.

- Teach your child not to engage in horseplay at the bus stop.
- Be sure your child's apparel does not have long drawstrings that could get snagged in the door of the school bus. Several children have been injured when a piece of clothing or drawstring became caught while exiting the bus that was already pulling away.
- If your child must wait for the bus in the dark, be sure he wears light or reflective clothing.
- Pick up and drop off your child on the same side of the road as the bus stop.

What to teach your child about school bus safety. Before your child begins commuting on a school bus, teach him the following rules:

- Wait for the bus as far from the street as possible.
- Never approach the bus until it has come to a complete stop and the door has opened.
- Never reach under or go beneath the bus. If a belonging falls beneath the bus, tell the driver. After all, if the object gets run over, it can be replaced.
- Never horse around or chase another child at the bus stop.
- Never chase the bus.
- Always look left, right, and then left again before crossing the street while approaching or leaving the bus stop.

When can you trust your child to walk across a neighborhood street without your supervision? Most youngsters have the skills necessary to cross a residential street safely at about ten years of age. Begin teaching the skills of pedestrian safety at an early age. Be sure your child is able to master the following rules before you let him go it alone:

- Always stop before entering a street.
- Look both ways before entering a street.
- Never walk in the street when it can be avoided.
- Obey all pedestrian signs.
- Never enter a street from between two parked vehicles.
- Always walk, never run, across a street.
- Use a crosswalk when available.

Continue to teach these rules for the next few years—repetition, repetition.

BURNS/FIRES

(See also "Home Fires," page 47; "Fourth of July" in "Holidays," page 52; and "Burns/Fires" in "Toddlers and Preschoolers," page 141.)

How They Occur

During the school years, your child will be less likely to get burned or scalded because he can understand the dangers of fire and heat. But some injuries to children at this age do still occur.

Experimenting with fire. Your older child might take an active interest in playing with fire. If this is the case, he will be more likely to suffer burns to the hands, arms, and face. Many house fires are caused by youngsters who play with matches and cigarette lighters. Boys suffer more burns than girls at this age because they are more likely to experiment with fire.

Flammable materials. Some substances are so flammable that they should always be kept locked up. Gunpowder, gasoline, candles, and other flammable fuels can get young "firebugs" into very dangerous situations.

Cap guns. Certain toys can also burn children. Cap gun caps, in rolls or strips, can ignite if chafing occurs while inside a pants or shirt pocket.

- Never allow your child to play with flammable or explosive materials.
- Keep all flammable items locked up.
- Closely supervise him when playing with cap guns.

Teaching Fire Safety

The toddler and preschool years were times of basic learning and preparation. Teaching fire and burn safety may have been overlooked. But during the early school years, it is imperative that your child learn about fire safety. If he does not learn it now, he may never learn it. First, teach him not to touch stoves, ovens, matches, candles, lighters, and outdoor grills. Teach him to dial 911 in the event of an emergency. Also, involve him in home fire drills and escape plans. As he gets older, he will become capable of learning more complicated fire safety techniques, such as using a fire extinguisher.

Be sure a fire safety course is provided in your child's school. If this is not being done, ask the school principal if you can help organize a class through the local fire department. Visit your local fire station for an exciting way to stimulate your child's interest in fire safety.

The following are some fire safety rules you can teach your child as early as first grade:

- Never play with fire, lighters, candles, matches, or other flammable materials.
- Never touch the stove, oven, outdoor grill, electrical outlets, or any flame.
- If a fire starts in the home, immediately begin screaming to alert others. Then go to the nearest exit.
- Stop, drop, and roll: If clothing is on fire, do not run. Stop and drop to the ground. Then roll about to extinguish the flames. This can be practiced together.
- If there is heavy smoke in the house and it is hard to breathe, crawl on the ground to the nearest exit.
- If smoke is coming from beneath the door, check to see if the knob is hot. If it is hot, do not open the door—use an alternate escape route.
- At least one window in your child's bedroom should serve as an alternate escape route. Teach your child to open this window in the event that he cannot escape through the door.

Electrical burns. Electrical injuries result in approximately seventeen thousand visits to emergency rooms every year. Nearly 50 percent occur in children less than six years. Ninety percent of these mishaps take place in or around the home. Severe electrocution can result if a child in a bathtub comes in contact with an electrical appliance, such as a radio, hair dryer, or lamp. Older children who play on housetops, tall trees, or telephone poles are in danger of electrocution from power lines. Of course, the most common electrical burns result from shocks caused by electrical outlets and appliances. Fortunately, these injuries tend to be minor. Electrically operated toys such as trains can also lead to shock injuries if not used properly.

- Never allow your child to use an electrical appliance in the bathroom.
- Never swim during a thunderstorm.
- Never use electrical appliances near water.
- Never go near a power line. Immediately tell an adult if a fallen line is found.
- Follow the manufacturer's instructions closely when setting up and playing with an electric toy.
- Never play with electrical cords.
- Teach your child to never stick anything into an electrical outlet.

DROWNING

Swimming
(See also "Fourth of July" in "Holidays," page 52; "Swimming Pools" in "Sports and Recreation," page 80; and "Swimming Lessons—When to Start," in "Sports and Recreation," page 82.)

Public and residential pools everywhere are teeming with little ones in the summer. Swimming is an activity that can be safely enjoyed by young children, but only if swimming lessons have been taken. Formal classes can teach respect for the water and improve your child's abilities. Your child's risk of drowning in a pool will decrease as she learns to swim and recognize the dangers that exist around water. Natural bodies of water (i.e., lakes, rivers, and oceans), however, become an ever-increasing danger.

- Enroll your child in swimming lessons.
- Always supervise your child closely when swimming in a lake, a river, or an ocean.
- Never allow her to swim in waters that are not sanctioned for swimming.
- No matter how good a swimmer she becomes, always be sure a qualified lifeguard is present to supervise your child's swimming at a public pool or beach.
- Be sure her swimming instructor is well qualified.

Diving

Certain water activities are known to be dangerous at this age and must be recognized. Diving into pools or lakes and jumping from a bridge are two of the more common ways that older children get hurt and drown. Diving can be a safe and enjoyable activity, but only when performed properly. If a diving board is used, the proper depth of water should be ten to twelve feet. But this depth depends upon the height of the board. Diving from boats is also dangerous. Many spinal cord and brain injuries have occurred to children while diving from a boat into murky water that turned out to be too shallow.

- Never allow diving from the side of a pool unless the depth of the water is at least eight feet.
- Never let a child dive from a boat.
- Strictly forbid diving from a bridge, a cliff, a pier, a dock, or any other shoreline point.

Who's Watching the Kids?

As your child's swimming skills improve and her time in the water requires less direct supervision, you might be tempted to let your guard down. But do not forget about the younger children in your area. Keep your attention on them, and don't expect your school-age child to do any supervising herself—she's too young. She may be a strong and responsible swimmer, but it takes a higher maturity level than she has reached to take on that kind of responsibility.

Boating Safety

When children are brought on board a boat of any size, special considerations must be given for their safety.

- Be sure a proper-size U.S. Coast Guard–certified life jacket is worn by every passenger in the boat. These personal flotation devices, or PFDs, are rated as type I, II, III, or IV. Type II life jackets are best for most children, as they are available in many sizes and are designed to float a person faceup.
- Don't make the common mistake of placing an adult-size jacket on a child; it will not adequately hold her head above water if the craft sinks or flips over.
- Have your child complete a boating safety course and swimming lessons before riding in a boat.
- Be sure you are proficient in water safety and rescue techniques. You never know when these skills might be needed to rescue yourself or your child.

Personal Watercraft Dangers

With the rising popularity of personal watercraft, we are beginning to see the dangers that they pose to children. Nearly a hundred people are killed each year on jet skis. Children are the most vulnerable to injury because:

- They are smaller and more likely to suffer internal injury.
- They don't have a full understanding of speed, acceleration, and the associated dangers.
- They don't understand their own mortality.

For these reasons, children simply have no business operating a personal watercraft. Treat these smaller recreational vehicles with the same caution you would operate a motorcycle. I recommend that children under the age of sixteen years not ride on personal watercraft.

DRUGS

By now your child has learned what substances are not safe to eat or drink. Indeed, there is very little risk that he will be poisoned by a household product or medication. But he will soon be exposed to another type of poison found at school and in your neighborhood—street drugs. Illicit drugs and alcohol are being introduced into elementary and middle schools earlier than ever before. I am even beginning to see school-age kids in the ER with drug problems. All youngsters, even yours, are at risk. His success in staying away from alcohol and other drugs will primarily be determined by you. How you approach the topic of drugs and alcohol will affect your child's understanding of this danger. Believe it or not, your early-school-age child is very capable of understanding and remembering what you teach him about drugs. You may not think it necessary to talk about drugs with him at such an early age. Many parents don't. But avoiding the issue now can be a huge mistake with deadly consequences later. So don't be afraid to have open, honest conversations with him about drug use, alcoholism, and intoxication. Chances are he really wants to hear what you have to say about this subject, so get his attention while you can. If you do, he will be more likely to say "no" when offered drugs or alcohol.

A Matter of Moral Conviction

Remember, drug awareness is not something instinctively learned or appreciated. Be patient; it may take years of discussions with your child before your wisdom about street drugs and alcohol is fully imparted. Children who stay away from drugs do so because they have developed a moral standard with strong convictions against their use. This conviction comes not from school or elsewhere in the community, but from family.

Your Battle Against Peer Pressure

As early as second grade, your child will begin to sense the intense peer pressure that other children exert. It is normal and healthy for children to do things that encourage friendship and respect from classmates. Your child will have a natural tendency to submit to peer pressure in attempts to conform and be accepted; be prepared for this. But in some situations peer pressure can be damaging and even deadly to children because it involves the use of tobacco, street drugs, or alcohol. Combating negative peer pressure is a matter of instilling confidence, self-esteem, and pride in your child. It also helps if your child has a few good friends who come from like-minded families that teach the same positive values you espouse. Teach your child to act independently and say "no" if others ask him to do something that makes him feel uncomfortable.

What a Parent Must Know

Before you can properly teach your school-age child about street drugs, you must first educate yourself on the subject. This means that for each type of street drug you must know:

- the street names
- what each drug looks like
- how each drug is used and what the effects, the side effects, and the overdose symptoms are
- how the drug gets into your community and how children might gain access to it

What a Parent Should Teach

It is important that what you teach your child fits his level of understanding and maturity. As early as first grade, children can understand such statements as, "It is not good to take drugs or alcohol because they can hurt your body."

Third and fourth graders are capable of learning about specific drugs and how they hurt people. Children at this age can learn what types of drugs are out there and why people use them.

Junior high school kids should be taught what specific drugs look like and how people abuse them. Also, it is important that they know where such drugs come from and how their peers might obtain them. Let your child know that he is likely to be confronted by classmates who want him to try drugs. Street names of various drugs are also important to know, so your child will recognize what a substance is when offered to him.

- Teach him to stay away from drugs and the people who use them.
- Be firm about your rule that drugs must never be used or accepted from someone else.
- Begin talking with him as early as fourth and fifth grade about marijuana, cocaine, crack, heroine, and methamphetamine.
- Explain how and why these substances are harmful to use.

Why a Parent Must Teach

The subject of street drugs and alcohol will be one of the most important you ever discuss with your child. A properly informed child will be less likely to fall victim to misinformation and will be better able to refuse offers of drugs and alcohol. The more you teach your child about drugs, the less impressed he will be with his peers who use them. The benefit of drug education during the early school years is that your child will be better prepared to face the challenges of avoiding drugs when he enters adolescence. Still, his education must continue as he gets older. As he enters junior high and beyond, get more specific when discussing various drugs. Explain how they are used and what harm they cause so that he can make the right decisions about drugs and alcohol when offered to him by other kids. In high school he will literally be bombarded with opportunities to use alcohol and other drugs. And it doesn't matter what school he goes to or what part of town you live in; all facets of our society are inundated with drugs. Learn to accept and live with the fact that drugs and alcohol are a way of life now and that teens and young adults everywhere are engaging in their misuse. Let this be the reason for launching an all-out campaign in your household against drugs and alcohol.

Don't They Teach This Stuff in School?

Yes and no. Alcohol and drug awareness programs are often taught in public schools, but that depends on your school district. When provided, these classes do help in the war against drugs. Just don't rely on them to teach your child what he must know about street drugs and alcohol. Not only do these courses lack complete information, they are too brief, too sporadic, and often too late. Classes at school also cannot provide your child the moral convictions that are necessary to avoid street drugs—this can only come from the family.

Drugs Every Parent Should Know About

National survey results on the use of street drugs by U.S. children indicate that overall usage continues to rise. Some drugs are increasing in popularity, while others are decreasing. Unfortunately, the problem is spreading to younger kids. Children as young as eight and nine years of age in some communities are being regularly exposed to drugs. The most common drugs on our streets today are cannabis, cocaine, amphetamines, depressants, opiates, hallucinogens, and inhalants. The following pages provide some basic information on each of these drug classes. Use this knowledge to help teach your child about the dangers of street drugs.

Cannabis. Cannabis is a plant that can be smoked or eaten. The immediate effects of the drug result from a direct action on the brain and include euphoria, passivity, and changes in the sensations of hearing, vision, and touch. These effects may last up to four hours after smoking a "joint." The long-term effects of regularly using cannabis are very real and well known, and include impairment of memory, learning, and motor skills, along with decreased motivation and responsibility.

Cannabis is sold on the street in four general forms: marijuana (pot, Mary Jane, grass, weed, dope, ganja); tetrahydrocannabinol (THC); hashish (hash); and hashish oil (hash oil). Marijuana looks like dried parsley and is usually rolled into cigarettes, but can also be eaten. Tetrahydrocannabinol comes in the form of soft gelatin capsules. Hash comes in the form of soft, dark-colored balls often covered in tinfoil—it is usually smoked in pipes or bongs, but can be eaten. Hash oil is usually mixed with tobacco and smoked.

Cocaine. Growing in the warmer climates of South America, the coca plant is harvested. From the leaves comes an extract that when purified into a white powder is known as cocaine. Its popularity in the United States has grown to extraordinary levels, with nearly 40 million Americans having admitted to using cocaine at least once in their lives. Cocaine is a very potent stimulant of the brain, giving the user a euphoric feeling.

Side effects of cocaine include rapid heart rate, elevated blood pressure, dilated pupils, and general excitability. The immediate effects of cocaine can also hurt or kill those who use it. Seizures, arrhythmias, heart attacks, and accidents due to impaired thinking are common ways that cocaine kills. Cocaine leads to more emergency room visits each year than any other illicit drug, but the most damaging effect of cocaine is its addictive potential. People who are addicted to cocaine will often stop at nothing to obtain the drug. Prostitution, burglary, assault, and murder are all frequent consequences of the irrational behavior exhibited by cocaine users. Addicts who commit crimes for the purpose of obtaining drug money cost our nation billions of dollars.

Cocaine is found in two primary forms on the streets: cocaine powder (coke, snow, nose candy, blow), which is inhaled as a white powder or liquefied by heating before injecting; and freebase cocaine (crack, rock, freebase), which is smoked. Crack usually resembles small, lightweight white rocks that are hard in consistency.

Amphetamines. Amphetamines give the user a sense of euphoria by stimulating the central nervous system, much like cocaine. True amphetamines come in the form of capsules, pills, and tablets and have many street names, including speed, uppers, ups, black beauties, pep pills, Benzedrine, and Dexedrine. Amphetamines were once widely prescribed for medicinal purposes, but the last forty years have seen a sharp decline in amphetamine prescriptions by physicians. However, similar compounds with much the same effects, known as methamphetamines, can easily be synthesized in homemade labs. Methamphetamine is usually sold in the form of a white or off-white powder or soft rocks, but may also come as pills. Both amphetamines and methamphetamines can be taken orally, injected, or inhaled.

Amphetamines and methamphetamines usually cause elevated heart rate and blood pressure, excitability, anxiety, and dilated pupils. Stroke, heart problems, and seizures can also result.

Depressants. The two most commonly abused depressants today are barbiturates and sedatives. Often prescribed by physicians for various medical and psychiatric conditions, these drugs make their way onto the streets by various routes. Depressants usually cause a person to be calm and relaxed and have the same effects of hindering one's coordination and driving skills as alcohol. When taken in larger doses or in combination with alcohol, depressants can cause a person to stop breathing. Depressants are also physically addicting, so a person who has regularly been abusing them might experience convulsions or even death if use of the drug is suddenly stopped.

Barbiturates (downers, barbs, blue devils, red devils, yellows) are usually found as red, yellow, or blue capsules and are taken orally. Sedatives (Valium, Ativan, Xanax, Librium) come in the form of various pills or capsules and are also taken orally.

Opiates. Opiates are a class of drugs that come from the opium plant. Abusers experience two or three hours of euphoria and drowsiness. Most opiates can be taken orally, smoked, or injected. The most common opiates are heroin (smack, horse, black tar, brown sugar), oxycodone (Tylox and Percocet), hydrocodone (Lortab and Vicodin), morphine, opium, and meperidine (Demerol).

Side effects include constricted pupils, watery eyes, itching, and nausea. An overdose on opiates can cause respiratory arrest, seizures, coma, and death.

Hallucinogens. These drugs cause the user to experience alterations in perceptions of reality, such as visual hallucinations. The tendency for violent outbursts in phencyclidine (PCP) users, combined with poor pain perception, makes the users highly dangerous to themselves and others. Other immediate side effects of hallucinogens include dilated pupils, increased heart rate, increased temperature, confusion, and loss of self-control.

The most common hallucinogens today include phencyclidine (PCP, angel dust, hog, killer weed), lysergic acid (LSD, acid, microdot), mescaline and peyote (mesc, buttons, cactus), and psilocybin (magic mushrooms, 'shrooms). Phencyclidine comes in all forms and can be swallowed, smoked, or injected, while LSD is usually in the form of residue on blotter paper, colored cubes, or liquid, and can be licked from the paper, eaten, or dropped into the eyes. Mescaline and peyote are usually in tablet or capsule form and can be chewed, swallowed, or smoked. Psilocybin is a natural compound found in certain wild mushrooms that are eaten.

Inhalants. Many household and industrial chemicals can be abused simply by inhaling the vapors they emit. Users experience a wide variety of sensations. The immediate and long-term injuries that can occur to the human body affect most organ systems and are too numerous to list. Most chronic abusers in this category suffer profound brain damage with very poor motivation, personality changes, and memory loss.

Some of the more commonly abused solvents include nitrous oxide (laughing gas or whippets), released from small metal cylinders sold for use as aerosol propellants, and amyl nitrite (poppers or snappers), a clear yellowish liquid in small glass ampules that is sometimes stolen from hospitals. Toluene is found in certain glues, gold paint, and paint thinner. Users will either "huff" the vapors from a moistened cloth, "sniff" from a small container, or "bag" from a plastic bag. Hydrocarbons (gasoline) can also be inhaled by users in need of a very cheap high.

Designer drugs. One of the greatest problems we face today in combating drug use is that a drug can only be made illegal based upon its unique chemical structure. Amateur chemists can easily produce a variation of an illegal drug and sell it on the open market without risk of prosecution because that particular chemical structure, although nearly identical to an illegal drug, has not yet been outlawed. Thus, the drug dealers are legally able to stay in business by keeping a few steps ahead of the legislative process. Several drugs related to various classes have found their way onto the streets during the last twenty years, with street names such as synthetic heroin, china white, MPTP, MPPP, Ecstacy, XTC, Adam, MDM, and PCE. Don't be fooled into thinking that because it's sold in a store or advertised in a magazine it's not a drug of abuse. Many designer drugs are legally marketed and sold.

Warning Signs of Drug Use

Common warning signs to look for include constant or recurrent fatigue, weight loss, poor hygiene habits, repeated complaints of illness, personality change, irritability, mood swings, depression, poor school performance or attendance, and trouble with the police. If your teen has friends who exhibit these warning signs, be alert—the dangers of drug use may be closer to home than you think.

FIREARMS

(See also "Firearms," page 45; and "Firearms" in "Toddlers and Preschoolers," page 161.)

Accidental shootings are all too common these days. Sadly, our nation has become desensitized to the fact that so many young children are being killed by guns. Every day we read about it in the newspaper, hear about it on the radio, and see it on television. Yet the problem only worsens. Would you believe that every two hours in the United States a child is killed by a gun?

MOTOR VEHICLE ACCIDENTS

Parents have a tendency to grow lax about automobile safety once their child outgrows the safety seat. But consider this: your older child will spend more and more time in the family car as you taxi her back and forth to school and other activities. Her risk of being involved in an MVA will be greater than ever before.

Recently, we have come to realize that early-school-age children are often not protected even when wearing seat belts. In fact, your child could suffer serious injury in an MVA if her neck is thrown against a seat belt that rides too high on her. Most experts now recommend that children ride in booster seats until about the age of six years, because they generally do not fit adult-size seat belts. Generally, children grow out of booster seats by the time they are six years of age. However, one manufacturer, Britax, sells a child safety seat large enough for children up to ten years of age. This is the only seat of its type currently on the market. I recommend that your child use this seat until she is at least eight years old. For more information, call Britax at 803-802-2022.

Where Should Your Kids Sit?
Due to their small size, schoolkids are more likely to suffer multiple injuries if involved in an MVA. Proper positioning is still very important. The impact of a deploying air bag against a young child can cause serious injury or even death. When sitting up front, a child is in danger of having a passenger-side air bag deploy against her head and neck, especially if she is too close to the dash. Air bag off switches are now available in certain car and truck models and for families who have numerous children and can't avoid putting them in the front seat. Off switches are particularly important in pickup trucks and sports cars in which there is no backseat for child passengers. *(See also "On/Off Switches" in "Automobiles," page 16, for more details on air bag off switches.)*

- Until your child reaches twelve years of age, have her ride in the backseat of the car.
- If she must sit up front, be sure the seat is placed as far back as it will go, especially when a passenger-seat air bag is present.
- If your child must sit up front, have an air bag off switch installed and use it whenever she rides in the vehicle until she is a teenager.

Be a Good Role Model

Your own behavior behind the wheel will serve as a valuable example to your child. If you consistently drive safely and wear your seat belt, you will set the stage for a lifelong habit of safe driving. Aggressive drivers are also more likely to be involved in motor vehicle accidents when their children are in the car, so take a defensive approach to driving for the immediate safety of your child.

School Bus Safety

(See also "School Bus Stops" in "School-Age Children," page 169.)

Generally there is no safer way for young students to travel than on a school bus. In fact, school buses are about two thousand times safer for children than your family car, according to the National Highway Traffic Safety Administration (NHTSA). The size of a school bus alone is a tremendous advantage—not only because visibility to other drivers is so great, but because the sheer mass of the bus protects its passengers from sudden deceleration and intrusion during impact. Well-trained bus drivers are yet another reason school bus injuries to children are uncommon. Still, some injuries do occur. Since 1985, nearly 150 child passengers have been killed in school bus accidents. Recent statistics show that approximately 9,000 children are injured (350 seriously and 15 fatally) each year in school buses.

Seat belts. Children less than four years or forty pounds should ride in booster seats that are held in place by seat belts—this we are sure of. But what about school-age children? On this subject experts are not so certain. A national debate has been launched over whether school buses should be outfitted with seat belts. Although most school buses today have high-backed, padded seats, many believe they could be made safer if children were properly restrained. Another argument for the use of seat belts on school buses is the teaching point that could be made. What a wonderful opportunity to teach young children the importance of wearing a seat belt. On the other hand, some experts suggest that children may be susceptible to other types of back and neck injuries if only a lap belt is used. The cost of installing lap and shoulder belts in every seat of every school bus would be astronomical, and many believe the money could be better spent for child safety in other ways. For the next few years the seat belt issue promises to be hotly contested in school districts and legislatures across the country. In the meantime, instruct your child to use a seat belt whenever one is present on the school bus. And remember, the greatest danger to your child is not on the bus, but at the bus stop. A child's likelihood of being struck by a moving bus or passing vehicle at the bus stop is much greater.

Small buses and vans. The inherent safety that has been shown to exist with school buses applies only to those that are full-size. Smaller buses sometimes used to transport children often do not meet federal safety standards requiring seat belts, emergency exits, flashing lights, and stop-arms. Ordinary vans are also sometimes used to transport children back and forth to extracurricular activities. These smaller vehicles can be driven by someone without special training. In some circumstances school districts are blatantly violating the law by using smaller vehicles that do not meet the required standards for child transportation.

- If your child travels in a smaller school vehicle, be absolutely certain that appropriately sized seat belts and other standard safety features are present.
- Look for a certification sticker on the windshield of your child's smaller school bus or van.
- If you suspect your school district is using vehicles that do not meet federal safety standards, call the National Highway Traffic Safety Administration at 800-424-9393.

PHYSICAL VIOLENCE AND ABDUCTION

Let's face it, we have become desensitized to violence. Youngsters watch it on television and in movies, listen to it on the radio, and hear about it from adults and other children. Hopefully your child will never experience it firsthand, but the fact is that many children do suffer violent injuries at home or in the community. Unfortunately, those who suffer from violence as children often live to perpetuate the cycle of violence to their own children: violence begets violence.

Two types of assault commonly occur to children: child abuse and random violence. Child abuse is extremely common and is discussed in the "Child Abuse" chapter earlier in this book (see page 26). Random violence is more likely to affect children as they get older and spend more time outside the home. They can be victimized by adults or other children around the neighborhood. If drugs are being sold in your neighborhood or in your child's school, the potential for violence increases dramatically. And if your child ever becomes involved with drugs, he will be in imminent danger. Children who belong to or interact with gangs are most prone to violent behavior and are likely to be victimized themselves.

Setting Limits

Your child's risk of being injured by violence can be dramatically decreased by setting certain limits on his activities. As your child gets older he will begin to use bicycles, skateboards, or in-line skates to get around the neighborhood, giving him the new-found ability to travel farther from home. Placing restrictions on the distance he travels is a must if you are to prevent him from straying into dangerous areas. Children mature at different speeds, making it impossible to set a definite age at which it becomes safe to play in the neighborhood without full supervision. Consider such factors as the area in which you live and your familiarity with neighbors, as well as your child's maturity level, when making these decisions and setting curfews.

- Familiarize yourself with your child's friends and their families to help ensure that his time is spent with people who are concerned about child safety.
- Place restrictions on where and how far away your child travels throughout the community.
- Enforce a strict curfew on the time your child spends away from home. Keep him indoors during the late-evening hours when violent crimes are most likely to occur. Based on your child's maturity and the neighborhood in which you live, set the curfew to ensure that he is indoors at an appropriate hour.
- If your neighborhood is home to roaming thugs, keep your child off the streets as much as possible.
- Search for extracurricular activities that involve athletics, music, or boys and girls clubs for the after-school hours.

Teaching Nonviolence

As emphasized throughout this book, education is paramount to child safety. Begin teaching your child about the dangers of drug use and criminal behavior as soon as possible. The earlier he learns about violence, the more likely he is to avoid it successfully. And remember, parents who live a nonviolent life set a terrific example for their children. Bringing about peaceful resolutions to your own conflicts will teach your child to do the same. Community role models are helpful, too. Introduce your child to local police officers to help him develop respect for the law and those who enforce it. Find an officer who is willing to take you and your child on an exciting field trip to the police station or jail.

- Be a peaceful role model to your child.
- Minimize his exposure to violence through television and movies.
- Introduce him to a local police officer.

Stranger Dangers

(See also "Halloween" in "Holidays," page 54.)

Few events tug at our heartstrings like the kidnapping of a child. Your child must under-stand that any stranger could be dangerous. It is important for him to realize that a stranger is not just a scary-looking person, but that a stranger can be anybody. A stranger is a grocery store clerk, the man who cuts the grass, a lady selling makeup door-to-door, or anybody else who isn't a parent or very close relative. Some youngsters grow up with a natural sense of stranger anxiety. Shy children tend to be in less danger because they are not easily approachable by strangers. These children will often run away in fear before ever speaking to a stranger. But some kids are friendly toward strangers, and it is these outgoing children who are at greatest risk. Child abductors have the ability to select quickly children who will be approachable and receptive to their advances. Child predators know to seek out friendly, less-anxious children as their victims. They know which child is more likely to accept a piece of candy or a ride home. Child abduction by a stranger is uncommon, but it does occur—and when it does, tragedy usually results. Some criminals target children because they are easy prey. Indeed, our little ones have an innocence and naïveté that make them vulnerable. Public schoolyards and playgrounds make successful hunting grounds for these child predators. A luring temptation followed by a sudden distraction is all it takes for a child to be grabbed and taken away. In a matter of minutes, an unwary child can be help-lessly trapped in a vehicle traveling down a highway.

Internet Danger

One of the newest ways that predators meet young children is through the Internet. Once again, predators are particularly cunning when it comes to identifying vulnerable children. After two simple questions—"Are you home alone?" and "What is your address?"—a child abductor can be on his way to your doorstep.

- Teach your child the importance of keeping personal and family information to her-self and never to give it out.
- Make the content and broad subject matter of the Internet off-limits to your unsu-pervised child.

Home Alone

Over 5 million youngsters in the United States come home to an empty house each day. How old must your child be before he can safely stay at home alone? Generally, chil-dren are not ready to be left unsupervised until they are at least ten years of age. But remember, children mature at different speeds. While one ten-year-old may be mature and responsible enough to stay at home alone, another twelve-year-old might not. You must decide for yourself precisely when your child is ready to manage a brief stay at home alone. He must be comfortable with being alone. A child who quickly becomes lonely and insecure is more likely to invite friends over or to speak with strangers who might call or ring the doorbell.

- Before leaving your child at home, be sure he understands the rules of home safety. He must have good judgment and the ability to make basic, intelligent decisions on his own.
- Teach him to keep all windows and doors locked at all times.
- Teach him to call 911 in the event of an emergency.
- Children tend to get themselves into dangerous situations more frequently when they are with other children. Never allow him to have friends over without adult supervision until he is at least twelve years of age.
- Teach him never to open the door unless he knows the person on the outside.
- Install a low-set peephole on your front door that he can reach without having to stand on a chair.

Door-to-Door Sales

Many worthwhile projects and organizations are partially funded by the efforts of children who sell cookies, candy, and other goods at the front doorsteps of neighbors and friends. This is yet another way your child could encounter a child predator. To avoid the dangers associated with door-to-door sales, be sure your child is always accompanied by an adult and approach only those homes of families you know well. The truth is that children would all be better off if the donations necessary to fund these organizations were collected by means other than through their own labor. Consider other ways to raise money besides door-to-door sales. Using our children to support community organizations in this way is really not in their best interest.

What to Teach

Never give a predator the chance to get near your child. Teach your child to interact with strangers as little as possible. You want him to be unapproachable by people he doesn't know. Although it may be necessary to interact with other people from time to time (i.e., in emergencies, or to ask for directions), teach your child *never to go anywhere with a stranger.* This is the golden rule of stranger safety for children. He should never enter the car or the home of a stranger. Teach your child how to react if a stranger ever does grab him. Teach him to immediately scream, kick, and bite in an effort to get away.

As soon as your child enters school, teach the following rules of safety:

- Never go anywhere with a stranger.
- Never let yourself be alone with a stranger.
- Always travel with a friend.
- Never get near a stranger's car. Run away if an unidentified car pulls up.

- Never answer a door to your home when a stranger knocks.
- Describe some of the tactics that might be used by an abductor, such as:
  - offering candy or money
  - offering a ride
  - posing as a family friend who is supposed to pick the child up
  - posing as an authority figure—a police officer, a fireman, or a school official
  - asking for help
  - posing as a door-to-door salesman

Sexual Molestation
(See also "Child Abuse," page 26.)

As unbelievable as it seems, there are individuals in our society capable of forcing children into sexual activities. This is an unfathomable crime against humanity. As a parent, you must acknowledge the harsh reality that these crimes do occur so you can teach preventive tactics to your child.

What do we know about pedophiles? First, the perpetrator is almost always male. Second, he is almost always known to the child. Sadly, the molester is often a father, an uncle, an older brother, or a cousin of the victim. And third, other family members all too often look the other way while an ongoing abusive relationship exists.

For more information on this vital issue, I recommend that you read *Protecting the Gift,* by Gavin De Becker (Dial Press, 1999).

CONCLUSION

Excellent work! You have once again reached a milestone. The early school years have been negotiated and high school is just around the corner. Believe it or not, you have already educated your child on the many dangers he will face during adolescence. In other words, he has a head start. But prepare for the possibility of stormy times as your child enters puberty and the world of adolescence. Stay on guard against alcohol, drugs, and motor vehicle accidents. Each of these entities is hazardous in its own right, but when mixed together, they can be deadly. Nearly ten thousand teens die each year from traumatic injuries, usually in motor vehicle accidents. Prepare for these years by reading up on adolescent behavior and psychology well before your child reaches high school. Plan your injury prevention strategies and implement them early. Consistency in your rules and good communication have been an important part of preventing injury up to this point, and that will not change. Keep up the good work and good luck with the teen years.

PART III

Product Recalls
and Resources

Product Recalls

*For more information on these or other possible product recalls, visit the Consumer Product Safety Commission (CPSC) web site at www.cpsc.gov. The following recall list is comprised of many products recently recalled by the CPSC because they were specifically harmful to children. Products such as general household items or any other type of item not meant for use by children are excluded.

(Company name)	(Number sold)	(Name & description of product)
**Key: Bell Sports, Inc.	5,800	Bicycle helmets

(Date of Recall Notice)	(Further details about the product and the nature of the problem leading to danger)
(4-29-99)	The chin straps are defective.

(Where the product was sold)	(How to reach the manufacturer)
Sold nationwide	(800) 456-BELL.

Bicycles

Bell Sports, Inc.—5,800 Bicycle Helmets (4-29-99). The chin straps are defective. Date stickers inside the helmets read, "October 1998 through March 1999." Sold nationwide October 1998 through April 1999. 800-456-BELL.

Dah Ken Industrial Co., and RST USA—3,300 Bicycle Front Suspension Forks, models RST Hi-5 and RST Hi-5 MOZO (3-17-99). The rider may lose control of the bike due to the forks breaking off. Sold nationwide February through October 1997. 800-227-6778.

Dynacraft Industries Inc.—500 Mountain Bikes Coleman CM 2100 (5-17-99). The quick-release mechanism may be difficult to tighten and consequently the front wheel could fall off while being ridden. Sold nationwide May 1998 through June 15, 1998. 800-551-0032.

GT Bicycles—10,000 GT Speed Series and Robinson Bicycle Frames (3-12-98). A rider may lose control of the bicycle and become injured due to the frames of the bicycles cracking and separating. The following models are part of this recall: 1995, 1996, 1997, and 1998 XL and XXL model GT Speed Series, Speed Series Team, and Speed Series Cruiser frames and bicycles. Also, 1997 and 1998 model Robinson Pro, Pro XL, Pro 24, and Amtrac frames and bicycles. Sold nationwide November 1994 through February 1998. 800-743-3248.

Hsin Lung Accessory of Taiwan—1,400 bicycle suspension forks, model HSF-350 installed exclusively on Huffy Bicycle Company "Verdict" full-suspension mountain bikes, serial numbers B98J, B98K, B98L, and B99A (8-10-99). These suspension forks can break apart during use when the upper crown weld fails, causing serious injury to the bicycle rider. Sold nationwide in mass-merchandise stores such as Shopko, Service Merchandise, Pamida, and TRU*SERV January 1999 to June 1999. Call Huffy Bicycles for a replacement at 800-872-2453.

Norco Products USA—450 Bike Passenger Trailers, models Norco Stagecoach, Norco Rambler, Norco Tot Taxi, Axiom Firefly, and Bike Mate Trailer with folding arm (3-31-98). Injury can occur to the occupant of the trailer. The hitch arm pivot bracket may fail due to metal fatigue and, consequently, the trailer will break loose from the bicycle. Sold January 1997 through February 1998. 800-521-9088. Washington residents should call 800-635-5550.

Performance, Inc.—3,650 Pairs of Performance Campus Bicycle Pedals (5-19-98). The rider may lose control of the bicycle and fall off, due to axles on some pedals breaking off. Written on the end of the pedals is "PERFORMANCE." Sold nationwide December 1996 through April 1998. 800-553-8324.

Raleigh USA—1,400 Ballistic LE300A suspension forks on the 1996 Raleigh M55 bicycle (3-3-97). The forks may separate, causing the rider to crash. Sold nationwide August 1995 through January 1997. 800-222-5527.

Rand/Ross Bicycle Co.—11,000 Mountain Bikes, models Rock Machine 2600, Rock Machine 3600, Tarantula MRX 1200, and Ross Mt. Washington (4-27-98). Riders may lose control and fall due to the front suspension fork separating from the frame of these adult bikes. These bikes are adult size. Sold nationwide February 1997 through March 1998. 800-338-7677.

SRAM Corp.—25,000 Bicycle Chains, model numbers PC-41, PC-51, PC-61, PC-80R and PC-91 (all have the date code "F") (5-14-98). The rider may lose control of the

bicycle, and become injured, due to the chain breaking. The chains were originally part of various Giant, Schwinn, and Specialized Bicycles.

GIANT BICYCLES	SCHWINN BICYCLES	SPECIALIZED BICYCLES
ATX-1100	Moab A2	Rockhopper
ATX-1200	Moab A3	Rockhopper FS
ATX-860	Moab A1	Rockhopper Comp FS
ATX-865	Moab A1-E	Ground Control
ATX-870		Ground Control FSR
ATX-890		Ground Control FSR Comp
ATX-970		Ground Control FSR extreme
CFR-2		
CFR-3		

Sold nationwide July 1997 through May 1998. 888-588-8140.

Sachs Bicycle Components—16,500 Diamondback mountain bikes, 1998 models Sherwood, Lakeside, Interval, Expert, Voyager I, Voyager II, Sorrento, Sorento SE, and Wildwood DX (11-12-97). The chains on these bikes can break during use, causing the rider to crash. Injuries have been reported. Sold nationwide July 1997 through November 1997. 800-343-8586.

Schwinn Cycling & Fitness—2,800 BMX Bicycles, model BMX Cruiser (3-3-99). Bicycle frames may crack during use. Sold nationwide February 1998 through December 1998. 800-SCHWINN.

Shimano—1 million Pedal cranks (7-1-97). The cranks can break, causing the rider to crash. The cranks have been installed on 49 various bicycle models. 800-353-4719.

Specialized Bicycle Components, Inc.—2,500 Bicycle Chains, 1998 models Stumpjumper M2, Stumpjumper M2 Comp, Stumpjumper M2 Pro, S-Works M2, Ground Control FSR Elite, Ground Control

FSR Pro, and Ground Control FSR Limited (6-9-98). The rider may lose control of the bicycle, and become injured, due to the chain breaking. Sold nationwide January 1998 through May 1998. 800-214-1467.

Specialized Bicycle Components, Inc.—4,000 Specialized 1999 Allez and Allez Sport model bicycles (7-20-99). The handlebars can come out of the stem during use. Sold through authorized Specialized dealers October 1998 through June 1999. Call 800-214-1468.

Bunk Beds

The CPSC, in cooperation with the following manufacturers, has issued bunk bed recalls for various reasons. For information on specific models recalled, call the manufacturers and the numbers noted below. This is only a partial list. For further bunk bed recall listings, see the CPSC web page at www.cpsc.gov.

Acme Trading Co.—July 96 through January 1997. 213-623-0000.

Bedder Bunk Co.—1984 through 1992. Out of business.

Chicken and Egg Furniture.—1987 through 1997. 206-623-6144.

Fine Pine—1190 through 1998. 800-874-5737.

Heartland Furniture—November 1995 through May 1997. Out of business.

IEM Furniture—1994 through 1998. 800-869-1688.

J.I.M. Manufacturing—1986 through 1998. 800-989-6141.

Kidron Woodcraft—1992 through 1997. Contact retailer.

Lewis Furniture—1989 through January 1997. 864-847-4281.

New England Woodcraft—1994 through 1997. 802-247-8211.

NewCo—January 1994 through September 1998. 877-865-5191.

Oakland Wood—September 1994 through October 1996. 510-536-4014.

P.J. Sleep Shop—1981 through October 1996. 503-232-5222.

Padilla's Furniture—1996 through 1998. 800-232-2310 or 213-232-2310.

Rosalco—1993 through 1997. 812-284-0027.

Silver Eagle Corporation—1995 through 1997. 916-925-6099.

Springhill Woodcrafters—1991 through 1997. 412-834-3037.

Stoney Creek—1980 through 1993. Out of business.

Temple Pine Furniture—1994 through 1997. 770-562-5910.

Wholesale Importers and Exporters—1984 through March 1996. 213-563-3346.

Child Safety Seats

The following child seats were recalled by the National Highway Traffic Safety Administration:

All Our Kids Juvenile Products—child safety restraints, model numbers 600 and 602. The nylon fabric in these child safety restraints does not meet the requirements of Federal Motor Vehicle Safety Standard (FMVSS) No. 213, "Child Restraint Systems." Produced April 1993 to September 1994. All Our Kids will treat the fabric with flame retardant agents; call 800-545-3265.

Babyhood Industries, Inc.—child restraint seat cushions, model number 820. The child restraint seat cushions do not adequately resist compression/deflection of the seat occupant's head when tested for crash worthiness. Produced March 1991. Babyhood will replace the seat cushion with a cushion that meets the compression/deflection requirements; call 508-845-4231.

Britax Child Safety, Inc.—belt buckle, Freeway model 101. The belt buckle can open by lifting up on the "push button" at less than the nine-pound minimum force required in FMVSS No. 213. This means that a child can more easily open the buckle. Produced June 1996 to April 1997. Britax will provide owners with a newly designed replacement buckle and installation instructions; call 800-683-2045.

Century Products—buckle, model numbers 4525, 4535, 4560, 4565, 4575, 4590, infant car seats; and 11-570, 11-597, 11-600, and 11-650 4-in-1 car seat stroller systems. Due to misassembly of the buckle assemblies, the buckles can release upon impact. Produced 1995 to May 1996. Century will provide a free replacement buckle kit and installation instructions; call 800-762-7463.

Century Products—buckle, model Smartmove and 4750. This child safety seat utilizes a latch assembly in which a variation in the components resulted in the potential for a buckle to release. This does not conform to the dynamic testing requirements of FMVSS No. 213. Produced November 1995 to February 1996. Century will provide a retrofit kit so owners can easily replace the latch assembly; call 800-762-7463.

Century Products—release button, model number 2000STE. The red release button can rotate upward in a crash or a sudden stop, making it possible for the buckle to release the shoulder harness. Produced December 1991 to April 1992. Century will provide a kit to retrofit the child safety seat with a modified release button assembly to consumers; call 800-762-7463.

Century Products—release button, model numbers 4353, 4365, 4366, 4367, 4368, 4369, 4380, 4450, 4460, 4470, 4475, 4476, 4480, and 4490. Some red buttons shipped to repair buckle release buttons recalled under NHTSA Campaign No. 92E017 were incorrect. Produced September 1989 to April 1992. Century has issued graphic instructions to all seat owners who may have received the wrong part. The instructions provide details on how to determine whether the previously shipped red release button is correct. If the wrong button was shipped and the owner notified Century of the problem, Century will ship the owner the correct button; call 800-762-7463.

Century Products—release button, model numbers 4353, 4366, 4367, 4368, 4369, 4380, 4450, 4460, 4470, 4475, 4476, 4480, and 4490. The red shoulder strap release button can rotate out of the frame in a crash or a sudden stop. In this event, the release button could not be activated with less than sixteen pounds of force as required by FMVSS No. 213. Produced September 1989 to March 1992. Century will provide a kit to retrofit the child safety seat with a modified release button and dress plate to consumers; call 800-762-7463.

Century Products—instructions, model numbers 4153, 4163, 4261, 4263, 4265, 4266, 4365, 4366, 4367, 4368, 4380, 4381, 4460, 4470, 4475, 4476, 4480, and 4490. The Spanish instructions on the positioning label are incorrect. Produced December 1990 to October 1991. Century will provide new labels with corrected Spanish instructions to owners; call 800-762-7463.

Century Products—instructions, model numbers 4580, 4581, 4583, and 4584. The directions for threading the shoulder straps through the metal retention slides are unclear. Produced July 1986 to December 1989. Century will provide owners with new instructions and a descriptive label so they can rethread the shoulder straps correctly; call 800-762-7463.

Century Products—buckle release, 3000STE models 4353, 4365, 4366, and 4368, and 5000STE Models 4450, 4460, 4470, and 4475. Buckle release force can exceed sixteen pounds when not used in appropriate forward latch position for a child weighing thirty pounds or more as required by FMVSS No. 213. Produced March 1987 to December 1990. Century will issue notification, and change instructions and labeling to indicate that the rear latch position is not to be used with children weighing thirty pounds or more; call 800-762-7463.

Century Products—harness assemblies, model numbers 4450GD, 4475GA, and 4460FE. These safety seats exceed the post-impact buckle release force requirement of sixteen pounds maximum during FMVSS No. 213 testing. Produced December 1988 to November 1989. Century will replace the harness assemblies with a new version that includes a modified latch tongue; call 800-762-7463.

Century Products—retaining screws, model numbers 4581, 4583, and 4585. The retaining screws on the handle to the shell can loosen, allowing the handle to separate from the shell. Produced June 1986 to October 1989. Century will provide owners with newly designed screws and installation instructions; call 800-762-7463.

Century Products—removable protective fabric pad, 3000STE models 4365DT and 4366. The removable protective fabric pad that is attached to the front tray shield with Velcro tabs has exposed urethane foam on the underside of the shield pad that children can pick at with their fingers, possibly putting small pieces of the pad in their mouth and creating a health hazard. Model 4365DT was produced March 1987 to October 1988 and model 4366 was produced February to October 1988. Century will replace the current pad with a pad containing two button fasteners that cannot be removed by a child. Also, tweed pads will be from foam that is covered with a nonwoven backing. Call 800-762-7463.

Century Products—shoulder strap, 2000STE models 4253, 4263, and 4265. The loop on the end of the shoulder strap is only glued together, rather than glued and sewn. Produced April 1986 to June 1989. Century will provide to owners new straps that have been glued and sewn, along with installation instructions; call 800-762-7463.

Cosco, Inc.—structural failure of belt path area, models Tourvia 5-Point and Tourvia Overhead Shield. When these seats were tested dynamically per the requirements of FMVSS No. 213, structural failure occurred in the belt path area of the shell in the forward-facing reclined position only. Produced August 9 to August 22, 1997. Cosco will provide inspection instructions to the owner. If the seat is involved in the campaign, a remedy kit will be provided to the owner. Call 800-221-6736.

Cosco, Inc.—latch-release housing assembly, model Arriva 02-741. Separation of the buckle latch-release button and spring from the latch-release housing assembly. Produced March 1 to May 31, 1995. Cosco will replace the entire latch release assembly; call 800-221-6736.

Cosco, Inc.—back angle requirements, model Dreamride Ultra. These seats do not meet the maximum back angle requirements of FMVSS No. 213. Produced April 1994 to June 1995. Cosco will provide a retrofit kit to owners of these seats which will include an easy-to-install metal plate that hooks over the base of the seat and is securely snapped in place by two plastic fasteners; call 800-221-6736.

Cosco, Inc.—buckle latch housing, model numbers 02-034 and 02-404. In a vehicle crash, at speeds greater than thirty miles per hour, the buckle latch housing mounted in the base of the shell can deform, causing the latch mechanism to fracture, allowing disengagement of the buckle tongue from the buckle housing. Produced May to August 1994. Cosco will send to owners a replacement buckle housing that can be easily replaced by removing the four screws attaching the original buckle latch assemble; call 800-221-6736.

Cosco, Inc.—seat cover, model TLC infant car seat, 01-188-ARQ. The ribbon quilt child seat cover has been tested and the material burns faster than the rate established for child seat material. The child seats do not comply with FMVSS No. 302, "Flammability of Interior Materials." Produced April to December 1993. Cosco will send owners a replacement child safety seat cover; call 800-221-6736.

Cosco, Inc.—pads, model Dreamride, 02-719-ARQ. The fabric cover of the pads on these seats do not meet the requirements of FMVSS No. 302. Produced January 1, 1989, to January 11, 1994. Cosco will provide a replacement pad for these child seats; call 800-221-6736.

Cosco, Inc.—foam seat pad, model Deluxe Commuter, 02-086. The foam seat pad on the child seat was not sealed at the seams, allowing the foam pad to be accessible to the seat occupant. Produced October 12, 1987, to February 2, 1988. Cosco will replace the unsealed foam pad with a sealed pad; call 800-221-6736.

Cosco, Inc.—harness retainer, Soft Shield Models 02-090 and 02-190 and Auto Trac Models 02-290, 02-790, and 02-890. The child seat failed to meet the head excursion requirements of FMVSS No. 213. Produced October 1989 to June 1990. Cosco will furnish a repair kit consisting of a harness retainer with installation and use instructions; call 800-221-6736.

Cosco, Inc.—plastic shell, model numbers 313, 323, and 423. Cracks develop in the plastic shell where the frame of the car seat is riveted to the shell. Produced January 1984 to June 1985. Cosco will send owners a brace assembly kit to preclude separation of car seat from belted position and installation instructions; call 800-221-6736.

Downunder—instructions, model Kangaroo Booster Seats. This is not a safety recall in accordance with Federal Regulation 573. However, it is deemed a safety improvement campaign by the agency. Misused Velcro seat belt guide for booster seat built prior to January 31, 1997. Downunder is providing revised instructions to all owners of the Kangaroo Booster Seat to help clarify shoulder belt replacement. For owners of the Kangaroo Booster Model Number 3 (models without the Velcro shoulder belt positioner), a Velcro shoulder belt positioner will be sent to upgrade these boosters. Call 800-459-5209.

Evenflo Juvenile Furniture Co.—red push button assembly, On My Way infant car seat/carrier model 207 and On My Way Travel System infant car seat/carrier with stroller base model 492. The red push button assembly on each side of the seat that is used to latch and adjust the carrying handle can unexpectedly release and cause the seat to flip forward. Produced December 15, 1995, to July 27, 1997. Evenflo will provide a free repair kit that includes stronger latch buttons and springs; call 800-203-2138.

Evenflo Juvenile Furniture Co.—booster seat, Sidekick booster seat, model 224. These seats do not comply with FMVSS No. 213, which limits the head injury criteria. In recent tests on some of these boosters seats, the head injury criteria scored more than allowed by this standard. Produced April 23, 1996, to May 20, 1997. Evenflo will reimburse owners either completely or partially, depending on whether the seat can be used by the owner's child. Owners are advised to use the Sidekick booster seat only as a belt positioner. When used as a belt positioner, the Sidekick must be used without its front shield and only in vehicles equipped with a three-point lap shoulder seat belt system. Call 800-233-5921.

Evenflo Juvenile Furniture Co.—harness, Champion, Scout, and Trooper, model numbers beginning with 219, 224, 225, and 229. These seats do not comply with FMVSS No. 213. Slippage of the harness webbing can result in loosening of the harness straps. Produced October 14, 1996, to February 6, 1997. Evenflo will provide a harness adjuster retrofit kit and detailed instructions to the owners; call 800-233-5921.

Evenflo Juvenile Furniture Co.—recline arm, Scout and Champion model numbers beginning with 224 and 229. These seats do not comply with the thorax acceleration requirements of FMVSS No. 213. Produced June 1, 1993, to December 16, 1996. Evenflo will provide a modified recline arm that will alter the restraint's angle and installation instructions for consumers to repair these seats. Meanwhile, consumers are advised to use these seats only in the reclined position until they receive the free modified recline arm. Call 800-233-5921.

Evenflo Juvenile Furniture Co.—instructions, Trooper model. Due to a printing error, the foldout instruction pamphlet providing information on toddler use was incorrectly labeled for infant use. Produced November 1995 to January 1996. Evenflo will send a new pamphlet to consumers; call 800-233-5921.

Evenflo Juvenile Furniture Co.—detachable autobase, On My Way model numbers beginning with 206. These seats do not meet the sled test requirements of FMVSS No. 213, when tested without the detachable autobase. Produced May 1994 to May 1995. Evenflo will provide a set of plastic inserts to all owners of the On My Way infant restraints. Evenflo recommends that owners use the restraint with the detachable autobase only until the plastic inserts are received and installed. Call 800-233-5921.

Evenflo Juvenile Furniture Co.—pushpins, model numbers 453, 454, 470, and 471. The black plastic pushpins used to attach the pads to the seat structure can be removed by children presenting a possible choking hazard. Produced February 1987 to August 1988. Evenflo will send owners newly designed replacement pushpins and installation instructions; call 800-233-5921.

Evenflo Juvenile Furniture Co.—seat shells, Ultara II model 227. These seats fail to comply with the head and knee excursion requirements of FMVSS No. 213. Produced January to June 1990. Evenflo will replace the seat shells on these seats; call 800-233-5921.

Evenflo Juvenile Furniture Co.—buckle tongue, Dyn-O-Mite, Evenflo Infant models 201, 202, 441, 442, 443, 444, 445, 446, 448, 456, and 458; One-Step models 221,

401, 402, 403, 404, 405, 406, 407, 408, and 409; **Seven Year Car Seat models 228, 453, and 454; Bobby-Mac models 411, 412, 414, 415, and 416; One-Step Deluxe models 222, 223, and 417; Evenflo Booster Seat models 242, 470, and 471.** Certain seat buckle and tongue assemblies do not properly engage when latched, failing to meet the requirements of FMVSS No. 213. Produced April to December 1985 and January 1986 to April 1990. Evenflo will provide owners with a replacement buckle tongue and installation instructions; call 800-233-5921.

Evenflo Juvenile Furniture Co.—harness, model number 420. These seats failed the post-impact buckle release force requirements of FMVSS No. 213. Produced September 1988 to July 1989. Evenflo will provide owners with a new harness and installation instructions; call 800-233-5921.

Evenflo Juvenile Furniture Co.—installation instructions and warning labels, Dyn-O-Mite models 441, 442, 443, 444, 445, 446, and 448 and Infant Car Seat/Carrier models 456 and 458. These seats failed to meet the seventy-degree maximum back support angle requirements of FMBSS No. 213. Produced January 1985 to January 1989. Evenflo will provide owners with new installation instructions. Also, the child seats are not to be used in the most reclined position with lap belts only. Warning labels will also be issued. Call 800-233-5921.

Evenflo Juvenile Furniture Co.—harness, model number 410. The single strap slide that is positioned on the right and left side of the upper harness can slip. Produced June 1988 to June 1989. Evenflo will send owners a double slide locking harness; call 800-233-5921. NHTSA recall number 89E017.

Fisher-Price—warning label, model number 9173. The seats have an incorrectly positioned label warning that any car seat used in the rear-facing position should not be installed in an automotive seat on which an air bag can deploy. This does not comply with requirements of FMVSS No. 213. Produced September to November 1994. Fisher-Price will send owners a new label with instructions to place the label correctly on the child safety seat; call 800-432-5437.

Fisher-Price—buckle assembly, model number 9104. The red button on the buckle of the child safety seat can dislodge from the casing, causing one of the appendages attached to the button to be on the outside of its protective casing. Produced June 15 to September 4, 1992. Fisher-Price will provide either a replacement child safety seat or a refund of the cost of the seat. The consumers will also have the option of receiving a new buckle assembly. Call 800-432-5437.

Fisher-Price—shoulder belts, model number 9101. The shoulder belts on car seats using a particular design of connector bar can come free of the connector bar after extended use. Produced February 8, 1991, to January 24, 1992. Fisher-Price is providing a plastic cover that fits over the opening on the connector bar that will prevent the shoulder belts from coming free of the connector bar; call 800-432-5437.

Fisher-Price—buckle shield, model numbers 9100 and 9101. The plastic laminate on the buckle shield can break after force is applied in repeated use. Produced May 1987 to January 1989 and February 1989 to October 1989. Fisher-Price will send owners a new shield and installation instructions; call 800-432-5437.

Fisher-Price—breast shield, model number 9149. The breast shield could separate from the tongue of the restraint assembly in crash conditions because of a faulty buckle frame.

Produced January to February 1991. Fisher-Price will replace the breast shield assembly; call 800-432-5427.

Fisher-Price—metallic label, model numbers 9100 and 9101. The metallic label glued to the breast shield of the seat can become loose over time, presenting a choking hazard to the seat occupant if the child removes the label and places it in his or her mouth. Produced April 1985 to June 1989. Fisher-Price is requesting owners to inspect the shield periodically, and if the label is loose, peel it off and discard it.

Fisher-Price—button on the shield strap, model numbers 9100 and 9101. The button on the shield strap can become loose and can be removed by a child, presenting a choking hazard if the child places the button in their mouth. Produced July 1988 to October 1990. Fisher-Price will send a replacement button and installation instructions to owners; call 800-432-5427.

Fisher-Price—seat metal laminate shield, model number 9100. The seat metal laminate shield, located inside the shield buckle, can break after repeated use. Produced April to August 1985. Fisher-Price is providing owners with installation instructions and a new shield; call 800-432-5427.

Fisher-Price—retractor assembly, model number 9101. The retractor assembly has a "tongue" used to engage the breast shield of the child restraint. A stamping die used on this tongue could cause the part to fail and completely separate in a crash. This does not meet the requirements of FMVSS No. 213. Produced February to March 1990. Fisher-Price is providing owners with installation instructions and a replacement retractor assembly; call 800-432-5427.

Fisher-Price—foam piece, model numbers 9100 and 9101. A car seat foam piece that is attached to the plastic seat shell located under the seat cover does not meet the flammability requirements of FMVSS No. 302. Produced April 1985 to January 1989. Fisher-Price will send owners a new piece of foam; call 800-432-5427.

Fisher-Price—shoulder belt retraction, model number 9100. A foreign object or substance can cause the white lock lever to be stuck in the down position at the time the chest shield is unbuckled to remove the child. The shoulder belt would retract too far, making it difficult to remove the child. Produced April 1985 to July 1986. Fisher-Price will provide owners with installation instructions and a new belt button that acts as a stop, limiting the retraction of the shoulder belt; call 800-432-5427.

Gerry Baby Products Co.—warning label, model numbers 626 and Secure Ride. The seats have an incorrectly positioned label warning that any car seat used in the rear-facing position should not be installed in an automobile seat on which an air bag can deploy. This does not comply with the requirements of FMVSS No. 213. Produced August 1994 to March 1995. A new label will be sent to consumers with instructions on how to correctly use the child seat in the vehicle; call 800-952-5552.

Gerry Baby Products Co.—buckle, model Gerry Guardian. The buckles on these child restraints are not stiff enough to prevent a child from releasing the buckle. Produced January 31 to May 3, 1990. Gerry is providing owners with a free buckle replacement kit; call 800-952-5552.

Kolcraft Products, Inc.—material, model Performa. The material used in these seats does not comply with the requirements of FMVSS No. 302, "Flammability of Interior Materials." Produced March 1 to October 31,

1996. Kolcraft will replace the material on these infant seats; call 800-453-7673.

Kolcraft Products, Inc.—buckle, models Performa and Secure Fit. These seats do not comply with the buckle release requirements of FMVSS No. 213. Produced January 26, 1996, to July 31, 1997. Kolcraft will provide owners with installation instructions, a replacement buckle housing kit, and the tools necessary to install the new buckle; call 800-453-7673.

Kolcraft Products, Inc.—crotch strap assembly, models Travel About, Plus 4, Plus 5, and Infant Rider (models 138xx, 368xx manufactured March 4 to April 30, 1996; July 17, 1996; July 25, 1996; and August 19, 1996) and Travel About, Plus 5, and Carter Travel 5 (models 13833, 13842, and 13852, manufactured May 1 to September 30, 1996). During compliance testing, a crotch strap assembly separated from the shell of an infant restraint. This does not comply with requirements of FMVSS No. 213. Produced March 4 to September 30, 1996. Kolcraft will provide owner with instructions to examine the crotch strap retainer clip and for realigning the clip if it has been misinstalled. A sticker will also be provided for installation on the child restraint notifying the user of the possibility of a misaligned strap retainer clip with simple instructions for its realignment. Call 800-453-7673.

Kolcraft Products, Inc.—buckle, model Traveler 700. During crashes involving speeds greater than thirty miles per hour and with the seat in a forward position, the buckle can unlatch. Produced November 1994 to August 1995. Kolcraft is providing owners with a new buckle mechanism, instructions, and the tools needed to replace the buckle; call 800-453-7673.

Kolcraft Products, Inc.—harness assembly, models Traveler 700, Automate, and Playskool. The tongue of the buckle assembly can corrode. This does not comply with requirements of FMVSS No. 213. Also, the label with use and safety instructions is missing from the Playskool model. Produced June 30, 1993, to October 1993. Kolcraft will provide owners with a free replacement harness assembly and installation instructions. Call 800-453-7673.

Kolcraft Products, Inc.—instruction sticker, model Traveler 700. The instruction sticker attached to the child seat is incorrect, since it was written for a different model child seat. This does not comply with requirements of FMVSS No. 213. Produced January to December 1991. Kolcraft will provide owners correct instruction stickers; call 800-453-7673.

Kolcraft Products, Inc.—seat cushion, model Perfect Fitt 180-200. The bottom cushion of the seat failed to meet the flammability requirements of FMVSS 213. Produced January 1988 to July 1990. Kolcraft will provide owners with new seat cushions; call 800-453-7673.

Kolcraft Products, Inc.—seat shell, model Dial-A-Fitt II 180-600. The seat shells failed to comply with the structural integrity standards of FMVSS No. 213. The plastic seat shells cracked during dynamic impact testing. Produced November 1990 to August 1991. Kolcraft will send owners a new seat shell; call 800-453-7673.

Kolcraft Products, Inc.—seat shell, model Traveler 700. The armrests of the child seat crack and splinter at the attachment to the seat back, leaving springs and sharp pieces of plastic exposed. Produced January 1991 to August 1991. Kolcraft will replace the seat shell with a new seat shell that eliminates the spring and strengthens the plastic of the armrest; call 800-453-7673.

Kolcraft Products, Inc.—seat cushion, Playskool models 140-155 and 180-400. The foam seat cushions fail to conform to the flammability requirements of FMVSS No. 302. Produced December 1989 to August 1990. Kolcraft will send owners a new seat cushion; call 800-453-7673.

Kolcraft Products, Inc.—seat shell, Perfect Fitt models 180-200 and 180-150. The seat fails to meet the head and knee excursion requirements of FMVSS No. 213. Produced March 1989 to October 1990. Kolcraft will send owners a plastic reinforcement tube kit to install in the rear of the seat shell; call 800-453-7673.

Kolcraft Products, Inc.—canoe clip, Dial-A-Fitt models 180-200 and 180-300, Perfect Fitt models 180-100 and 180-150, and Rock-N-Ride model 131-101. The polypropylene fasteners (canoe clip) used to attach the seats can develop hairline cracks or weaknesses that can cause the clip to break. Produced January 1987 to August 1989. Kolcraft will send replacement clips to owners; call 800-453-7673.

Kolcraft Products, Inc.—buckles, Dial-A-Fitt models 180-200 and 180-300. These seats exceed the post-impact buckle release force requirements of FMVSS No. 213. Produced April to June 1989. Kolcraft will send a new harness to owners; call 800-453-7673.

MCP Enterprises, Inc. (World Toys Discount)—head and knee excursion requirements, model Lin Lih. These seats do not meet the occupant head and knee excursion requirements of FMVSS No. 213.

Produced January 1987 to July 1989. MCP will refund the purchase price upon return of the car seat; call 213-626-1847. NHTSA Recall Number 89E024.

Porsche Cars—air bag deactivation, Porsche Carrera, 911, and Boxter model vehicles equipped with the child seating system air bag deactivation kit, 1997 and 1997 models. Due to a manufacturing problem, the contact buckle does not deactivate the air bag. Dealers will install a modified airbag deactivation kit. Call 800-545-8039.

Renolux (FBS, Inc.)—model GT7000. The wiring used to connect the child seat to the cigarette lighter overheats and melts the plastic wire covering. Produced May 1989 through June 1993. FBS, Inc., is no longer in business.

Renolux (FBS, Inc.)—models GT2000, GT4000, GT5000, and GT7000. The seat cover fails to meet the minimal flammability requirements. Produced May 1989 through June 1993. FBS, Inc., is no longer in business.

Renolux (FBS, Inc.)—models GT2000, GT4000, GT5000, and GT7000. The padding behind the head of the seat occupant does not have sufficient compression deflection resistance. Produced January 1992 through January 1993. FBS, Inc., is no longer in business.

Renolux (FBS, Inc.)—model GT5000 Turn-A-Tot. The seat cover fails to meet the flammability requirements and the seats fail to meet the head excursion requirements. Produced February 1990 through April 1991. FBS, Inc., is no longer in business.

Renolux (FBS, Inc.)—model GT1000 and GT2000. The seats failed to meet the pre-impact buckle release force requirements and back support angle requirements. FBS, Inc., is no longer in business.

Virco Manufacturing Corp.—model 832 Pride Trimble. These seats fail to meet the head excursion requirements. Produced January 1988 through April 1989. Consumers can remove the optional shield attachment or return the car seat for a full replacement. Virco has sold the child safety seat manufacturing portion of the company and there are no new seats available for replacement.

Child Safety Seats (Integrated)

Chrysler Corp.—1996–1997 Chrysler Town and Country, Dodge Caravan and Grand Caravan, and Plymouth Voyager and Grand Voyager. The shoulder harness restraint can become difficult to extract, thus trapping a child in the seat. Produced January 1, 1995, through July 31, 1997. 800-992-1997.

Chrysler Corp.—1998 Plymouth Voyager and Grand Voyager, Dodge Caravan and Grand Caravan and Chrysler Town and Country. Children may not be properly restrained in the child safety seat due to a defect in the harness restraint system. Produced November through December 1997. 800-992-1997.

Chrysler Corp.—1996 Plymouth Voyager and Grand Voyager, Dodge Caravan and Grand Caravan, and Chrysler Town and Country. The bolts that secure the integrated child seat modules to the seat frame can break. Produced June through July 1996. 800-992-1997.

Evenflo—800,000 On My Way Infant Car Seats/Carriers, model numbers 207 and 492 (3-5-98). While the seats are being used as infant carriers, serious injuries can occur to children due to defects in these seats and carriers. Manufactured December 15, 1995, through July 27, 1997. Sold nationwide January 1996. 800-203-2138.

Ford Motor Co.—1998 Windstar. The headrest mechanism on the child safety seat is defective. Produced January 1997. 800-392-3673.

General Motors Corp.—1996–1998 Chevrolet and GMC ML model vans. Some of these vehicles may be missing seat belt parts. Produced May 1996 through September 1997. 800-222-1020 (Chevrolet) or 800-462-8782 (GMC).

Clothing

Bentley Lingerie—30,000 "Esleep Juniors" robes, GPU numbers 9816, 9817, 9818, 9885, 9886, 9890, and 9891 (8-19-99). The robes fail to meet federal flammability standards for children's sleepwear. Sold nationwide in JCPenney stores July 1998 through April 1999. Call 888-330-3803.

Catton Brothers—13,200 Disney Babies romper sets for boys and girls, style numbers 1168 and 1169 (4-15-97). Romper's crotch snaps have exposed prongs which may cause injury. Sold nationwide October 1996 through February 1997. 800-357-6343.

Deckers Outdoor Corp.—65,000 Children's Teva Sandals (10-8-98). Falls can occur to children due to the straps attached to the footbed of the sandals coming apart. Sold nationwide December 1997 through August 1998. 800-781-9928.

Elegant Headwear Co.—150,000 Infant and Toddler Hats (1-14-99). If the chin strap gets caught on playground equipment, riding toys, or other catch points strangulation can occur. Sold nationwide 1985 through 1998. 800-689-9237.

GapKids—127,800 Kids' Spring/Summer Anoraks (6-3-98). The zipper pull contains lead. Sold worldwide January 1998 through June 1998. 800-333-7899, ext. 75000.

GUESS? Inc.—78,000 liquid-filled bubble patch T-shirts "GUESS? Girls" or "Guess USA" (8-31-99). The bubble patch contains a petroleum distillate. If the patch is punctured or leaks, the petroleum distillate can be harmful if ingested. Sold nationwide in GUESS? Inc. and other clothing stores June 1997 through March 1999. Call 800-347-1466.

Gymboree Corp.—7,000 toddler boys 5-pocket denim jeans "GYMSPORT' (6-30-99). The snap on the waist of the jeans can come off, posing a choking hazard to young children. Gymboree stores sold these jeans March 1999 through June 1999. Call 800-558-9885.

Hardwick Knitted Fabrics—16,800 fleece garments, mostly for children (1-5-98). These items were sold at the following stores:

- JCPenney—"Winnie the Pooh" Infants and Toddlers Vests, RN 19109
- JCPenney—"Winnie the Pooh" Infant and Toddler Pants, RN 19109
- Kohl's Department Stores—"Winnie the Pooh" Infant Shirt, RN 19109
- Chocolate Soup retail stores—"Chocolate Soup" Girl's Jumper and Boy's Shirt

Sold nationwide August 1996 through July 1997. 888-424-8223.

Kid's Patrol—12,000 Athletic Team zippered vests (11-13-97). Sold as part of a three-piece set. The zipper "pulls" can slide off the top of the vests, creating a choking hazard. Sold nationwide in Wal-Mart stores June 1997 through October 1997. 800-562-5373.

Levi Strauss—86,000 Short-Sleeve Western Dress, Long-Sleeve Western Dress, Long-Sleeve Plaid Blocked Dress (6-2-97). Snaps on the dresses may become detached, creating a choking hazard. Sold nationwide April 1996 to February 1997. 800-USA-LEVI.

Limited Too, Inc.—390,000 Children's Satin Sleepwear Pajama Sets (9-16-98). The pajamas do not meet federal flammability standards for children's sleepwear, which presents a risk of burn injuries to children. Sold nationwide in Limited Too stores December 1995 through July 1998. 800-934-4497.

Limited Too, Inc.—17,600 Children's Fleece Robes (1-20-99). The robes present a risk of serious burn injuries to children because they fail to meet federal flammability standards for children's-size sleepwear. Sold nationwide in Limited Too stores September 1998 through December 1998. 800-934-4497.

Little Laura of California, Inc.—2,000 Sweet Suzana brand infants' shirt and pant sets, RN 41601 (5-28-97). The tulip-shaped buttons may break off, creating a choking hazard. Sold nationwide in Kids R Us stores January 1997 through March 1997. 800-213-1994.

Little Me—7,200 Mini Fruit Girl's Rompers for newborns and infants—RN 20864- (7-27-99). The garments have ornamental cherries on them that pose a choking hazard to young children. Sold nationwide in major department stores and children's clothing stores March 1999 through July 1999. Call 800-843-8460.

NIKE—110,000 of Infant's Little Air Jordan XIV Sneakers, model number 132549 102 (3-5-99). The red trim paint on these shoes contains lead. Sold nationwide January 1999 through March 1999. 800-344-6453.

Payless Shoe Source—6,000 child's novelty purses (5-18-98). The decorative liquid in the purse flap contains a petroleum distillate that may be dangerous and possibly fatal if ingested. Sold nationwide February 1998 through May 1998. 800-444-7463.

Payless Shoe Source—80,000 children's sneakers, COASTERS brand (6-23-98). Young children can choke on the detachable teddy bear or metal heart clasps found on the zippers of these shoes. Sold nationwide in Payless Shoe Source stores March 1998 through June 1998. 800-444-7463.

Reebok—140,000 children's side zip sneakers, styles: toddler sizes 81-46353, 81-46354, 81-46395, 81-47286, 81-47287, 81-47288, 81-47289, 81-48115, and 81-48116; child sizes 71-46351, 71-46352, 71-46394, 71-47282, 71-47283, 71-47284, 71-47285, 71-47438, 71-47439, and 71-49204 (7-15-99). A side pocket on the sneaker has a pull tab on the zipper that can be twisted off, presenting a choking hazard. Sold nationwide in shoe and sporting goods stores September 1998 through June 1999. Call 800-648-5550.

Shopko Stores Inc.—68,000 Peek-A-Babe newborn and infant "creepers" (7-29-99). The creepers snaps can detach, posing a choking hazard. Sold nationwide in Shopko Stores December 1998 through June 1999. Call 800-791-7333.

Spiegel Catalog, Inc.—4,200 velvet baby garments, item numbers 82-5609 baby cardigan with snap front, 82-5604 baby coveralls with snaps at shoulders, 82-5610 long-sleeve baby tee with snaps at shoulder (4-7-99). Young children can choke on metal snaps that might come off. Sold nationwide by Spiegel November 1998 through February 1999. 800-443-4856.

Target—106,000 Utility fleece sweatshirts for men and boys (3-24-97). Material is flammable. Sold in Target stores nationwide June 1996 through February 1997. 612-304-6000.

Tommy Hilfiger U.S.A., Inc.—38,000 infant cardigans (5-26-99). The snaps on the cardigan can detach, posing a choking hazard to infants. Sold nationwide in upscale department stores August 1998 through October 1998. Call Tommy Hilfiger Consumer Relations Department for an exchange or full refund. 877-TOMMYCARES.

Wear Me Apparel Corp.—30,000 Little Miracles Rompers, SN 9448, 9449 (3-11-97). The paint on the cap snaps contains lead. Sold nationwide in K-Mart stores October 1996. 800-223-0777.

Cribs and Playpens

On November 24, 1998, the CPSC announced multiple play yard recalls due to protruding rivets that pose strangulation hazards to children. The brand names of these playpens are Bilt-Rite, Evenflo, Gerry, Graco, Kolcraft, Playskool, Pride-Trimble, and Strolee. These products have been sold nationwide from 1985 to the present. For more information call 800-794-4115.

All Our Kids—13,000, model number 742 and 762 (11-21-96). The crib/play yard may collapse and entrap a child in folded top rails. The CPSC recommends that you destroy the crib/play yard immediately due to the fact that the firm is out of business.

B&B Stores (also known as Velasco Alonso, Inc.)—400 mesh-sided cribs (12-18-97). Multiple dangers are present with this crib that could result in choking, strangulation, and entrapment injuries. Sold in B&B stores in Puerto Rico August 1996 through January 1997. 787-878-0980.

Baby Trend—"Home and Roam" or "Baby Express" portable playpens (1-10-95). The sides of the playpen may collapse onto a child inside, leading to strangulation or suffocation. Sold 1992 and 1994. 800-421-1902.

Baby's Dream Furniture—13,000 Generation oak cribs, number 194 (2-10-98).

These cribs have a drop gate that folds down at the front of the crib, rather than a rail that slides up and down, presenting a danger to an infant who might get fingers or toes pinched as the drop gate is used. Sold nationwide December 1994 through June 1997. 888-866-4217.

Bedside Cradle (W. C. Redmon Co., of Peru, Ind.)—1,800 Cuddle Me Close Bedside Cradles (11-12-98). The legs on the cradles can become loose and can separate, causing the cradle to tip. Sold nationwide February 1998. 765-473-6683.

C & T International—Tracy model wooden sleigh crib (item 800) and Christine model crib wooden rocker crib (item 210) (6-24-97). The side rails may separate, creating a danger of strangulation. Sold on the East Coast from February 1994 through March 1996. 888-470-1260.

Century Products—212,000 Fold-N-Go travel play yards, models 10-710 and 10-810 (11-21-96). The playpen can collapse onto an infant. Sold nationwide at Toys R Stores February 1993 through November 1996. Century is offering a free Posi-Lock kit, which will prevent such collapses. 800-541-0264.

Century Products—cribs, various models (2-10-95). There have been reports of five entrapment incidents and one death associated with defects in the side slats of Century cribs. 800-541-0264.

Century Products—50,000 Fold-N-Go Care Centers, models 10-750 and 10-760 (9-3-98). An infant can become entrapped and suffocate because the care center's bassinet may have loose fabric that can create a pocket near the floorboard. Sold nationwide March 1998 through August 1998. A free repair kit is being offered. 800-583-4092.

Coaster Company of America—1,856 full-size medal baby cribs, item numbers 2364 and 2368 (5-15-97). Slat spacing in the cribs is greater than $2\frac{3}{8}$ inches, creating a strangulation hazard. Also, the plastic end caps may separate, creating a choking hazard. Sold nationwide June 1996 through April 1997. 800-221-9699, extension 157.

Cosco—390,000 full-size metal baby cribs, model numbers 10T01, 10T04, 10T05, 10T06, 10T08, 10T14, 10T84, 10T85, 10T94, 10T95, 10M96, 10M84, 10M85, and 10M94 (7-9-97). The spacing between the rail slats is greater than $2\frac{3}{8}$ inches, creating a strangulation hazard. Sold nationwide beginning in 1995. 800-221-6736.

Cosco—190,000 full-size cribs, model numbers 10T01, 10T04, 10T05, 10T06, 10T09, 10T11, and 10T14 (12-6-96). The side rails have attached spindles that can separate and create gaps, allowing the infant to fall from the crib or become strangled. Sold nationwide January 1991 through April 1994. For a free repair kit, call Cosco at 800-314-9327.

Cosco—62,000 crib mattresses (2-17-99). Twelve incidents of babies becoming entrapped between the crib bars and the platform have been reported. One baby boy was killed when this occurred. Sold nationwide. 800-221-6736.

Draco Corp.—190,000 All Our Kids Portable Cribs/Playpens, models 741, 742, 761, and 762 (11-21-96). The playpens (also known as travel yards) can collapse onto an infant or young child, leading to strangulation. Seven deaths have been attributed to this mechanism. Sold nationwide 1992 through 1995. Draco Corp. is currently out of business and therefore a recall is not in effect. These playpens should be destroyed.

Evenflo—1.2 million Happy Camper, Happy Cabana, and Kiddie Camper play yards (6-25-97). The play yard can collapse onto a child inside. At least three deaths have been associated with these play yards. Sold nationwide January 1990 through 1997. To receive free hinge covers to correct the problem, call 800-447-9178.

Evenflo—205,000 Houdini Portable Play Yard, model numbers beginning with 332 (12-18-96). Presents hazards due to small parts and sharp edges. Sold nationwide 1994 through 1996. 800-490-7549.

Generation 2 Worldwide—6,600 Next Generation Pisces Baby Cribs, model number 67-8100 (5-10-99). Infants can become entrapped in the side rails due to large openings created by the slats on the headboard and footboards coming loose. Sold nationwide March 1997 through December 1998. 800-736-1140.

Gerry Baby Products—17,043 cribs, models 8200, 8300, and 8500 (10-5-95). These cribs may collapse onto an infant inside. Sold nationwide May 1994 through August 1994. The cribs may be adjusted to prevent this occurrence. 800-525-2472.

Graco—133,000 Playyards, manufacture dates 11-13-95 through 1-12-96 (10-30-96). The mesh on these play yards may come undone, posing a potential strangulation hazard to infants. Sold nationwide. 800-423-9078.

JCPenney—6,000 Francisca Full-Size Baby Cribs, Model numbers 343-3935 and 343-4065 (9-30-97). The cribs' side rail spindles are too short and may allow the bars to fall out, creating a space greater than 2⅜ inches. This could allow an infant to become entrapped between the bars and strangled. Sold in JCPenney catalogs August 1996 through April 1997. 800-709-5777.

Kolcraft Inc. and Playskool—11,000 Playskool Travel-Lite Portable Cribs, model numbers 77101 and 77103 (2-17-93). These cribs have rotating top rail hinges that may collapse, entrapping children and suffocating them. Six deaths have been related to these cribs. There is a $120 Child Saver Reward for the return of each crib. This is a nationwide recall which has been in effect for approximately five years. Sold between 1990 and 1992. 800-453-7673.

LaNacional—2,288 styles CAMA CUNA R.N.C., CAMA CUNA No. 2, and Crib with Drawers (12-5-95). They fail in numerous ways to comply with U.S. safety standards. The crib slats are greater than 2⅜ inches apart and corner posts are greater than 1 inch high. Identification markings are lacking except for the words "Made in the Dominican Republic" printed beneath the mattress support. These cribs were distributed in Puerto Rico from January 1994 through April 12, 1995. For a full refund, call LaNacional at 809-758-3606.

Okla Homer Smith Furniture Manufacturing Co.—cribs made between April 1992 and December 1993. Slats may be loose or missing, creating a risk of entrapment in the side rail of the crib. For replacement rails, call 800-647-3876.

Furniture

Allen Manufacturing—42,000 recliner chair number VA-9300 Tn (5-23-96). Small children can get trapped or strangled in the recliners if caught in the space between the seat and footrest. Sold nationwide January 1988 through December 1995. Call 888-338-0550.

Bucky Products—3,800 Baby Bucky baby pillows (3-28-96). The pillows, for use in car seats and strollers, pose a potential suffocation hazard to infants. 800-692-8259.

Bush Industries Inc.—100,000 television carts, model numbers 5414 in black and 5014 in brown (7-14-99). These carts can tip over and cause serious injury to young children. Sold nationwide in discount, home, and furniture stores June 1992 through August 1998. Call 800-950-4782.

Crate & Barrel—7,00 toy chests (7-22-98). The lid of the chest may fall onto a child's head or neck due to a possible failure of the chest's lid support. This may cause entrapment and lead to strangulation. Sold nationwide from September 1994 through March 1998. 800-352-0688.

Crate & Barrel—4,300 children's tables (6-21-99). Has a six-inch hole cut in the center of the table where four children have become entrapped; two required emergency personnel to free them. Sold nationwide by Crate & Barrel September 1998 through February 1999, in stores and catalogs. Call or stop at Crate & Barrel for a free repair disk. 800-897-5919.

Golden Chair Inc.—100,000 recliners, License number NY 58770 (5-23-96). Small children can get trapped or strangled in the recliners if caught in the space between the seat and foot rest. Sold nationwide January 1987 to December 1995. 800-965-1277.

IRIS U.S.A.—100,000 plastic toy storage chests, model numbers WT-80, WT-120, and WT-175 (12-3-98). The chests do not contain a necessary lid-support device, do not have enough ventilation when the lid is closed, and have latches that keep lids closed. This may cause entrapment and suffocation of children. Sold nationwide since January 1996. 800-320-4747.

K-Mart—205,000 sling garden chairs (11-3-97). The chairs can collapse during use. Several fingertip amputations and crush injuries have been reported. Sold in K-Mart stores nationwide February 1997 through September 1997. 800-63KMART.

Keysheen International—children's folding chaise lounge chairs (3-25-97). A child's fingers can get trapped between the support leg and metal frame, causing pinching or amputation. Sold nationwide from 1994 through 1997. 888-539-7436.

Lane Furniture—38,300 cedar chest (9-4-96). Approximately 12 million cedar chests that automatically latch when closed were manufactured by Lane from 1912 to 1987. These chests have been associated with suffocation injuries to children who became trapped inside. 888-856-8758.

Meri-Jon Artist Colony—150,000 beanbag chairs (4-2-96). Any beanbag chair which can be easily opened poses a choking risk to children, as the pellets inside can easily fit into a small child's mouth. Fifteen other manufacturers have recalled over 12 million such chairs during previous years due to this risk. Meri-Jon has made these chairs since 1980. 800-476-4618.

Now Products—20,000 foam children's chairs (7-25-96). When unzipped, the fabric cover exposes a plastic liner that can cause suffocation in infants and young children. Sold at Ames Department Stores January 1994 through June 1996. For a free repair kit, call Now Products at 800-535-3218.

PJ Toys—8,300 units of children's furniture sold at Target (9-3-98). The furniture contains lead in the paint. The furniture is decorated in either a circus or a princess theme. The following furniture items have been recalled:

CIRCUS THEME

Seal Wall Mirror (#097-02-0049)
Circus Rover (#097-02-0052)

Circus Table and Chair Set (#097-02-0053)
Clown Coat Hook (#097-02-0057)
Circus Wall Shelf (#097-02-0056)
Clown Stepping Stool (#097-02-0051)
Clown Tot Stool (#097-02-0090)
Banana Coat Tree (#097-02-0054)
Rocking Elephant (#097-02-0055)

PRINCESS THEME

Princess Step Stool (#097-02-0058)
Princess Rocker (#097-02-0059)
Crown Wall Hooks (#097-02-0061)
Princess Table and Chair Set (#097-02-0062)
Crown Mirror (#097-02-0063)
Crown Wall Shelf (#097-02-0065)
Crown Tot Stool (#097-02-0060)
Crown Coat Tree (#097-02-0060)

Sold nationwide in Target stores April 1998 through July 1998. 800-935-5060.

Playskool—287,000 1-2-3 High Chairs, serial number TX 51321–TX 61442 (10-12-95). Chairs may collapse due to cracking at the joints or the restraint bar may crack or break off. Sold nationwide May 1994 through May 1996. For a free refund, call Playskool at 800-752-9755 or 800-555-0428.

Primo International—1,600 futon mattresses (4-28-97). Flammable material. Sold nationwide January 1994 through August 1996. 800-267-7746.

Ridgewood and Charleswood—309,000 four-drawer dressers, model numbers 80813, 88813, 80413, and 88413 (1-16-96). *This is only a warning, not a recall.* The children's dresser may become unstable and tip over if heavy items are placed in the top drawers. Consumers are urged to remove the feet from the dresser in order to diminish this risk. Sold nationwide in 1991. 800-314-9327.

Sauder Woodworking Co.—2 million television carts, brown oak model 5155, black oak model 5055, and white oak model 5251

(5-24-99). These carts tip over easily, causing the television to fall off. One three-year-old was injured this way. Sold nationwide in discount stores, home centers, and furniture stores March 1989 through September 1998. For a free repair kit, call 888-800-4590.

Southern Sales/Marketing—900,000 plastic lawn chairs Perla, Althea, and Malibu Styles (8-1-96). The chairs' rear legs lack rubber feet and may spread apart and break, causing the chair to collapse during use. Sold nationwide January 1992 through September 1995. 800-729-5033.

Step 2—350,000 Big Storage Chests, model numbers 7511 and 7211 (1-12-98). The lids of these chests can fall onto the heads and necks of young children. At least sixteen incidents of such injury have been reported. Sold in Toys R Us, K-Mart and other retail stores nationwide February 1992 through November 1997. 800-347-8272.

Go-carts

The CPSC and various go-cart manufacturing companies recalled for repair over 400,000 go-carts with exposed rear axles. These axles can injure or kill riders if clothing or hair become entangled. At least two children have already died this way. Sold nationwide from January 1972 through August 1997. The following manufacturers are involved in the recall of these go-carts.

Avenger—83 Yellow Jacket go-carts, model SST (5-6-97). Call collect at 318-322-2007.

Bob's Kart Shop—7,000 Grasshopper, T.C. Go-Fur and Ground Hawg go-carts (5-6-97). Call collect at 815-496-2820.

Carter Brothers—5,000 Superwheels, Hotbodies, Kartwheels, Master Karts, and Desert Storm go-carts (1-22-97). Call 800-523-5278.

Kartco—750 Kartco and Raodboss go-carts, model number 445 (5-6-97). Call 800-621-2789.

Ken-Bar—75,000 Streaker, Sand Dog, Salute to America, Scorpion, and Mud Hog go-carts, model numbers DD7, DD8, D680, D710, D720, D780, D790, D810, D840, S465, SC7, STA8, STA9, and SD11; and serial numbers 001-100,000 (5-6-97). Call 800-241-3557.

Manco Products—300,000 Fox, Phoenix and Sears go-carts (7-16-96). Call 800-293-0795.

Minat—200 U.S. Eagle Series go-carts, models Eagle I and Eagle II (5-6-97). Call 800-350-8739.

T&D Metal Products—39,000 Klipper Karts, ProKart, Pathwinder, Kook Kart Campout and Bird Mfg. go-carts, serial numbers EM001–EM029 and 0030–39126 (5-6-97). Call 888-465-2780.

Tiger Industries—1,800 Tiger II, Tiger II EL, Tiger III, and Black Max (9-10-98). Call collect at 602-668-1077.

Hammocks

Academy Broadway, Algoma Net Co., Avid Outdoor, Coghlan's, EZ Sales, Nelson/-Weather-Rite, Twin Oaks Hammock, Rothco, Safesport Manufacturing, Schwarzman Export Import, Standard Sales, and Texsport—These manufacturers are recalling over 3 million similarly made hammocks, which do not have spreader bars at the ends. These spreader bars hold the hammock open, helping to prevent the hammock from twisting about a child's neck or other body parts. About twelve children have died in this manner. The hammocks have been sold nationwide from 1979 to 1991. These hammocks should be returned to the stores where they were purchased for a full refund or replacement.

Household Items

American Hua Mao—139,000 cigarette lighters, models Windproof #L2 and #L3 (12-23-98). The child-resistant mechanisms on these lighters do not work. Small retail stores and souvenir shops in New York and Maryland sold these lighters March 1997 through November 1998. 212-244-1692.

BRK Brands—First Alert True Fit Safety Gates, model CSSG1 (9-30-97). Small pieces of the gate can break off, presenting a choking hazard. Sold nationwide beginning October 1996. 888-777-5599.

C & H Trading—40,000 disposable and novelty cigarette lighters (6-3-99). The lighters do not have child-resistant mechanisms. Sold in small retail stores in Louisiana, Massachusetts, Minnesota, Nevada, Texas, and Washington October 1998 through March 1999. 504-456-9251.

ERA Intermarketing—840,000 Elite-2 Disposable Cigarette Lighters, bar code 16229 12001, date 3/97 (4-9-98). The lighters do not meet the requirement for child-resistant mechanisms. The lighters are composed of clear plastic which is tinted in assorted colors. Sold nationwide June 1997 through March 1998. 888-682-2388.

Gerber—300,000 LIL' SPORT Spill Proof Sport Bottles (7-2-99). A valve inside the cap can detach, posing a choking hazard to young children. Sold nationwide February 1999 through July 1999. Call 800-4-GERBER.

Golden Bay Enterprise—50 3-WAY FLASHER CHRISTMAS LIGHT SET (12-17-96). Fire hazard. Sold in Florida October 1996 through December 1996. 800-791-2960.

Kikkerland Designs, Inc.—20,000 novelty lighters (4-13-99). Child-resistant mechanisms are not present on the lighters. The lighters resemble lamps and flying saucers. Sold nationwide March 1997 through February 1999. 800-869-1105.

North States Industries, Inc.—3,200 Stairway Gates, manufacturers ID number 8675 (6-3-99). The locking mechanism can release if the gate is shaken, allowing a child access to the unsafe area. Sold nationwide at Ames, Ann & Hope, Hambleton & Carr, and Value City department stores March 1999 through April 1999. Return to store where purchased or call 800-848-8421.

Papel Freelance—28,000 pencils with miniature pacifiers found on the eraser end (5-22-97). The pacifier may detach from the pencil, creating a choking hazard. Sold nationwide September 1996 through April 1997. 800-634-8384.

Playskool—273,000 spillproof cups, models 6 oz. and 8 oz. Spillproof Cups, 6 oz. Spillproof Trainer Cup, 7 oz. and 10 oz. Easy Grip Spillproof Cups, 8 oz. Spillproof Trainer, and 6 oz. Spillproof Cups with Teletubby character decals (7-8-99). The spout on the cup can tear between the slit opening, causing a small piece of material to come loose, posing a choking hazard to young children. Sold nationwide by major retailers, including Walmart and Target January 1998 through July 1999. Call 888-690-6166.

Schweiss Distributing Co., of Fairfax, Minn.—500 bottom-operated bi-fold doors (10-20-98). Door operators and bystanders can become entrapped in moving door parts, such as the drive drums and cables, causing serious injuries such as amputations and fractures. The doors lack a safety shield, which allows accidents to occur. These bi-fold doors were not manufactured or designed by Schweiss Distributing Co. They were manufactured by a predecessor company. Sold nationwide January 1984 through August 1993. 800-746-8273.

TV Guard, Inc.—70,000 TV Guards (9-28-98). Children can sustain bodily injury by pulling on the TV Guard and tipping the television over. Sold nationwide April 1993 through September 1998. 877-TVGUARD.

Walgreens—Smoke Tote Cigarette Lighters (9-24-97). These lighters have child-resistant mechanisms that can fail. Sold in Walgreen stores August 1996 through August 1997. 888-899-0538.

ZNY Enterprises, Inc.—10,600 novelty and disposable cigarette lighters (6-15-99). The lighters do not have child-resistant mechanisms. Sold nationwide in small retail and souvenir stores January 1999 through April 1999. 917-373-4289.

Note: Numerous importers and distributors have been forced by the CPSC to recall lighters because they either do not have child-resistant mechanisms or they have defective child-resistant mechanisms.

Infant Carriers

Century Products—166,000 TraveLite SPORT Strollers, model numbers 11-171, 11-181, and 11-191 (4-16-97). These models have faulty restraint buckles and fold locks. These defects create a danger of an infant falling from the stroller and of the stroller collapsing. Sold nationwide February 1995. 800-944-0039.

Century Products—125,000 infant swings, Lil'Napper model (9-2-97). If the shoulder straps loosen or are unbuckled, a child can become entangled and strangle. Sold nationwide beginning in 1991. For repair, call 800-231-1448.

Cosco—355,500 Quiet Time infant swings, model numbers 08-975 and 08-977 or a date code of 0593-4095 (beneath the seat) (4-24-97). Screws in the frame may loosen, causing the seat to fall. Forty-four injuries have occurred. Sold nationwide February 1993 through September 1995. 800-221-6736.

Cosco—6,000 Voyager Car Seat/Strollers (12-16-97). The car seat can be snapped into a frame that allows it to be used as a stroller. The seat can fall from the frame during use, causing the child in it to be injured. Sold nationwide September 1997 through November 1997. 800-221-6736.

Cosco—57,000 Geoby Two-Way Tandem Strollers, model numbers 01-644 and 01-645 (2-17-99). The stroller locks might fail, causing the stroller to collapse. More than two hundred babies have been injured when this occurred. Manufactured February 1997 through February 1998. Sold nationwide. A free repair kit is available. 800-221-6736.

Cosco—670,000 Arriva models 02-665, 02-729, 02-731, 02-732, 02-733, 02-751, 02-756, 02-757, and Turnabout models 02-758, 02-759, 02-760, 02-761, 02-762, 02-763, 02-764, 02-765, 02-767 infant car seats/carriers (7-8-99). When used as a carrier, the handle locks on each side of the seat can unexpectedly release, causing the seat to flip forward. The infant could fall to the ground if this happens, causing serious injuries. There have been 151 reports of such incidents resulting in 29 injuries. Sold nationwide March 1995 through July 1999. Call 800-221-6736.

Evenflo—800,000 On My Way Infant Car Seats/Carriers, model numbers 207 and 492 (3-5-98). While the seats are being used as infant carriers, serious injuries can occur to children due to defects in these seats and carriers. Manufactured December 15, 1995, through July 27, 1997. Sold nationwide January 1996. 800-203-2138.

Evenflo—22,000 Hike 'n Roll Child Carriers, model numbers 522101 and 522102 (9-8-98). Strangulation may occur because there is the potential for a child to slip sideways into the leg openings. Sold nationwide June 1996 through June 1998. 800-649-0071.

Evenflo and Hufco-Delaware, Inc.—327,000 soft infant carriers model 075 and 080 Snugli Front & Back Pack (6-24-99). Infants can slip through the leg openings and fall; babies under two months are at greatest risk. Thirteen infants have been reported to have slipped through the openings. One suffered a skull fracture and two others suffered bruises when they fell to the ground. Sold nationwide January 1996 through May 1999. 800-398-8636.

Gold Bug—5,400 Carter's infant carriers, style number 89000 (3-25-97). The carrier's shoulder strap may separate from the buckles, creating a danger that an infant may fall. Sold in JCPenny stores nationwide June 1996. 800-942-9442.

Grayco Children's Products—564,000 carriers and carrier/swing seats, model numbers 1300, 1301, 1310, 1350, 1501, 1502, 1530, 1723, 2788, 5510, 8108, and 36264 (12-19-97). The handle on these models can unlock unexpectedly and cause an infant to fall out. Four skull fractures and two concussions have been reported. 800-281-3676.

L. L. Bean, Inc.—10,000 Backpack Child Carriers, model number AC25 (12-10-98). Strangulation can occur to small children if entangled in the carrier's harness. Children can also fall through, topple out, or escape the harness. Sold nationwide January 1997 through October 1998. 800-555-9717.

L. L. Bean, Inc.—13,000 Backpack Child Carriers, model number W695 (4-19-99). Head and body injuries can occur to small children because it is possible for them to work their way out of the harness and fall through a leg opening or topple out of the top of the carrier. Sold nationwide January 1993 through March 1995. 800-555-9717.

MTS Products—18,200 J. Mason infant carriers (12-8-97). The handles on these carriers can break, causing a child inside to fall to the ground. Seven reports of injuries have been made. "J. MASON" is imprinted on the handle. Sold in K-Mart, Rose, and State Enterprise stores nationwide April 1996 through August 1997. 800-242-1922.

Regal + Lager—240,000 Baby Bjorn Infant Carriers (1-21-99). Infants can slip through the leg openings and fall. Sold nationwide January 1991 through October 1998. 877-242-5676.

Monitors

Gerry Baby Products—86,000 rechargeable baby monitors, Clear Choice brand, model 618 (4-8-98). The rechargeable battery may cause the monitor's "parent" unit to smoke and flame if an electrical short occurs. Sold nationwide April 1996 through March 1998. 800-273-3521.

Safety 1st—25,000 nursery monitor batteries model number 49226, date codes 00097 through 03097 (10-28-97). The batteries that accompany the monitors may rupture, leading to a malfunction of the monitor and a skin-irritant hazard to your infant. Sold in retail stores nationwide June 1997 through August 1997. 800-964-8489.

Pacifiers and Bottles

Atico International USA—13,000 pacifiers sold at Bath & Body Works (10-1-98). The nipples on these pacifiers may separate from the base, posing a choking hazard to children. Sold nationwide by Bath & Body Works stores. 800-395-1001.

Binky-Griptight—13,000 Binky Newborn Orthodontic Pacifiers (1-15-97). The pacifier nipple can detach, presenting a choking hazard to young children. Sold in Target stores nationwide August 1994 through August 1995. 800-526-6320.

Walgreens—40,000 Kid's Sipper Bottle. (4-29-99). Children may choke on the bottles' caps, which can be pulled off. Sold nationwide March 1999 through April 1999. 800-934-4768.

Playground Equipment

Hedstrom—180,000 Star Cruiser Swings on backyard gyms (4-24-96). Children can cause the swing to flip over while swinging in it. Sold nationwide 1994 through April 1994. 800-233-3271.

Pool Equipment and Toys

Dive Sticks—19 million (6-24-99). These dive sticks are used in swimming pools and in shallow water can cause serious injuries to children because they stay vertical in the water. There have been six impalement injuries, four of which required hospitalization and surgery, and one facial injury. Sold nationwide at many stores, many of which do not have brand names printed on them. The sticks are either cylinder or shark-shaped, and should be thrown away. For more information on these products, go to the CPSCs web site at www.cpsc.gov.

Hydro-Air Industries—206,000 main drain covers in spas, hot tubs, and swimming pools, model number 10-6200 (2-3-97). A bather's hair can become entangled in the drain cover, causing the bather's head to be held under water. This drain cover was available for installation from 1980 to 1995. 800-230-9560.

K-Mart Corp.—114,000 Splash Club Deluxe Baby Floats, UPC numbers 016438897266 or 016438100267 (10-8-98). Children may drown due to possible tearing at the seam on the seat of the pool toy. The floats were sold by K-Mart stores nationwide September 1996 through August 1998. 800-63KMART.

K-Mart Corp.—90,000 Splash Club Deluxe Inflatable Kiddie Boats, UPC numbers 016438897204 or 016438100205 (8-13-98). Children may drown due to possible tearing at the seam on the seat of the pool toy. Sold by K-Mart stores nationwide September 1996 through July 1998. 800-63KMART.

Sta-Rite Industries—135,000 floor inlet fittings for gunnite and concrete pools and spas, model 08417 (1-16-97). If used improperly, these fittings may allow a bather's hair to be drawn in and become entangled, creating a potential for drowning. Two such drownings have occurred. 888-446-8285.

Swim N' Play—1,465 aboveground ledge covers (3-11-96). The triangular caps on the ledge covers do not completely cover the metal ledges on the pools, posing a risk of injury to swimmers. Sold with aboveground pools from 1980 to 1994. 800-631-3483.

Sporting Goods

Irwin Sports—8,400 baseball catcher's mask and face guard, number CL87 (6-26-96). The masks can be adjusted so that a ball could enter through the wire face guard, leading to facial injury. Sold nationwide October 1995 through May 1996. A free wire face guard replacement is being offered. 800-268-1732.

Nike—250,000 NIKE sport water bottles (7-20-99). The drinking valve on the cap can detach, posing a choking hazard. Sold nationwide in major sporting goods and department stores April 1999 through July 1999. Call 800-344-6453.

Ohio Art, Little Tikes, Today's Kids, and Fisher-Price—10.1 million toy basketball nets (12-22-98). Children can strangle on loops or openings in the nets. This is caused when nets come unhooked from the rim, or have knots that slide. Sold on basketball sets nationwide since 1976. The manufacturers will help consumers determine if the nets need to be replaced. 800-528-3328.

ProCourt—29,800 portable Basketball Systems (backboard, rim, pole, and base), date codes 970101 through 970873 (4-30-97). Water can leak from the base, allowing the set to fall down. Sold nationwide January 1997 through April 1997. 800-225-3865.

Rawlings Sporting Goods Co., Inc.—45,000 slow-pitch softball bats, model numbers SBZ2, SBZ3, SBZ4, SBB3, SBB4, SBB5, SBB6, SBB7, SPT-PK2, and DUAL-E (5-20-99). The top of the bats can shear off during use. Sold nationwide September 1997 through May 1999. 800-367-3455.

Schutt Manufacturing Co.—12,000 Baseball Striker and Softball Striker Batting Aids (4-27-98). Serious injuries can occur to users and bystanders during normal use. The ball can become separated from its cable when struck. Sold nationwide January 1994 through April 1998. 888-325-3978.

Toys

A. of America—recalling over 5,300 sets of twelve bracelets in various shapes, such as hearts and flowers on elastic string sold as party favors; the package label reads "FUN TIME PARTY FAVORS" (10-6-97). The jewelry can break into small parts that present choking dangers. Sold nationwide through March 5, 1997. 908-613-8555.

Al-Dan Trading—747 crib toys, which consist of four plastic balls and plastic animal figures on a piece of elastic; UPC number beginning with 69658 (7-16-97). The toys are not labeled as being a risk of strangulation to infants and young children when strung across a crib. Sold by Daniel Club Wholesalers and Swamis Trading in Miami, Florida, March 1996 through June 1997. 800-446-7091.

Al-Dan Trading—5,800 wooden vehicle toys (10-7-97). Small parts can come apart and become choking hazards to young children. The toys include small trucks, trains, race cars, motorcycles, airplanes and cranes. Sold in All for 99 Cents, Always 99 Cents, Dollar Store, Dollar Dave's, Daniel Club Wholesalers, and Swamis Trading in Florida, June 1996 through June 1997. 800-446-7091.

Almar Sales—8,600 matching children's necklace and bracelet sets with plastic beads in the shapes of balls, hearts, and teddy bears on elastic strings (10-6-97). The beads can break off the strings, leading to the danger of choking. Sold nationwide through March 1997. 800-251-2522.

Almar Sales—28,000 children's jewelry sets, Expressions brand, style numbers NB104, NB113, NB114, NB118, and NB136 (7-28-98). The jewelry may break, causing possible choking and aspiration haz-

ards. Sold nationwide January 1994 through June 1998. 800-251-2522.

Arby's—220,000 toy saxophones (5-7-98). Small parts of the toy saxophone may separate, causing children to choke. Distributed with Arby's meals nationwide January 1998 through March 1998.

Atico International—329,000 Halloween Floating Eyeballs and 100,000 Smiley Face Floating Balls (4-8-98). Young children may easily become poisoned due to the ball cracking and leaking kerosene that is contained within the balls. Children may also choke on the smaller balls. Sold nationwide June 1885 through October 1997. 800-645-3867.

Brass Eagle, Inc.—42,300 paintball masks, Brass Eagle's Xtreme Vision 280, item number 7472 (8-18-98). The lens on the mask can crack when struck by a paintball, presenting the possibility of an eye injury to the paintball player. Sold nationwide July 1997 through April 1998. 800-354-8841.

BRIO—79,000 wooden toy clowns (11-6-97). The hat can fall off and present a choking hazard. One toddler was killed when he choked on the hat and suffocated. Sold nationwide 1977 through September 1997. 888-274-6869.

Century—125,000 Lil' Napper Infant Swing, model numbers 12-344, 12-345, 12-347, 12-475, and 12-476 (9-2-97). Infants can become tangled in the shoulder harness straps. Three deaths and one near strangulation have occurred to infants using this mechanism. Free repair kits are being offered. Sold nationwide since 1991. 800-231-1448.

Chariot Victor Publishing—44,000 Veggie Tales' Dave and the Giant Pickle Playset, model SPCN 9834501358 (3-8-99). This playset poses a choking hazard to children.

Sold nationwide September 1998 through February 1999. 800-743-2514.

Charming Shoppes—4,800 metallic heart-shaped medallion necklaces (5-12-97). The necklaces contain high levels of lead. Sold nationwide through Fashion Bug Stores October 1996 through January 1997. 800-478-2918.

Colorbok—3.8 million Blue's Clues Handy Dandy Notebook (3-25-99). Children may choke on small parts that can break off the ends of the notebook coils. Sold nationwide June 1998 through January 1999. 877-677-4725.

Cosco—355,500 Quiet Time Wind Up Infant Swings, model numbers 08-975 and 08-977, date codes 0593 through 4095 (4-24-97). The seat can fall off and injure a child. 800-221-6736.

Creative Designs International, Ltd.—7,000 Magic Doll Feeding Sets, Binky, number 8221 (6-15-99). The nipple on the orange baby bottle separates, posing a choking hazard to children. Sold in California, Connecticut, Kentucky, New York, Washington, and Puerto Rico in toy and variety stores January 1998 through December 1998. 888-869-7234.

Creative Products—28,000 toy jewelry sets that include necklaces, bracelets, and earring clasps (7-10-97). The jewelry pieces can break, releasing small beads and pieces, creating a choking hazard. Sold nationwide August 1995 through November 1995. 800-366-6686.

Dairy Queen—150,000 toy water batons (1-6-97). The baton end cap may come off if a child sucks or chews on it, creating a choking hazard. Provided to customers who received kid's meals at Dairy Queen stores nationwide June through October 1996. 800-956-9565.

Determined Productions—Felix the Cat roller fun balls (3-10-97). The balls may break open, releasing small plastic toy fish that create a choking hazard. Distributed with kids' meals at Wendy's restaurants nationwide February 10, 1997, through March 4, 1997. 800-443-7266.

Division Sales—26,000 Baby Buzz crib toys, containing plastic balls and animal figures on an elastic string (1-15-97). Not properly labeled to warn of the dangers of infant strangulation. Sold nationwide in Dollar Value and other discount stores December 1995 through December 1996. 800-621-8134.

Division Sales—6,300 wooden toy trucks (4-17-97). The toy trucks have wooden balls and figures in the cab that can be removed, presenting a choking hazard. Sold nationwide October 1993 through November 1996. 800-621-8134.

Effanbee Doll Co.—2,500 miniature rocking chairs (1-29-98). The chairs were painted with lead paint. Sold nationwide in JCPenny catalogs and by the Effanbee Collector's Society June 1996 through December 1996. 800-226-3647.

Etna Products—13,200 wooden toy cars (4-17-97). The toy parts may separate, creating a choking hazard. Sold nationwide 1994 through March 1997. 800-841-1007.

First Years—108,000 High Chair Gyms (2-19-98). Two plastic balls, each approximately one-inch wide, are suspended from the frame; they have choked at least two infants, both of whom survived. Sold nationwide January 1995 through November 1997. 800-533-6708.

Fisher-Price—17,000 toy police cars of the Little People Roadside Rescue set (5-19-97). The cars may break apart, creating a choking hazard. Sold nationwide since February 1997. 888-407-6479.

Fisher-Price—10 million Power Wheels ride-on battery-powered vehicles (10-22-98). Electrical components on the vehicles can overheat, causing fires. Also, wiring problems can prevent the vehicles from stopping. Consequently, children may suffer injuries from fires and malfunctions, and house fires can occur. Numerous battery-powered vehicles have been recalled. Consumers should remove the vehicle's batteries right away and not let children use the vehicle until the appropriate repair has been made. Toy and mass merchandise stores have sold the vehicles nationwide since 1984. 800-977-7800.

Fisher-Price—21,000 Cookie-Shaped Refrigerator Magnet Toys, Refrigerator Activity Magnet Set, number 71126 (3-2-98). A choking hazard is present to children due to the magnet coming apart and releasing small plastic pieces. Only cookies with the date codes from 224 through 228 are part of this recall. Sold nationwide beginning September 1997. 888-407-6479.

Fisher-Price—49,000 Crib Mobiles, Magic Motion Mobile, number 71153 (3-2-98). Part of the mobile can detach and fall into the crib, presenting a choking hazard. Sold nationwide beginning June 1997. 888-407-6479.

Franco Manufacturing Co., Inc.—4,800 beanbags with Barney Hopscotch Game Towels (6-7-99). The seams on the beanbags can come loose, spilling the plastic pellets inside and posing an aspiration hazard to young children. The game towels were sold nationwide in Ames, Meijers, and Wal-Mart stores March 1999 through May 1999. Return only the beanbags to the company for a refund. 800-631-4663.

Gamo USA—1,335 precompressed air pistols (BB gun), model AF-10 (6-9-97). The BB gun has been reported to discharge unexpectedly. Sold nationwide June 1994 through April 1997. 888-872-4266.

Graco—19,000 Stationary Entertainers, model numbers 4118RA, 4118C, and 34429 (9-28-98). The screw securing the clicker toy to the Entertainer's tray can come out, presenting a choking hazard. Sold nationwide April 1998 through September 1998. 800-281-3676.

Graco—100,000 Graco and Children on the Go brand Stroller Snack and Activity Trays, Bathtime Activity Trays, Bathtime Activity Trays, and Bathtime Toy Netting products (8-27-99). The suction cups can detach, presenting a choking hazard. There have been four reports of children starting to choke after putting the suction cups in their mouths, including one that required use of the Heimlich maneuver. Sold nationwide in discount, department and juvenile product stores including Toys "R" Us and Sears January 1998 through August 1999. Call 800-446-1366.

Great American Toy Co.—18,700 Stuffed Crab Toys (10-20-98). The crab's antennae have a sharp wire that present a puncture wound hazard to children. Only stuffed crabs that have antennae with wires and that have the letters "BSW" on the Great American Toy Co. label. The crabs were given away as prizes at traveling fairs and carnivals. 888-767-3443.

Gymboree—6,500 children's umbrellas (8-5-97). The outer coating of the umbrella contains high levels of lead. Sold nationwide September 1996 through May 1997. 800-558-9885.

Gymboree—727 wooden toy trains, number 1103-0028 (2-4-98). Small pieces of the toy can come off, causing a choking hazard. Sold in Gymboree stores nationwide October 1997 through November 1997. 800-558-9885.

Hasbro, Inc.—618,000 Star Wars Lightsaber toys, the Darth Maul and the Qui-Gon Jinn (6-24-99). The batteries can overheat or rupture, causing burns. Sold nationwide May 1999 through June 1999. For a free repair kit, call 888-690-6141.

Hedstrom—1.5 million Glide Rides sold with backyard gym sets (1-5-98). This is a two-person ride commonly referred to as a teeter-totter. It has a defective J-bolt that can break and cause the rider to be dropped to the ground. Seventeen reports of injured children have been made. Sold nationwide April 1993 through December 1997. 800-233-3271.

IKEA—8,000 various stuffed animals (5-12-97). The stuffed animals' eyes may detach, creating a choking hazard. Sold nationwide January 1997 through May 1997. 800-455-IKEA.

IKEA—28,000 Stacking Ring Toy, Mula (5-11-99). Young children can choke on the red ball that tops this toy. Sold nationwide October 1991 through April 1999. 800-793-5408.

In-Mar Trading—various squeak toys, including gopher, penguin, rabbit, tiger, bear, and mouse (7-9-98). The squeak toys contain a squeaker on which children can choke. Sold in Puerto Rico January 1997 through June 1998. 787-796-1560.

In-Mar Trading—10,000 jet fighter toys (7-9-98). The jet fighter toy contains small parts that may become separated from the toy, presenting a choking hazard. Sold in Puerto Rico January 1997 through June 1998. 787-796-1560.

Isaac Morris, Ltd.—Tonka Toy Trucks (grader trucks) (6-7-99). The trucks contain small parts, presenting a choking hazard to young children. Only those trucks distributed with Tonka toddler T-shirts are being recalled because the toy parts are dangerous to children under three years. Sold nationwide with Tonka T-shirts as package deal November 1998 through March 1999. 800-248-6652.

K•B Toys—500 Bubble Beauties floating balls (6-8-98). These floating balls may be harmful or fatal if ingested. The ball contains a petroleum distillate that is similar to kerosene. Sold nationwide in K•B Toy stores May 1998. 800-877-1253.

Klutz—66,000 Chinese jump ropes sold with a children's book entitled *Chinese Jump Rope* (6-19-97). The ropes are connected by metal crimps that have been reported to break apart. This may injure children during play. Sold nationwide beginning March 1997. 415-857-0888 (call collect).

KMC USA, Inc.—190,000 cans of Party Time Happy String (1-21-99). This spray string is flammable when sprayed near an open flame and could result in serious burns. Sold nationwide in Dollar Tree, Dollar Bills, and Only $1 stores October 1998 through January 1999. 800-876-8077.

Laiko International—2,400 Knock-A-Block Wooden Toys, Knock-A-Ball item number 785 (6-29-98). Children may choke on the balls. Sold nationwide from August 1997 to June 1998. 888-280-0280.

Mazel Co.—835 Teddy Precious Indian girl and boy stuffed bears (5-1-97). The beads from the bears' costumes can break off, creating a choking hazard. Sold nationwide July 1996 through December 1996. 800-443-4789.

Menard, Inc.—8,000 Henry Gym Sets, model number 68 (11-12-98). The glider support tube on these gym sets may bend or break if assembled incorrectly, causing children to fall or be thrown from the glider. Sold in Menard retail stores in the north-central

United States July 1991 through August 1998. 888-215-3349.

Mermaid International—28,000 Kiddie Necklace Bracelet Sets, NB2490, NB2491, NB2492, or NB2493 (10-6-97). Matching toy necklace and bracelet sets with beads in the shapes of hearts, multicolored disks, and bows and fish pose choking hazards. 800-876-7581.

Michael Friedman Corp.—2,000 rattles, Hobby Horse (6-29-98). Infants and young children may choke on small parts of the rattles that may break off. The rattles resemble roses. Sold nationwide March 1997 through May 1998. 718-257-7800.

Nadel & Sons Toy Corp.—8,000 stuffed bears (10-14-97). The eyes can become detached, leading to a danger of choking. The bears were distributed as prizes at game booths and machines by entertainment centers, including Busch Gardens Theme Park in Tampa, Florida, Dutch Wonderland in Lancaster, Pennsylvania, and Play Day Amusements in Seaside Heights, New Jersey, October 1995 through May 1997. 800-234-4697.

Nancy Sales—4,000 beanbag crab toys (1-27-98). The material can separate, causing the release of small plastic pellets that can cause young children to choke. Sold nationwide January 1997 through October 1997. 800-626-2947.

OddzOn Products—5,000 Starfish swimming vests (7-14-97). The vest's buckles may detach, releasing the child into the water unexpectedly. Sold nationwide May 1996 through March 1997. 800-755-6674.

Ohio Art Co.—67,800 Splash Off Water Rockets (7-17-97). The toy rocket may break apart under high water pressure. People nearby may be injured by flying parts. Sold

nationwide April 1997 through June 1997. 800-641-6226.

Oscar Mayer—16,000 decals on pedal cars (6-2-98). The decals on these cars contain high levels of lead. Distributed nationwide in various grocery stores and through special promotional ads June 1995 through May 1998. 800-433-9361.

Peg Perego—274,000 battery-powered children's riding vehicles, models Corral 270, Diablo, Dragon, Gaucho, Gaucho Grande, Gaucho High Torque, Gaucho Sport, Magica, Magnum, Ranger GT, Thunderbolt, Thundercat, and Tornado (3-24-99). Fire and injury hazards can occur to children due to pedals sticking and electrical components overheating. Sold nationwide 1990 through 1997. 888-893-7903.

Playskool—116,000 Weebles Tractors, item number 5242 (4-16-97). The red plunger on the toy may break apart, creating a choking hazard. Sold nationwide January 1996. 888-377-3355.

Playwell Toy—mallets from 200,000 individually sold xylophones, item number 044073; 150,000 Little Ones Infant Three-Piece Musical Gift Sets; and 1,800 Little Ones Infant Five-Piece Musical Gift Sets (10-15-98). The xylophone mallets can get stuck in the throats of children because the rounded ends are smaller in diameter than the 1.75-inch standard for small balls. This may cause choking and could possibly lead to death among young children. The musical instrument has "MADE IN CHINA" printed on it. Sold nationwide in Target, K-Mart, Right Start Stores, and other various retail stores. 877. PLAY-WELL.

Pyramid Accessories, Inc.—3,700 Mulan Backpacks and 1,800 units of Rolling Luggage (8-18-98). High levels of lead is in the artwork paint on these items. Sold nationwide June 1998 through July 1998. 800-543-4327.

Restoration Hardware, Inc.—12,000 Sock Monkey stuffed animals (6-16-99). Pins and sewing needles have been found in the stuffing of the monkeys, presenting a laceration hazard. Sold in Restoration Hardware's stores, catalogs, and through their web site October 1997 through May 1999. 877-747-4671.

Rite Aid—12,000 Cyber Fighter and Flying Angel Dolls (2-17-98). The dolls have wings that can break off during use and injure the eyes of young children. Sold in Rite Aid drugstores nationwide February 1997 through January 1998. 888-468-4356.

Rubbermaid, Inc.—60,800 Icy Rider Toboggans, model number 2108 (12-1-98). The front of the toboggan may break away, placing the rider in danger. Sold nationwide September 1997. 800-567-2112.

Rubie's Costume Co.—6,000 Children's Vampire Capes (style number 50282) and 6,000 Witch Brooms (style number 85) (10-28-98). The capes and brooms do not meet federal mandatory standards for flammability and could ignite readily, presenting a serious risk of burn injuries to children. The capes are black vinyl and the edges of the cape are scalloped. The brooms are twenty-seven inches long with a bamboo handle and a brush made of twigs. Sold nationwide September 1997 through October 1998. 516-488-0484.

Safari, Ltd.—10,200 Toy Puzzles, number 9536-12 (3-18-99). Children may choke on two of the puzzle pieces. Sold nationwide April 1998 through February 1999. 800-615-3111.

Safety 1st—106,000 Bouncing Buggy Toys, product number 45606 (6-11-98). A sharp plastic edge can be created by the breakage of the cat "stop" sign and dog "go" sign toys that are attached to the snack tray. Sold nationwide May 1997 through April 1998. 800-723-3065.

Sanrio, Inc.—29,000 Stuffed Mascot Plush Animal Toys, item numbers 014388, 0143389, 014390, and 014391, names Hello Kitty (cat), Keroppi (frog), Pochacco (dog), and Badtz Maru (penguin) (4-28-98). Children can choke on small bells that might detach from the stuffed toys. Sold nationwide October 1997. 888-311-6720.

STK International—15,800 baby rattles, Turning Ball with Whistle (6-24-98). Infants and young children can choke on the handles of these rattles. The handles of the rattles are oddly shaped and, if inserted in the throat, pose a threat of blocking a child's airway. Sold nationwide December 1997 through May 1998. 800-536-7855.

STK International—24,400 clock tambourine toys (11-5-97). Small pieces could break off the toys and become choking hazards. Sold nationwide June 1995 through June 1997. 800-536-7855.

Summer Infant Products—5,000 Crib Rail Toys, UPC number 0 12914 05802 2 (12-14-98). When bent, the plastic flower toy stem can break. This may cause cuts and puncture injuries due to its sharp edge. Sold nationwide February 1998 through November 1998. 800-426-8627.

Tara Toy Corp.—670,000 Flying Warrior Dolls: Rotor, Blades, Gyro, and Spin (9-2-98). Serious injuries to children may occur if the wings of the flying dolls break off. Sold nationwide April 1995 through December 1997. 888-669-7087.

Tiger Electronics, Ltd.—202,000 Pooh Poppin' Piano toys, only pianos with serial numbers starting with "WT" or "CO15D"

(8-5-99). The green "leafy" top section of the carrot-shaped microphone attached to the piano toy can break off, posing a choking hazard to young children. Sold nationwide in toy and discount stores August 1997 through August 1999. Call 888-748-2860.

Tonka—1 million Soft Walkin' Wheels toy vehicles, model 90165 (1-29-97). The wheels may separate, creating a choking hazard. Sold nationwide January 1994. 800-524-8107.

Toys "R" Us—4,000 Baskets of Bubbles craft sets, SKN number 668192, manufacturer number 7, UPC 7-31346-00707-0 (12-24-97). The package insert instructs the user to microwave the soap disks for ten minutes—it should have read ten seconds. If the instructions are followed, a fire hazard results. Sold in Toys "R" Us stores nationwide November 1997 through December 1997. Any Toys "R" Us store will provide a full refund.

T.S. Toys—4,000 Activity Block Sets, item number 38329 (7-16-98). Rods on the blocks could break, releasing small hollow cylinders. Young children may choke on these cylinders. Sold in the East and Midwest May 1997 through June 1998. 800-543-3704; 800-257-4101, ext. 159; 606-261-6962; or 800-621-4245.

Toys "R" Us—71,000 Bathtub Baby doll sets, BATHTUB BABY, WHAT A DOLL!, FISHEL, and MADE IN CHINA appear on the hangtag (8-3-99). These sets come with a small ball that presents a choking hazard to children under three years old. Sold nationwide in Toys "R" Us stores October 1998 through July 1999. Call your local Toys "R" Us stores for information.

United Tradeline—4,400 Hot Pet Cars, model number HK-736 (10-1-97). Small pieces can break off and become a choking hazard. Sold in Los Angeles April 1997 through May 1997. 888-898-9296.

Warner Bros. Stores—2,500 Tweety Water Timer Game Key Rings (4-8-98). Young children can become poisoned if they swallow ethylene glycol, a chemical that may leak from the key rings. Sold nationwide by Warner Bros. April 1996 through April 1997. 800-795-9277, ext. 43288.

Zany Brainy Inc.—220 Miffy Wooden Shape Sorters (5-5-99). Children can choke on wooden pegs that can break off. These toys resemble small wooden houses and are composed of various shaped and colored blocks that can be inserted in the roof. Sold nationwide October 1998 through March 1999. 888-969-5437.

Lawn darts—all brands. *Effective December 19, 1988, the CPSC banned all lawn darts because they could cause brain injury or death to children. Destroy all lawn darts immediately.*

Child Safety Resources

Alliance to End Childhood Lead Poisoning
227 Massachusetts Avenue, NE
Washington, DC 20002
202-543-1147
www.aeclp.org
Information on lead poisoning.

American Humane Association
63 Inverness Drive East
Englewood, CO 80112-5117
303-792-9900
800-227-4645
www.americanhumane.org
Distributes professional publications regarding child protective services and child abuse and neglect.

American Association of State Highway and Transportation Officials (AASHTO)
444 North Capitol Street, NW
Suite 225
Washington, DC 20001
202-624-5800
800-231-3475

800-525-5562 (Fax)
www.aashto.org
Information on bicycle safety and facility design.

American Automobile Association (AAA) Foundation for Traffic Safety
1730 M Street, NW
Suite 401
Washington, DC 20036
202-775-1456
www.aaa.com
Educational materials and reports on bicycle safety and facility design and other traffic-related issues.

American Red Cross (ARC) National Headquarters
2025 E Street, NW
Washington, DC 20006
202-728-6531 (or call your local chapter)
www.redcross.org
Provides information on a wide variety of safety instruction materials and cardiopulmonary resuscitation (CPR) classes.

American Society for Testing and Materials (ASTM)
100 Barr Harbor Dr.
Conshohocken, PA 19428-2959
www.astm.org
Standards on playground surfacing, sports equipment, and protective equipment.

Association of Home Appliance Manufacturers (AHAM)
20 North Wacker Drive
Chicago, IL 60606
www.aham.org
For more information on how to safeguard your refrigerator or freezer.

Automotive Safety for Children Program
Riley Hospital for Children
575 West Drive
Room 004
Indianapolis, IN 46202
317-274-2977
Provides material and reference information on the transportation and occupant protection of children with special needs.

Bicycle Helmet Safety Institute
4611 Seventh Street South
Arlington, VA 22204
(703) 486-0100
www.helmets.org

Boys and Girls Clubs of America
Government Relations Office
611 Rockville Pike
Suite 230
Rockville, MD 20852
301-251-6676
www.bgca.org
Has 1,200 clubs nationwide serving over 1.6 million boys and girls. Offers a child safety curriculum.

Bunk Bed Kit
P.O. Box 2436
High Point, NC 27261

Child Accident Prevention Foundation of Australia
26 Liverpool Street
Suite 5
Melbourne 3000, Victoria
Australia
General information on child safety.

Child Accident Prevention Trust (CAPT)
28 Portland Place
London WIN 4DE
England

Child Help USA
National Child Abuse Hotline
P.O. Box 630
Hollywood, CA 90028
800-422-4453
800-222-4453 (for hearing impaired)
Provides comprehensive crisis counseling by mental health professionals for adult and child victims of child abuse and neglect, offenders, and parents, who are fearful that they will abuse or who want information on how to be effective parents. The Survivors of Childhood Abuse Program (SCAP) disseminates materials, makes treatment referrals, trains professionals, and conducts research.

Cocaine 24-Hour Hotline
164 West 74th Street
New York, NY 10023
800-COCAINE
www.drughelp.org
Provides crisis intervention, counseling, and referral services to parents and children.

Consumer Product Safety Commission (CPSC)
5401 Westbard Avenue
Washington, DC 20207
800-638-2772
www.cpsc.gov

The Danny Foundation
P.O. Box 680
Alamo, CA 94507

800-83DANNY
www.dannyfoundation.org
Educational materials on safe cribs.

Education Training Research (ETR) Associates

P.O. Box 1830
Santa Cruz, CA 95061
800-321-4407
www.etr.org
Nonprofit organization that distributes child safety materials.

Environmental Design Research Association (EDRA)

1800 Canyon Park Circle
Suite 403
Edmond, OK 73013
405-330-4863
www.telepath.com
Information on safety in children's environments.

Farm Safety Association

340 Woodlawn Road West
Suite 22
Guelph, Ontario N1H 7K6
Canada
519-823-5600
www.fsai.on.ca
Educational materials, fact sheets, and videotapes.

Farm Safety for Just Kids

110 S. Chestnut Avenue
P.O. Box 458
Earlham, IA 50072
515-758-2827
www.fs4jk.org.
Information on farm and animal safety.

Highway Safety Research Center

University of North Carolina
CB #3430
Chapel Hill, NC 27599
919-962-2202
Educational materials and reports pertaining to car safety.

Humane Society of the United States

2100 L Street, NW
Washington, DC 20037
202-452-1100
Information on animal-control ordinances.

Injury Prevention Center at Harvard University

Harvard School of Public Health
677 Huntington Avenue
Boston, MA 02115
617-732-1080

Insurance Institute for Highway Safety (IIHS)

1005 North Glebe Road
Suite 800
Arlington, VA 22201
703-247-1500
www.highwaysafety.org
Information on occupant protection and vehicle and roadway design.

Juvenile Products Manufacturers Association

Two Greentree Center
Suite 225
P.O. Box 955
Marlton, NJ 08053
www.jpma.org
An independent company that test and evaluates products on the market.

National Center for Missing and Exploited Children (NCMEC)

2101 Wilson Boulevard
Suite 550
Arlington, VA 22201-3052
703-235-3900
Hot line: 800-843-5678
TDD: 800-826-7653
www.ncmec.org
To report a suspicion of child abuse or the sighting of a missing child or to report a child who is missing.

National Child Care Information Center
243 Church Street, NW
2nd Floor
Vienna, VA 22180
800-616-2242
www.nccic.org
General information on child health and safety.

National Clearinghouse for Alcohol and Drug Information (NCADI)
P.O. Box 2345
Rockville, MD 20847-2345
800-729-6686
www.health.org
For a variety of government publications on the prevention of drug use by children.

National Clearinghouse on Child Abuse and Neglect Information
P.O. Box 1182
Washington, DC 20013-1182
800-FYI-3366
www.calib.com/nccanch
Publications on child abuse.

National Committee for Prevention of Child Abuse (NCPCA)
332 South Michigan Avenue
Suite 1250
Chicago, IL 60604
312-663-3520
800-835-2671
Has sixty-eight local chapters (in all fifty states). Provides information and statistics on child abuse and maintains an extensive publications list. The National Research Center provides information for professionals on programs, methods for evaluating programs, and research findings.

National Fire Protection Association (NFPA)
1 Batterymarch Park
Quincy, MA 02269
(617) 984-7274
www.nfpa.org
Educational materials, including Learn Not to Burn *curriculum, and information for design and construction of buildings.*

National Highway Traffic Safety Administration (NHTSA)
400 7th Street, SW
Routing symbol NTS-23
Washington, DC 20590
Auto Safety Hot Line: 800-424-9393
Technical Reference Library: 800-445-0197
(1300-1500)
www.nhtsa.gov
Educational materials and reports on traffic safety, safety seat promotion, and bicycle safety and facility design.

National Lead Information Center
EPA, CDC, and National Safety Council
800-532-3394
800-424-LEAD
www.nsc.org/ehc/lead.htm

National Safe Boating Council
U.S. Coast Guard Headquarters
Commandant (G-BBS)
Washington, DC 20593
800-336-BOAT
www.boatus.com/courseline
Information on boating safety regulations and classes.

National SAFE KIDS Campaign
111 Michigan Avenue, NW
Washington, DC 20010
202-939-4993
202-338-7227
www.safekids.org

National Safety Council
1121 Spring Lake Drive
Itasca, IL 60143-3201
630-285-1315
www.nsc.org

National Society to Prevent Blindness
500 E. Remington Road
Schaumburg, IL 60173
800-221-3004
www.Preventblindness.org
Information on nonpowder firearm injuries.

National Sudden Infant Death Syndrome Resource Center
2070 Chain Bridge Road
Suite 450
Vienna, VA 22182-2536
703-821-8955
www.SIDS@circsol.com
Provides general information on SIDS.

National Transportation Safety Board (NTSB)
800 Independence Avenue, SW
Washington, DC 20594
(202) 341-6100
www.ntsb.gov
Information on various studies and crash investigations.

Parents' Resource Institute for Drug Education (PRIDE)
800-853-7867
A national resource center that can provide referrals to counselors and parent support groups.

Partnership for a Drug-Free America
405 Lexington Ave.
16th Floor
New York, NY 10174
212-922-1560
www.drugfreeamerica.org
Provides free information about various drugs and tips to help your kids stay away from them.

Poison Prevention Week Council
P.O. Box 1543
Washington, DC 20013
Materials for community activities to promote poison prevention.

Royal Society for the Prevention of Accidents (RoSPA)
Edgbaston Park
353 Bristol Road
Edgbaston, Birmingham, B5 7ST
United Kingdom
+44 (0) 121 248 2000
www.rospa.co.uk

Safe and Drug-Free Schools
800-624-0100
www.ed.gov/pubs
To order the free booklet, Growing Up Drug Free: A Parents' Guide to Prevention.

SafetyBeltSafe USA
P.O. Box 553
Altadena, CA 91003
800-745-7233
www.carseat.org
Free information about child safety seats.

Snell Memorial Foundation
P.O. Box 493
St. James, NY 11780
516-862-6545
www.smf.org
Information on safety helmet standards.

Toy Manufacturers of America
200 Fifth Avenue
Suite 740
New York, NY 10021
212-675-1141
www.toy-tma.org

On-line Child-Safety Stores

You can call these companies for free catalog:
Baby Guard: 703-821-1231 or
    www.babyguard.com
Baby Protectors: 800-859-0657 or
    www.babypro.com
Childproofers USA: 888-723-3230 or
    www.childproofing.com
Perfectly Safe: 800-837-KIDS or
    www.kidsstuff.com
Safe Beginnings: 800-598-8911 or
    www.safebeginnings.com
The Child Safety Company: 800-708-1648 or
    www.childsafetyco.com
Safety 1st: www.safety1st.com
Safety Matters: 800-9-SAFE-06 or
    www.safetymatters.com

Index

About the Author

Mark A. Brandenburg, M.D., his wife, Kelly, and their son live in Tulsa, Oklahoma. He is a practicing emergency physician at the Trauma Emergency Center (TEC) of Saint Francis Hospital in Tulsa. The TEC is the busiest emergency department in Oklahoma with approximately 70,000 patient visits each year. It is also the regional pediatric trauma center.

Dr. Brandenburg received his undergraduate degree in biology from West Virginia University in Morgantown, West Virginia. He attended medical school at the University of Oklahoma in Oklahoma City, graduating in 1992. His emergency medicine residency took place at the University of Oklahoma in Oklahoma City at University Hospital and Children's Hospital of Oklahoma.